George Rufus Harman is an actor, dancer, life model and writer. An unconventional Anglo-Australian bloke who has been fortunate to earn his crust in the performing arts. With his attitude of never looking back nor planning his future and only living in and enjoying the present, he suddenly came to realize that any understanding of his path in life requires a sense of the ridiculous! This is personified in this his first book describing his life as a male life model.

I am dedicating this book to the countless truly amazing kaleidoscopic creative female figurative artists of past and present in the UK, both non-professional and professional, who grace the art world with their creative energy.

George Rufus Harman

Naked Truths: Adventures in Art

The Life & Times of a
Male Life Model

Austin Macauley Publishers
LONDON * CAMBRIDGE * NEW YORK * SHARJAH

Copyright © George Rufus Harman 2025

The right of George Rufus Harman to be identified as author of this work has been asserted by the author in accordance with sections 77 and 78 of the Copyright, Designs and Patents Act 1988.

All rights reserved. No part of this publication may be reproduced, stored in a retrieval system, or transmitted in any form or by any means, electronic, mechanical, photocopying, recording, or otherwise, without the prior permission of the publishers.

Any person who commits any unauthorized act in relation to this publication may be liable to criminal prosecution and civil claims for damages.

All of the events in this memoir are true to the best of author's memory. The views expressed in this memoir are solely those of the author.

A CIP catalogue record for this title is available from the British Library.

ISBN 9781035879496 (Paperback)
ISBN 9781035879502 (ePub e-book)

www.austinmacauley.com

First Published 2025
Austin Macauley Publishers Ltd®
1 Canada Square
Canary Wharf
London
E14 5AA

I am eternally thankful for the inspiration of my closest friends and artists who have encouraged me to write this book, especially Colin, Joan, Dierdre, Mark, Penelope and Mona, along with their discreet humour and interest in my adventures in art.

"Creativity takes courage."
– Henri Matisse

"What is erotic, like taste in art, is subjective."
– Kelly Borsheim

"Why should I be ashamed to describe what nature was not afraid to create."
– Pietro Aretino

Chapter One

Why did I write this book?

How did it happen? Something must have formed the idea a catalyst for putting pen to paper. In my case, 'pencil to paper', to record my adventures as a male life model. Not only to record them but to make them available for public entertainment! The personal adventures and experiences in this book focus on me and the people I have met, the places and venues where I have modeled, the artists who have drawn me naked in many media of their choice, and importantly, the humorous, bizarre, and erotic situations in which I have found myself as a male life model.

However, experiences necessarily include situations that are not the usual fodder for public consumption. So for the most part within this book, I will also be conveying my most vivid unconventional experiences sometimes as 'confessions'. 'Confessions' is a word that conjures up thoughts of sin, secrets, sexual and erotic events, and fantasies that people in society have been conditioned, if not legally required, to keep secret, except in the most exceptional and trusting circumstances. To this end, the names, places, and chronology of events in this book have been changed to protect identities. The descriptions concerning myself, my upbringing, my background, and the actual adventures and confessions are all true.

Have I written this book of adventures for any purpose? Yes! For your entertainment, of course. An insight into over 20 years of life modeling while also earning my living as a professional dancer and jobbing actor. This book could be assumed to be a non-stop recollection of sexual experiences, but when put into the context of more than twenty years, it hardly equates. This book, necessarily by default, compresses time and gives the impression of pure debauchery! Have these confessions been secret? Yes, they have until now! You see, as a professional, working in the performing arts, I learned at an early age that my 'secret life' as a child when growing up led me into a lifelong belief that being discreet has always been the best policy! Keeping secrets has always worked to my advantage. I am not a gossip, never have been. People tell me stuff and I don't pass it on!

Do any of these confessions include descriptions of sexual encounters? Definitely and in explicit detail, so if you are of a sensitive persuasion, then put this book down right now! Remember, if you are offended, offense is only accepted, never given. Are any of these confessions pure fantasy? Certainly not, but they would certainly feature in some peoples' sexual fantasies. Remember that truth is stranger than fiction, and in this book that is certainly the case. As a professional life model, my sole intentions were few, namely, to act professionally in all situations, to earn an extra few bob as a 'penniless performer' and to indulge in my first love from my earliest memories—my lifelong love of art and artists, both dead and alive.

Have I been the object of sexual fantasies as a life model? If you consider that I have always been an extremely physically fit dancer who has appeared naked in front of people, the vast majority of them being female, then it is highly likely that some of them had the courage and opportunity and the uninhibited sexual desire to engage in sexual activity with yours truly! (Breathe!). Was I a willing participant? Of course I was! I take full responsibility for my actions alone. I take no responsibility for the actions of others, and I have never encouraged the actions of others to be against their will. I do have regrets though, as we all do in life, but #hashtag 'more of that later' #MOTL. I have, in short, just gone with the flow.

As a professional performer about to go on stage, waiting for that red light to go green or music to start to indicate it's your cue to go on stage, you bloody well go! Despite your nerves, doubts, or excitement, you are confronted with a willing, waiting, and wanting audience. The audience expects to be entertained. You step out there and play your part. It's theater. Theater is fantasy. I become the object of others' fantasies. Can you refuse to do it? Yes, but your first duty is just to go for it. That is in fact the first rule. Just 'go for it'. If you don't, especially at an early age, you will simply not become a performer. So when I have been confronted by an adoring, gorgeous female who desired me in the course of my work, I just 'went for it'! Like all good 'improv classes', just say "yes… and!" Could I have said, "Thank you, but no!"? Well yes, I could, and I have done so on a number of 'creepy' and undesirable occasions. But on the whole, I said yes, otherwise, there would not be any detailed confessions and no book!

So back to the initial question. Why did I write this book? Well, later on in the next chapter, I will describe my background and upbringing, which has a large bearing upon it, and how I became a dancer, an actor, and a life model. I would describe myself first and foremost as a 'performance artist' within the performing arts, stage, film, and TV. My sisters referred to me as 'The Cosmic Dancer', the T-Rex song written by the inspirational Marc Bolan. Listen to the lyrics and witness a rare compliment from my four older female siblings! I wrote this book first and foremost to entertain you.

I have never restricted myself to any particular type of performing art. I have willingly always said yes to performing whatever was available and offered to me at the time. This has included straight acting, musical theater, theater generally, TV, and film. This has included dancing in many genres with dance companies and solo, and I've worked as a performance coach, mainly for the gratification of my creative soul and, of course, the money to pay my bills, but mainly for my soul! I love it all. I've even worked front of house, as an ASM, I've even sold popcorn and ice cream! My experiences as a life model materialized out of my need and opportunities to immerse myself in my first love, as I stated earlier, art and the art world. To mix socially and professionally with artists is an addiction for me. I'm talking here about the 'visual arts' that we traditionally find in museums, galleries, artist's studios, and exhibitions. Of course, art exists all around us if we only open our eyes and look! But #MOTL

There I sat in a cold industrial unit on the outskirts of Manchester, England, waiting to be called in to an audition for a commercial, for which I had been 'called back' to audition in person after my 'self-tape' had been accepted. These days, actors 'self-tape' initially, which means you are sent a script by your agent for a particular role. You sit or stand at home with your back to a suitable backdrop and in front of your smartphone camera, which in turn is firmly clamped to a 'ring light'. You then perform and record your audition and email the video to your agent. Your agent sends it onwards to the casting agent for the producers to assess. If it is liked by the casting agent, directors, and producers (whatever mystical, unfathomable, ineffable process that is), you are offered a 'call back'.

During this Manchester audition, there were five other actors sitting and waiting to be called in. Not speaking much, we all sat, just politely nodding with quick smiles to each other. There was the usual useless quiet 'cool' non-binary looking teenage 'receptionist administrator', sitting in front of an iPad with 'ear pods' firmly implanted! There were three female actors waiting there, plus myself and one other male actor. I assumed correctly that a third male actor was already auditioning on the other side of the industrial-looking steel door and bare breezeblock wall in front of me.

Two seats from me sat an extremely attractive, slim young woman of about 28 years old with flame-red hair, called Sarah, as I was to learn after introducing myself. We were separated from the others by quite a distance in that cavernous, high-ceilinged cold space, which made it easier to strike up a one-to-one conversation without much chance of being overheard.

"Hello, I'm George, George Harman!" I said to her, smiling.

"Hi, I'm Sarah Wxxxxx" she willingly replied in a friendly tone. "You here for the audition… obviously?" she asked with feigned intrigue while swishing her hair. I was beginning to like her already, yum!

"Yeah!" I replied, laughing and proffered my hand, which she took without hesitation.

We shook hands, and we connected easily. She was quite happy to break the overbearing silence in the space and also to be distracted by talking, as I was. As is usual with actors, I asked her…

"What else are you working on…? At all…? At the moment?" with that knowing look that actors show each other to convey 'fuck all at the moment'!

"The usual, anything non-creative to keep the wolf from the door," she cheekily grinned conspiratorially in reply.

"I know what you mean," I said, "What do you do for reddies to pay the rent?"

"Oh jeepers!" she grinned wide-eyed, "I dress up like a hoe and hostess in a casino! What about you?" she continued, "Not a private income then?" she asked me, joking…

We both laughed and connected some more. Others in the room looked up with mild interest except the dopey teen receptionist lost in TikTok!

"Nope, I wish. I kinda think I'd actually be Hugh Grant if that was the case… Nooo, I take my clothes off as a life model!" I answered. Sarah quietly laughed.

"Woooo, that takes some courage!" she exclaimed.

"It makes auditioning with your clothes on seem like child's play," I laughed back at her.

Any of our residual hesitancy had melted completely now since we'd started chatting.

"We definitely have something in common at the basic level then, I think," Sarah continued. "We both earn a crust from awkward, unconventional social situations entertaining people."

"That we do. I could write a book," I prophetically replied!

And there, right there in that moment, my initial idea to write this book pinged into life.

Sarah paused the conversation and looked away, then slowly looked back at me, fixing her eyes on mine, and spoke suddenly in a lower octave, sounding sexy.

"… you'd look great naked, such poise," she slowly and coyly spoke. "I might even take it up!"

Never to be taken in by a teasing female, I asked.

"What, life modeling?"

"No, drawing you!" She quickly interjected, and she meant it because she quickly moved to sit in the seat right next to me, moving toward me in a half-standing, half-sitting shuffle, and sat on her hands. I feigned a blush.

"Thank you, Sarah," I said, slowly looking at her.

I'd used her name for the first time to cement the closer physical and mental connection between us, while at the same time not exaggerating the fact that I was excited and intrigued by her. I continued.

"Thanks, I could say the same about you too, but men can't say that to a woman these days even though we think it and mean it!"

"Yeah, we women are bitter and twisted these days!" she said, smiling.

She then pursed her lips together, squeezed them sideways, and lifted her eyebrows in an ironic, big-eyed, playful stare at me.

"… and that's why we resort to seeking validation and gratification from men on Instagram and OnlyFans for fuck's sake," she continued, remaining relaxed and playful.

"We women are our own worst enemies, we've forgotten how to attract men or refuse to attract them due to the insane brainwashing of bitter and twisted fourth-generation feminists! In real life, we want men to pay us compliments, but somehow, we have banned them, yet we parade ourselves like modern whores to any stranger on social media; one perpetuates the other," she said without rancor.

"You on either… Insta or OnlyFans?" I cheekily enquired.

"Oh, both of them," she said, "I don't claim to be anything but a hypocrite," she giggled, "You know, needs must," giggling more with venomous mirth!

This made everyone else in the space look up at us in unison.

"Okayyyyyyyy!" I replied quietly, dragging out the word, "allow me to tweak the nose of the thoroughly modern woman then… you'd look fuckin' ace naked!"

Sarah looked at me intensely and said, matter of factly, "Thank you, kind SIR," (emphasizing the 'SIR') "maybe you could teach me a few things that I'm completely ignorant of?"

You are now getting the gist! You have to love actresses. Well, some of them! All those finely tuned drama school improv classes certainly pay off. Well (I repeat) for some of them! Our rapid conversation then ran into chatting about how my life modeling stories of being naked in front of strangers is mainly fun, funny and entertaining for me. The tone of our extended chat was friendly and familiar. We were getting on like a house on fire! Sarah's stories of her 'hostessing' satisfied her alter ego as a scantily clad classy vamp in the casino world, her 'face on show' lingerie and bikini wearing Instagram account, and her anonymous erotic performances online, often less than partially dressed, cavorting on her OnlyFans account was proof of this!

"OnlyFans can only be described as either narcissistic at best or definitely seedy or both…" her words!

"You know, girls once had to meet one guy to access a million dollars, now you can access a million guys for a dollar each!" We both laughed at this fact. "You performing as a life model is juxta opposed to my escapades," she said genuinely and intelligently, "whereas mine are defo seedy and undignified, yours are creatively invigorating. I could never appear naked in a real-life situation with a real-life, in-the-same-room, closed group of people. I don't give a damn doing it online!" she said, thinking out loud whimsically, looking at nothing in particular.

Certainly, this was the first time she broke eye contact with me. I suddenly wanted to hug her to comfort her, but just as quickly she returned her eyes to mine and continued, her humor returning,

"Well, not without the right makeup, lighting, and filters," she added.

We both laughed again, easily.

"Just like insta and OnlyFans then? … you know your audience well, I reckon!" I said teasingly, hoping not to seem callous, and thankfully we both laughed some more.

There followed a long silence as we stared at each other. I wasn't going to break that silence even though my inner self-doubt screamed at me to say something, any bloody thing, but I didn't. The theatrical 'power of silence' method; life imitating art! Sarah broke the silence.

"You've got to be an actor to hide your disgust from the creepy, often inebriated gamblers, both men AND the women!" she exclaimed. "Energy-sapping. Unlike you, when life modeling. It has to be energizing easily as much as it is to be on stage?"

"Yeah, life modeling is energizing" I answered, agreeing with her. "Especially as I am a lifelong art lover in all its forms and guises, but I have come across one or two creeps" I added.

By now my subconscious was kicking in, connecting into ideas for action! The growing idea and affirmation to write this book became the conscious thing to do, firming up in my mind as we continued to share and laugh about 'creep stories'. Sure, Sarah had far more definitive and obvious creep stories than I did, but they made me realize that my own experiences of them, although few, were far more covert than the overt gropers and gobshites she encountered in her world. In fact, most of Sarah's experiences outside traditional acting were creepy, and I admired her fortitude under constant adversely draining situations. Her parody of the creeps kept her going. I further realized my life modeling confessions were far more diverse. In fact, the interesting, entertaining sheer erotic stories far outnumbered the creepy experiences in the extreme. My stories formulated again in my mind as 'confessions' and that word alone made me realize that to write about them would readily be transferable entertainment for an audience of adult readers. Certainly, they would intrigue in a fun and yet illicit way. #MOTL

So thank you, Sarah. This book was born because of your interaction with me. We created what my mum used to call "the creation of happy coincidences." So away I go, unleashed. The 'red light' turns to 'green'. Get on this new stage!

But what happened next, with you and Sarah after your auditions, I hear you ask? Go on, finish this bit off, give us the details then? I hear you, I hear you! Well, I'm not telling because my experiences with Sarah after the audition led to a relationship! So, no confessions here, as it wouldn't fit within the context of this 'book of confessions and adventures as a life model'. Also, Sarah wouldn't like it! Like many professional performers, we like to maintain a private life. Going back to the audition, I can tell you that Sarah was called in just before me. Twenty minutes later, she emerged, smiling my way.

"How'd it go?" I asked.

"Fuck knows!" she shrugged her shoulders playfully, "the usual eristic duplicity and equivocation from a 'director' younger than I am." I adored her even more. "Frankly, my dear, I don't give a fuck!" She continued with her unaffected conspiratorial sense of humor, and we laughed again. She was so entertaining.

"Listen!" I said quickly, expecting to be called in to audition very soon.

To be called in quickly would be a sign that they'd picked their chosen male actor already, so they would be going through the motions rapidly out of courtesy.

"Here's my card; stay in touch…" I gathered my courage, "or better still, I've got my car outside if you want to wait. I can give you a lift to the train station if you like."

"Ok" she said.

That's all, just 'OK'! I was happy. Then, as expected, I was called in to audition.

Sarah did wait. And we drove toward the train station in an easy mood together, not even mentioning the audition once, which suited us both. In fact, we drove straight past the train station I had fully intended to drop her off at after she asked me…

"Which part of the south did you say you lived?"

"I didn't say!" I replied, and then proceeded to tell her.

She listened carefully, looking straight ahead through the windscreen at the darkening, damp Manchester city streets. There was another silence before she said,

"My heart is racing right now at my bubbling recklessness, but it's been quite a while since I visited that part of the world… do you have your own place?"

"Yes, I do, and I've nothing planned for the next few days," I replied.

"Me neither!" she raised both hands as she spoke and flipped them over into a loose palm-up resigned gesture. She then 'shimmy-shrugged' her bottom as though trying to imbed herself further into the passenger seat and then began gently to shadowbox the air in front of her with delicate, clenched fists. She swished her loose, flame-red hair and said, "Then let's go and write our own book at your place! Oh, and I'll need to borrow a T-shirt and some joggers," she said laughing, and I knew she was being serious!

It was as if she had been reading my thoughts about me writing a book, and I knew that all along, as I had hoped, if not suspected, that we were on the same wavelength.

"Huh huh, why not!" I replied, and off we drove into the sunset… well, the darkening Manchester rizzle anyway.

Let the story continue. Don't fret though, darling! Even now as I write, I have a niggling doubt about wanting this book to be a success because that might lead to the sort of fame and notoriety that could damage my prized private life. There is plenty of naughtiness as well as many risqué activities to recount herein to entertain you if that is what I expect you are expecting. Also, I can tell you here I will be contending with the farcical, the ridiculous, the hilarity, the wonderful characters and situations that have arisen over more than twenty years to date. Certainly, they are unlikely ever to be part of most civvy-street jobs. So what can you expect from my adventures in art? There's definitely a slant, if not a definite leaning, toward the erotic sexual nature of my near and actual sexual encounters—not just erotic but also bizarre! Also, there are confessions of encounters with some of the strange and wonderful artistic people I have met and grown to like and the not-so-wonderful 'drains' I've encountered while life modeling.

However, I know what you want, really, I do, so I will endeavor to tease you and then serve up the 'dirt'! Be warned, right here that some of the confessions will 'make your hair curl' and for any Americans reading this, that means you might be shocked, but hopefully all of you will be entertained. So, fair dinkum, let's get into what makes George Rufus Harman tick, eh?

Chapter Two

A small boy in outback Australia

I'll commence with a description of what was, when I was a small boy, my unconventional upbringing and background. It definitely forms the basis, the foundation of why and how I have led such a colorful and adventurous life in the arts. I say 'arts' because although I didn't set out to work in the performing arts, it was inevitable. It was also a complete coincidence, or as a result of my mum inculcating me with her mantra to "go out and create happy coincidences," that I began working with visual artists such as painters and sculptors as a dancer and life model. This, I know, came about because I have always loved art for art's sake; my first love! #MOTL

I describe myself not as an actor, dancer, or life model but as a 'performance artist.' Robert Lindsay, for instance, describes himself as an entertainer, although we all recognize him as a superlative character actor in film, on TV, and as a lead actor on the stage, especially in stage musicals. When I first moved to London just before my 21st birthday, I was fortunate to meet with an established and successful female artist; I'll call her Ellie. She lived her life in the same way and with the same hedonistic gusto as the bohemian artist Nina Hamnett. Chatting with Ellie one day with a brew on in her gorgeous art studio, I told her how satisfying it has been for me to have found a way to include and dovetail the performing arts with the visual arts.

"My darling!" she gasped flourishingly, "We are ALL visual artists!"

And you know, she was right, and I absorbed that instantly. It has allowed me to fertilize and inspire all of my work by indulging myself in the art world. Previously I had compartmentalized art and the performing arts, keeping them separate in my mind. I'd come to think of art as my hobby and the performing arts as my vocation. From that very moment of realizing that we are all visual artists, my mind opened up, and I've never been left wanting for creative inspiration, a creative way of thinking. Not from that moment has my mind ever been blank, and never have I been a negative 'overthinker'. I have always found myself thinking 'what next' and conditioning myself to draw inspiration from the art world, always looking to improve, to do the new and the different, not 'more of the same'. 'Do your work by building on the shoulders of giants' is one of my mottos. I suppose I'm an adventurer too, looking continually at how to be creative and take the next steps. It's all out there in the art world. Go look for yourself, you can find art anywhere; absorb it. Art energizes your brain. In the words of Sir Patrick Stewart from his memoir 'Making It So'…

"Never doubt the capacity of art to bring about moments of profound emotion and reflection."

Without for one second undermining such a wonderful meaningful quote I would only add "and creative inspiration"!

I was born in the gulf country, Queensland, Australia, and lived there until I was nearly 21. I was an active child. I was walking on my own two legs unaided by the time I was nine months old. My mum told me my 'static verbosity' turned into "silent gone walkabout"! I always went missing. Not missing in the sense of going missing in the modern world requiring a police search, but missing in the inherently socially safe area in which I grew up. My four older sisters were told by mum to keep an eye on me all the time. I must mention here that my mum was nearly 48 years old when I was born. My older female siblings always said,

"Yes, mum, no worries."

But when mum was out of earshot, my sisters told me to,

"Just fuck off and leave us alone, you little 'ranga'!"

That was just bonzer for me! I was then free to go walkabout, or should I qualify that as 'run-off-about'? I ran everywhere until something grabbed my interest. Also, in Queensland, the spiders, snakes, and other creepies held no fear for me, just fascination. Qualifying my sisters' pejorative nickname for me, "Ranga"! It was due to the dark red hair I was born with, but which faded away into brown by the time I was three years old, or so I'm told. Ranga is short for orangutan and is a pejorative Aussie nickname. Orangutans have red fur. Redheads are called ranga in Aus! Also, I was christened 'George Rufus' (as in 'Rufus the Red') because of the shock of thick, dark red hair I was born with. In the Aussie sunshine, my hair became lighter too with sun-bleached blond streaks! On the occasions I had all my hair shaved off as part of the remedy for head lice, fleas, and the impetigo outbreaks; that my wandering and adventurous outdoor lifestyle bestowed upon me, my hair would begin to grow back dark red once again, only to go through the same process of going blondie brown again!

I was a boy, who these days would be called 'hyperactive'. I was never still for sure, even when sitting. I'm still the same today. I've spent my life on my feet unless forced to sit or lie down by circumstances. I only learned about the usefulness of 'stillness' as an actor and performer and most certainly as a life model! It is quite literally something I have to think about consciously in order to accomplish! 'Hyperactive' is a ridiculous description for mentally and physically curious children. Kids these days are even to a greater extent than ever before, categorized and labeled by the plethora of modern-day 'qualified' child psychologists, for fuck's sake! Even the 'disapproving' twats in society (the sheeple) comment on kids who are 'different' in any way compared to the boring, conforming oppressive norms. 'He must be this or that' labeling; what bollocks! These days inclusivity means conformity or exclusion!

In the days before the internet, all kids were seen to be different from each other, especially in the small community in which I was brought up. Everyone knew everyone else, and everyone had a unique personality, and this was implicitly understood and accepted. Sure, there was piss-taking, but that's life! No one ever said I was 'hyperactive' for fuck's sake! Since the advent of the internet and especially social media (which is the biggest most grotesque oxymoron ever), every Tom and Dick has a say about everything, and people have become sheep (or, as I previously referred to them as 'sheeple'… baaaa!). It's ironic that the greater access to information made easily available to people by modern technology, the fewer and less informed freethinkers there are in modern society.

As a small boy, my mum told me, and anyone else who saw us together, that my only waking 'still-time' that she could predict was when I was reading books, and I mean art books; I would have up to ten books around me at any one time! I was an early reader of books at school; in fact, I am still a prolific reader of books to this day. My bedroom was piled high with books, and I especially loved illustrated books. I was an early member of my local library; I can't remember joining, but I just remember being at the library a lot, especially on really hot and humid days in Queensland. If I ever went 'missing' mum would drive her 'ute' over to the library, to check if there was a red triangular flag hanging up in the window. The librarians would hang it there as soon as I entered as a sign to my family, I was ensconced in and absorbed by books, quiet and still! Mum couldn't ring as we had a shared telephone line for emergencies only in those days.

The other activity that mum discovered for me at the age of 6 years old was inadvertently to introduce me to ballet! This came about because I would accompany mum to pick up one of my sisters from her ballet class twice each week during term time. This was fun for me because mum would let me ride along on the flatbed in the back of the ute. I would begin the journey by sitting and holding tight, then I would let go with my hands and balance on my bum with my hands and feet raised. I would therefore, unbeknown to me, be using my abdominal muscles to keep my balance. With my back toward the direction of travel, I eventually learned to anticipate every curve and bend in the road and even when mum was about to apply the brakes. Great fun! I called this 'belly bum balancing'! Sometimes I would stand up, and by spreading my feet and using my arms to help me balance, I would travel along, keeping my balance. I became very good at balancing!

On these occasions, if mum saw me, she would bang on the back of the cab and shout, "George Rufus, sit down, you'll injure yourself!." I did sit down but I took my time doing so! I mention this because it stood me in good stead to take up the physical demands of ballet.

Arriving at the ballet classes early to pick up my sister, I would kneel down next to the dance studio door and look at the girls doing ballet through the lower glass pane in the door. The upper pane was covered with black paper precisely to stop people peering in and making the girls feel self-conscious. I was therefore very careful not to be too conspicuous! I noticed there were no boys doing ballet in the classes. Mum said that I would sit and be quiet for a full 15 minutes before the class ended, and then I would jump up and mimic the ballet positions and movements that I had observed. Mum recognized that I was very quiet and absorbed as I watched the girls in class, and this observation struck a chord with mum. I was very focused, and I would ask lots of questions about ballet, none of them remotely explained by my sister! But mum had an idea to teach me more focus and, importantly, discipline in a form I would enjoy rather than rebel against!

"Do you want to learn how to do ballet properly, George Rufus?" she asked me one day.

I remember her asking me that, but I do not remember my answer to her question, which she often quoted on many embarrassing occasions for me as I grew up!

"Yeah, but I don't want to wear a bathing cossie!" I replied.

By 'bathing cossie' (costume), I was referring to the leotards that the girls wore! So my mum enrolled me in ballet class at the age of six years old. By the time I was 16 years old, I was so advanced that I had passed every ballet exam possible that 18-year-old dancers achieved if they stuck at it that length of time. This also simultaneously inspired me to take up every opportunity to become involved in all sorts of dance and drama at school and local community events, so I was introduced to performing by default. Also, I loved to dress up in costumes! Very odd for a prospective life model!

Where am I going with this? Well, the other reason and possibly the main reason for me personally wanting to take up ballet as a small boy was a stirring within me when watching those graceful female creatures with elegant poise taking ballet class! They were beautiful clones of each other in maroon leotards, white tights, and their hair scraped up into tight buns. They were absolutely gorgeous. I fancied each and every one of them, and I just wanted to mingle with them in the ballet classes! To be in class with these beauties was very appealing to me. However, as I became more and more involved and absorbed by the challenges of learning ballet, as everyone who has taken up ballet will know, it takes an enormous amount of concentration and time, and 'ogling the girls' takes a back seat! Although I have to say being the only boy in ballet class was an object of fascination for the girls.

I received a regular cascade of female attention within the safe confines of ballet classes. As I grew and developed my ballet technique as well as developing physically, the girls became extremely appreciative of my ballet physicality and especially the image of a developing young man wearing ballet tights!

The older I got I developed an intense fascination, if not an erotic visual appreciation, of dancers' backs! Ballet leotards are cut low at the back and wide on the shoulders to allow ballet mistresses to see that correct posture is activated and maintained. As I stood and exercised at the ballet barre in class, I would be confronted by lines of gorgeous girls in front of me wearing leotards that consciously entranced me, especially how their gorgeous and delicious toned slender back muscles added to their mystery of graceful movement and my personal desire for them! So I can say for sure that I became a surefire one hundred percent red-blooded heterosexual male because of ballet! That's even more odd!

The majority of my male friends and colleagues I have met and worked with in dance and theater have been gay! Some camp, but certainly not all. Although it has often been assumed that I am also gay due to my ballet training, I am not remotely gay. Not one cell in my body is remotely sexually attracted to other males! Growing up influenced by classical ballet, music, and art has put me in contact with many gay men, and as such, I just accepted that is their preference. It never bothered me, and I never once felt threatened. I have never held any prejudices against gay people and never had cause to distance myself verbally or physically to protect myself. Gay men soon realize when a man is straight and make jokes about 'wasted talent'! To be honest, I prefer my male friends to be gay! Most are in fact, but I am not.

So as a result of ballet, I became what could be described as a 'backs, legs, and bums man'! Never have I been attracted to nor lusted after women with big boobs unless they are a size and firmness to be near self-supporting! A woman who can wear a bra as an outfit fashion accessory rather than a 'hammock of support' is my kinda turn-on, and together with lean toned and well-developed tight upper gluteal muscles and narrow deep thighs, then I am bowled over by her, at least physically! At this point I will state here that I kissed many of the girls I did ballet with growing up, or should I say they kissed me back more often, once the ice was broken!

Chapter Three

Juliet and Alison

At the age of nine years old, during that Aussie springtime shortly before my tenth birthday, things came to a head with one of the girls I knew from ballet. Her name was Juliet. Juliet was 15 years old and taking ballet in one of the senior girl's classes. My mum and Juliet's mum were close friends. One of my sisters was three years older than Juliet, and her class started too late for her to walk with me to ballet class, meaning she would be waiting around for two hours.

"No way am I taking him!" was her mantra on this subject.

She got away with that because she was 18 years old and not a kid anymore! This meant that I had no one to walk to ballet class with. So my mum arranged for me to be met by her best friend's daughter, Juliet, outside our school, and we would both walk together to Juliet's house not far away.

On almost every occasion when we reached Juliet's home, her mum would not be there. Juliet was an only child and lived in a beautiful, spacious Victorian house (the era, not the Australian state!). It had a huge sitting room with a piano in it. The floor was polished wood, and within a 'horseshoe' of sofas and comfy chairs was a large, patterned, thick rug that almost reached the large open fireplace. Juliet and I would each literally jump onto a sofa and wallow there, resting and chatting about ballet, school, and the shit youngsters chat about. This older girl chatted to me unlike my sisters and made me feel special. I did more listening than talking because Juliet was this comparatively tall, elegant, mysterious enigma growing in my nine-year-old brain. We wouldn't change into ballet gear until we reached the class, but we had a full hour before Juliet's mum would return home, prepare a snack for us, and then we'd walk off together to ballet class, or Juliet's mum would drive us there if time was pressing.

The usual unspoken arrangement in Juliet's sitting room would be for her to roll back the large rug toward the fireplace, and this would open up the floor for us to dance on. She'd still be wearing her school skirt and blouse, and I'd be wearing my school shorts and shirt. We would practice plies, tendus, and pirouettes, mostly having fun and laughing, having little ballet contests such as who could stay on demi-pointe in relevé the longest before losing balance. On one occasion out of the blue, Juliet unbuttoned her school blouse revealing her small white bra and proceeded to remove the blouse, and then the bra, too! I was transfixed! Of course, I'd seen my sisters naked fleetingly from time to time, but this was different. She then took off her skirt and socks and stood in front of me just in her dark blue knickers! I was sitting on one of the sofas resting and found myself staring at this surprising, unexpected, beautiful apparition!

"Would you like to watch me dance?" she asked quietly. I nodded without speaking.

Juliet then began a wonderful, dreamy ballet repertoire she had been learning for exam time, and I could not take my eyes off her. The beauty of her form connected with all of the figures in the art books I had read avidly. Here was a 'real and moving' work of art, a new dimension in my mind. Art, dance and the human form are personified. We said nothing to each other, but there was no need in that magical atmosphere. I responded by taking off all of my own clothes automatically, slowly as she danced. It was what I wanted to do instinctively. When she elegantly finished her piece remaining in a long extended classical pose, revealing all of her long balletic lines, all of her stretched moist abdominal muscles, in that sunny room I knew something special was about to happen. Juliet slowly and elegantly returned to a *'port de bras'* ballet position, and she stood in front of me again. She showed no surprise at my tanned nakedness sitting there. Her long, dark, straight hair in damp locks caressed her shoulders. She then asked,

"Georgie, have you ever seen a girl naked? You know, with no clothes on?"

"Yeah, my sisters, but they just tell me to fuck off, but I'm not interested in them anyway." I replied.

She then simply and slowly bent down and took off, her knickers! Juliet was now also completely naked in front of me! Whether she did this because I'd gone one stage further to be completely naked first, I don't know; it was like a visual contract. She initially stripped as far as she'd dared, I suppose, keeping on her knickers to protect her modesty. As I had stripped completely naked, she saw this as my acceptance of the 'nakedness contract'! A rather sophisticated 'you show me yours and I'll show you mine' sort of thing! She was beautiful. It wasn't sexual for me; it was simply exciting. It felt completely natural to be naked with her.

It was the first time that I was conscious of being naked. It felt natural and wonderful. I suppose from that moment on it formulated in my mind that I did not equate nakedness with sex. I can gaze for hours at the naked female form in any medium of art and appreciate that I am excited, but it isn't first and foremost sexual excitement. It is an artistic appreciation of form, movement, and expression. I feel a need to talk about it, to write about it, and fundamentally to create stories through the imagery of the human form by observing it in detail.

"You can touch my tits if you want to," she said quietly and slowly.

This comparatively tall and slight brunette 15-year-old girl fascinated me, and I knew that something exciting was definitely about to happen! I really wanted to touch her tits! She then walked over to the rug and rolled it back out flat again with a few delicate, elegant balletic flicks of her feet, and then she lay down on it on her back. She looked at me.

"Go on, you can touch them if you want to," she said again quickly.

I didn't need any more encouragement, and I was distinctly aware that my cock was hard but had no idea why! Obviously, as a prepubescent boy I had no understanding nor inclination to fuck her. I had no idea that men and women did that for fun. Fucking was a mysterious thing boys sometimes mentioned at school a lot less than they would chat about cricket and 'Aussie Rules' footie! If anything, I was excited by this opportunity with Juliet; this felt overwhelmingly naughty, and that appealed to me mostly! So I kneeled down next to her and began to feel her small, delicate breasts. Her eyes were closed, but I noticed mostly how those tits felt completely different from how they looked. They were firm and even and warm yet ever so soft. I could detect Juliet's breathing through her nose becoming slightly louder and longer! This progressed to her suggesting I should suck her tits, and I did! I massaged one while sucking the other and then swapped over. I was beginning to get the hang of this! I caressed, kissed, and sucked those pert tits for goodness knows how long, and I was enchanted by how much pleasure she was showing through her body too.

This is how twice weekly, during that spring and summer, things carried on between us. The same thing happened in the same way each time in an unspoken process of quiet enthusiastic naughtiness. Juliet never once touched me sexually, but she did teach me how to kiss passionately. She taught me how to snog with tongues like in the movies! I loved it and I still love snogging today! I just loved the freedom of being naked, and I especially liked the feel of her skin on mine when I lay close enough to her for our thighs and torsos to touch and the times when I just lay on top of her as she hugged me! #MOTL.

One day, Juliet suggested I stroke her pubic hair. I did. I gently stroked it for quite a long time with my fingertips, and I noticed that she parted her legs wider as I did so. After a while, Juliet took hold of my hand and placed it in hers against her pussy and drew up her knees. Using my hand, she demonstrated how she would like me to 'cup' my hand over her pussy. She then demonstrated the speed and pressure of the touch she wanted until, as I eventually came to notice, she would begin to moan softly and place her fingers of one hand in her mouth and moan and breathe through her fingers. Her breathing became deeper until she would arch upwards, balancing herself onto her heels and shoulders, really arching her spine.

The first time she did this, I stopped what I was doing, thinking she was going to be sick or something. I'd stopped rubbing and looked at her in wonder, but she just told me to carry on and not to stop, so from then on, I didn't stop until she touched my hand again. After she had calmed down and became still, she would lie there, quivering and jerking, and that's when she suggested I lie on top of her. She would then hug me. This happened every time after the first time. We'd lie there until we felt it was time to get up and put our clothes back on. Juliet rarely spoke afterwards, but she always smiled at me, and she would touch me on my face and arms like she was fond of me. I loved every second.

Juliet had by default introduced me to the female orgasm! I knew that in ballet music could 'climax' but this was different! I had no idea about the female orgasm and no idea that other girls would react like Juliet. I thought that it was unique to her. As a small boy, I didn't think to transfer this knowledge to other girls. It was a secret, and I loved that! I did enjoy the pleasure of how I began to have control over her, eventually she didn't have to put my hand into hers to show me what to do. I also liked the buildup of her breathing and the little suppressed squeaks and squeals she made, and the deep panting rumble in her chest when she climaxed. Her wetness as I touched her intrigued me and in no way repelled me. I learned how to make Juliet 'cum.' I had no idea what it was! Juliet never once explained about her orgasms! Not that I'd have understood if she had.

It never struck me to tell anyone about our secret sessions. My sisters never found out. If they had, I'm pretty damn sure they would have blurted it out at every opportunity or at least told mum! It was special between Juliet and me. She never once told me not to tell anyone. She must have sensed that I was a discreet little fella. I had many secrets and lived out secret lives when playing on my own like most kids do. If Juliet had told any of her few friends that she might have had, I never found out, but I doubt she told anyone. On reflection, Juliet came across as a 'happy loner'. At our ballet school in town, she often left her class on her own and walked home. My class finished before Juliet's, but I had to wait for my sister's class to finish later on. She would say 'hi' to my mum as she walked past, and not once, did she accept a lift from my mum even though mum offered every time. Many of the other girls hung around waiting for their lifts home or gathered in little chatty groups to walk home together. Not Juliet. I never saw Juliet's mum pick her up to take her home either.

Juliet and I were never caught, but it came close one day. Oh, my word! On just one single occasion, her mum came home early. Juliet and I were naked together on the rug, and we were not aware her mum had arrived home much earlier than usual. We only realized when we heard her mum's car door slam shut! We didn't hear the car approaching on the rough, stoney driveway as we normally did after we had gotten dressed. On this occasion, Juliet was in one of her 'trances' and breathing hard, and I was obviously concentrating on her! I remember Juliet and I suddenly looking in horror at each other; her eyes were wide and watery when that car door slammed. Without a word she jumped up and she had her skirt and blouse back on in a jiffy.

She scooped up her socks, knickers and bra and stuffed them in her school bag, and as she was doing this, she simultaneously and quickly rolled up the rug with her foot and pushed it up against the fireplace to make it look like we had been doing ballet on the wooden floor. I was back in my clothes as quickly as you could crack a whip! We both plumped down on separate sofas opposite each other, literally five seconds before her mum walked into the room! Juliet's mum spoke straight away.

"Gudday, yous twos," she said in a jokey happy tone, "Crickey, Jules, you look hot and flushed, you want a drink? You been practicing ballet, you two?"

"Yeah, to both," replied Juliet, as cool as a cucumber. I spoke up too.

"Hello, Mrs Jay. Yes, we have. I'd love a drink," trying to sound as cool as Juliet.

Juliet stared at me with wide eyes! Juliet's mum had now walked out of the room, and we could hear her doing things nearby as she carried on talking, raising her voice so we could hear her.

"Hey Georgie, how are your mum and dad?" Juliet's mum shouted from another room.

"Bonzer!" I replied.

I looked at Juliet, who had by now laid down flat on her back on her sofa, holding the hem of her short school skirt down and straight between her legs. Juliet's mum continued, "Jules, you could have gotten you and Georgie a drink, you know; you should take more care of each other."

"Yeah, OK!" said Juliet, grinning at the ceiling.

Juliet and I eventually looked at each other shortly before she got up to leave the room to fetch the two cold drinks her mum had prepared for us. When she came back, she handed me one of the cold drinks. We started laughing into our drinks. Our bond had not been damaged one little bit! Juliet grabbed a cushion from her sofa as she sat down with her drink and pretended to throw the cushion at me in fun and then buried her face into it, obviously laughing with relief! All the time this was happening, I had noticed too that Juliet was indeed flushed, like her mum had commented. Her flush went from her cheeks down the nape of her neck in a clearly defined patch and also across the front of her breastbone that I could see. I knew her small breasts would be pinky-red because that's what happened to them with all the touching, squeezing, and sucking I gave them!

These experiences with Juliet need to be put into context. Was my time with Juliet child abuse? Some of you reading this might say so! What about asking the adult me now? Or asking me, the nine-year-old, that question? I wouldn't have understood as a boy. All I remember is that my feelings during those occasions with Juliet were delicious and exciting! I absolutely loved it. Did I feel uncomfortable in any way? No, I did not! I still don't! I certainly didn't feel abused, I felt privileged. Juliet and I never repeated our secret liaisons at any other times nor anywhere else during and after that spring and summer in her sitting room. She was also kind to me and fun at all times.

She was my special friend. We never discussed what we did in any way at any time, not then and not since. In my adult experience, 15-year-olds do not discuss anything with nine-year-olds, they are more likely to 'explain' things from their older perspective, but Juliet didn't do that either. We were both instinctively connected. In fact, we still are to this day, and we still do not discuss what we did on those occasions. We don't have to, we just know how we felt and feel still, and that secret is still ours. We were connected physically and spiritually without words. Juliet never forced me, and I never once felt coerced.

That spring and summer passed and our 'sessions' simply stopped. I wasn't upset nor jealous or anything. A nine-year-old boy lives in the moment every moment; well, I did. I didn't think of the future in any way apart from wanting to play cricket for Queensland and Australia and then be an astronaut! No one found out at the time about Juliet and me and I'm pretty sure that anyone who knows us doesn't know either. Am I damaged in any way? Not that I would think. I learned about the wonderful and beautiful female body. I learned about the exquisite feelings of private intimacy. Neither Juliet nor I became sexual predators. I have always formed healthy relationships with women, but I often wonder whether my adult sexual adventurousness could have something to do with my early sexual experiences with Juliet.

When I say 'adventurousness', it is more precisely defined as 'confidence'. I do not watch pornography; I never have and yet I am completely sexually uninhibited with the opposite sex as a heterosexual man. I have never gone out to 'pull' a woman in a bar and never gone out looking for nor expecting sex. In fact, all of my sexual experiences with women have come about because I have by default mixed with women in situations of common interest. 'Safe spaces' as they are called today. Women are more comfortably confident in environments in which they feel safe and in control. When you have a woman's confidence, and she feels safe, they become more daringly adventurous. That can develop over time but precisely at the moment of their choosing.

I grew up in a world where girls far outnumbered boys within the circles of interest I enjoyed. Mum and four older sisters, female dance and drama teachers, most schoolteachers, and the vast majority of other kids doing dance and drama were girls. My male childhood and teenage friends were a breed apart from me socially. By comparison they were crude, blunt and coarse toward girls, certainly when referring to girls when in the company of other boys. I disliked this intensely. I was never like that and with boys being emotionally dense they never discovered my uncomfortable feelings toward other boys' attitudes toward girls when growing up. Also, I was good at sports which I believe distracted other boys from bullying me about my ballet classes and mixing with girls. I did know that I would never grow up and become a typical 'blokey bloke'. My time with Juliet fermented and cemented that in my mind. I simply grew up adoring all women and enjoying being in their company, all of them, any age, with very few exceptions! #MOTL

Juliet and I were children together, that is for sure. Looking back, as I have done many times since those days, she was a lovely girl especially toward me. She was never nasty nor cruel (as my sisters were on many occasions, kids being kids). She was never coercive nor devious with me. She merely as I see it now, created an opportunity to explore her sexuality as her biological changes developed her sexual awareness. She indulged herself with someone she trusted and took full advantage of the situation and opportunities, not me as a person. I know now that my early sexual experiences with Juliet set me free from sexual inhibitions. I learned that sexual feelings were to be enjoyed in private between two consenting people. If I think about it now, I kind of instinctively thought that at the time, as a kid, that if you do things you enjoy, exciting things happen and grow from that! In my adult life I've been described as a slave to hedonism mainly by people who work 9-5 in offices day in, day out! The arts are by definition a complete mystery to them.

I have spent my life by default without planning, without objectives, pursuing and indulging myself in artistic creativity, my own and that of others. It has though been a priority for me, looking everywhere in every moment to find creativity even if this has resulted in me being a contrarian thinker and doer even under the pressure of immediate circumstances. As a result of that, coupled with the fact that I have worked in essentially female dominated environments I have unconsciously attracted those deep and wondrous creatures called women! They have been attracted to me for many reasons unfathomable for men! The nearest description if not definition of this phenomenon was spoken out loud by the late great actor Peter O'Toole…

"I've never looked for women. When I was a teenager perhaps, but they are looking for us, and we (men) must learn that very quickly. They decide. We just turn up. Never mind the superficialities, how tall and handsome and all that. Just turn up."

I didn't look for girls even as a teenager hence Peter's use of the word "perhaps." I have certainly *put myself out there* but not for the purpose of attracting women. Women though have more often than not been discreet pursuers of me. I would say that to "turn up" for me has been turning up within the right mutually safe and familiar places and environments in which women have felt comfortable and confident to release their doubts and inhibitions when choosing me! Juliet chose me. She eventually took up advanced training to become a ballet dancer and the world of ballet brought us together. (Juliet eventually became a senior soloist ballerina with two globally renowned ballet companies until injury brought her career as a performer to a halt).

Safe to say here, that my childhood clearly opened up a wonderfully creative world that most men cannot even imagine. The world that women occupy was for me opened up for me to enter without consciously knowing it. I was easily accepted and included. The misogynists in this world for whatever reason have at best only tapped into half of the creative world that is on offer, by becoming self-denied through prejudice and therefore separated from the female creative world on every level. (I will mention here that I too have been labeled a *misogynist* by a 4th generation feminist I had the misfortune to date for a while! That taught me a simple lesson… 'red flag' never again. What a creative drain she was. She was all about 'smash up', 'break it' and 'destruction', and she accused me of living in 'La La Land'! She was a 'shit dumper'!)

So let my *naked truths* move on a little. I lost my virginity when I was 15 years old to one of the female 17-year-old school prefects on a school trip. Her name was Alison or Ali as she was known. This part of the story is relevant to the previous couple of paragraphs above because she *chose me* on the very first evening of the trip during the very first evening meal in the dining room filled with 40 students. She, like everyone else, was away from her parents for the first time. The opportunity for her to spread her wings (or should I say legs) for seven whole days and nights was something she and most of her friends had probably planned, at least verbally. At that first meal, Ali was one of the prefects assigned by the teachers to be 'head of table' for the younger kids at the table. Each table sat 12 diners. I remember waiting for her to tell the rest of us sitting at the table, when to go up to the self-service counter to grab our tucker. I noticed Ali slowly gazing around at each and every one of us at the table. Then her eyes settled on mine, and she smiled, and I suddenly felt like she and I were alone in the room, like everyone had suddenly disappeared! I immediately felt that same excitement I had felt with Juliet; the first time since Juliet!

Ali, I suspect spent much of her time exploring the large sprawling venue buildings and had familiarized herself with all the potential private places which were out of bounds to the students! The first of those secret off-limits places played their part in a seven-day sexual journey with Ali that started within an hour of finishing the meal. We *escaped* together at every improvised opportunity and prearranged occasion to have sex. You'd think it would have been a tentative one-off fumble, but I clearly remember getting naked with Ali the instant we were safely and privately located in an unoccupied chalet, even cupboards and a flat roof! Ali took the lead, but I reenacted my time with Juliet in detail and then some! Except that I willingly and spontaneously ventured into giving Ali oral sex! I didn't know how long it should have taken but I really enjoyed it both from my perspective and her reactions. I ate her pussy using the kissing, licking, and sucking techniques Juliet had encouraged me to do with her breasts! I ate Ali's pussy for so long and so many times that the sides and the underneath of my tongue became sore! I was amazed to experience that Ali reacted in the same convulsive way as did Juliet in her excitement but also altogether differently! She sounded different, smelled and tasted differently, and climaxed differently. Women I gleaned on that trip were all the same and yet unique!

Ali became the lead on every occasion. Our secret code word between us to arrange sex together was for Ali to say to me, "What are you eating later?" to which I would reply quietly, "Your pussy," and she would then tell me when and where we were to meet! I first experienced penetrative sex with Ali after she deliciously sucked my cock and then straddled me; a position she told me was called *cowgirl*.

The exact moment she took hold of my cock as she straddled me and positioned me to enter her pussy lives in my memory indelibly! The tight yet luxurious gentle pressure/push/pop sliding into her, the warm wet texture of her pussy, the envelopment of my rock-hard cock overwhelmed my senses completely. She sat upright on me with her arms completely outstretched with her hands flat on my chest. She was looking upwards all the time, thrusting her pelvis forwards and backward slowly and hard. I could feel her pubic bone pressing against my own. I was completely inside her and I was as hard as concrete, harder than I'd been to that point! I automatically reached up and squeezed her tits and pulled on her nipples as she rode me. I can also remember pausing while doing this and she told me not to stop! So I carried on.

"Pull them really hard," she whispered, "you won't hurt me I promise."

Ali did all the fucking, occasionally I would thrust upwards compulsively to maintain my deep connection inside her. She climaxed differently compared to Juliet. Each time she grew into an increasingly faster frenzy, breathing deeply flexing the lips of her mouth into a 'w' shape whispering "shit, shit, shit, shit, shit" until the moment she flung herself forwards onto me, her tits, much larger than Juliet's, squashed onto my chest, and there was a hot gush of wetness flooding all over my groin area. She would wiggle her pelvis making long 'Mmmmm Mmmmm Mmmmm' sounds and I came inside her. I'm not saying we fucked for hours, and it might have been very quick, I just don't remember. I remember the sights, sounds, smell and feel of her with no reference to time at all. I do remember cumming inside her and carrying on thrusting into her as much as I could, remaining hard until I finally slipped out of her with a gush of wetness that blobbed out of her all over me! This was a thick hot wet feeling, contrasting against the cooling wetness from her *squirting* on me previously. My cock became so sensitive I was unable even to have any pressure on it! The hot wetness slowly dribbled around my balls over my asshole and onto the thin mattress when we used a bed. I'd discovered what I later learned is called the *wet patch*! I also found out very quickly that the extreme sensitivity of my cock after cumming passes and you can become hard again!

I'm glad that my first experience of sex was in the cowgirl position because it taught me a woman's pace. Of course, over the week we had sex in every position known to man and never once used a condom! It never dawned on me to ask her about condoms, but she did at one point tell me she was *on the pill*. For me sex wasn't solely physical nor a physical need. It was and still is a delicious and exquisite seeing, hearing, touching, tasting, and listening experience. All five senses interplay to create through a sixth sense, a work of sexual art that for me is created and remembered with intense clarity.

Chapter Four

Moving to the UK, performing arts and life modeling begins

At the age of 18 I finished my school education when I passed my subjects for the Queensland 'Senior Certificate' (now the QCE, Queensland Certificate of Education) which is equivalent to 'A Levels' in the UK. To be honest I've lost touch with what exams exist now. I didn't exactly hate school but leaving was certainly a feeling of *'I'm free'* for me and I left school not just physically but completely, mentally and spiritually. During my final two years of school, I'd kept up with ballet after passing my Advanced Level Two ballet qualifications by the time I was 16 years old. Quite an achievement I was told.

I spent nearly two years working with dad on the cattle stations living an 'outback' lifestyle which I utterly enjoyed, but with dad's words in my ears I felt like I was treading water in a bygone era. At 20 the opportunity to travel to the UK and stay with friends and or relatives was the next step. I had a choice, to stay with relatives in the north of England or with friends of one of my sisters in London. Having a gap year before returning to Australia was very appealing. Little did I know that a 'gap year' was about to become a 'new life, new country' for me! By the age of 16 I began to sense that I wanted to earn my living in the performing arts but in small-town outback Australia the opportunities were limited to say the least!

As with many Australians in their late teens and 20s, it is almost traditional to fly off to the UK, find a part-time job, become settled within that enticing and fascinating young and temporary expat way of life and use the UK as a base to travel around Europe. The opportunity to visit the capitals of Europe like Berlin, Paris, Barcelona, the Greek Islands and Rome were the top destinations on every young Aussie's bucket list. The feeling of freedom and expanding your life becomes imbued in your Aussie soul as you approach the age of 18.

Some go backpacking, taking trains and some buy a cheap campervan to travel around the European mainland in the hotter European northern hemisphere months from March through to the end of September. There seems to be a constant conveyor belt of Aussie youngsters into London; as some leave to go back home or beyond, others arrive maintaining a kind of 'production line' of contacts. Friendships are often established well before actually meeting up in London. Modern communications have made that even more possible with websites and Facebook communities.

The Aussie penchant for gregarious networking is legendary. In my case my sister, Amy, who had already completed her European walkabout and returned to Aus, let me know that two of her Uni friends were staying in a flat in London for a year while working there. The flat was 'south of the river' in what was then a very unfashionable part of London called Stockwell. The advantage of Stockwell however was that rents were cheap, and it borders the vibrant Brixton. Many Aussies lived in the area at the time in and around Clapham, Streatham, Tooting Bec and Wandsworth. Of course, traditionally gay Australians had gravitated to Earls Court but for me to have a place to go to, a place to sleep and branch out from, was just what I needed.

I had no interest in traveling around Europe or working in a bar. I wanted to find every opportunity to perform on stage and London was and is famous for its West End theaters and productions. I felt pretty confident I could wangle my way into auditions for stage musicals based on my ballet qualifications and experience and hopefully at some point find myself in a show! Also, I had the added bonus of having 'dual nationality'. In other words, an Australian passport, and a UK passport. This then introduces my dad. Dad was English, born and brought up in the north of England and then took the opportunity to move to Queensland as a young man to work on the cattle stations in the Gulf Country. He became a very successful stockman and cattle breeder and eventually sold up his business and moved out with mum to Perth in Western Australia where they lived out their contented retirement.

My dad was a wonderful man. He always encouraged me in my interests and also took an interest in me personally. Being the only boy in the family I felt no paternal pressure to become a caricature of the hard drinking outback Aussie male. He was warm and solid in my life, and I spent many happy extended days working with him outdoors, learning to ride horses and corral the cattle for branding and slaughtering for example. I spent many nights under the stars on the massive cattle stations learning by osmosis the Aussie Outback way of life, an understanding of the flora and fauna and that developing indelible Aussie character for teamwork, self-confidence, and self-reliance in the face of adversity as well as an indestructible sense of humor.

On the day of my departure to the UK my dad approached me as I chucked my backpack into the back of mum's ute and he put his hand on my shoulder. He half turned to shield us both from the others waiting to wave me off and pushed his fist into my hand and passed me a roll of cash, $3000 Aussie dollars! A lot of dosh in those days and then he said to me,

"Take this George, it'll get you started. I'm very proud of you. I always knew you'd earn your living far easier than it has been for me but like me you'll earn a living doing what you love the most."

This made a huge impression on me. My dad was a man of few words and not at all tactile except that we'd always shake hands, and I'd kiss him on the cheek whenever there was an unspoken need to bond together such as when he traveled away or I started something new or achieved something. He is the only man I ever kissed. There was never any fuss but on special occasions I'd look up and there was dad with his hand out and a grin on his face and a little imperceptible wink of his left eye. It brings tears to my eyes as I type this. God knows I love my parents! This was a special thing I had with dad, and it was manly and connecting between us. Over the years I have often thought about that day and that special moment between dad and me. It became clear to me that dad knew in his head and in his heart that I'd be leaving Australia for more than a 'gap year'. Dad kept this from mum; I know that now. Whereas mum was the emotional loving parent, dad was the loving quiet parent who looked deeper than emotions to understand people. When I grew up, he repeated the same advice whenever I needed reminding until it took hold and its relevance to my life has pervaded my soul!

"Never make decisions based on emotions. Let your emotions calm down however long that takes and let them percolate into ideas. Then act on the ideas. And never forget that men of principle are but one short step from hypocrisy." Thanks dad x.

I hugged everyone and my mum drove me into town to take the bus to travel the 1800 km (about 1200 miles) to Brisbane to fly via Singapore to London. Why did I take the bus to Brisbane and travel for almost 24 hours? The reason for that is that there was a train, but it would have taken nearly two days to travel to Brisbane by train with long waiting connections! Europeans have no concept of the distances and time that we Aussies accept and understand, that's for sure! I was sad to say cheerio to everyone but as an independent spirited young fella I was extremely excited too. Also, I knew I had the support of a loving family and both mum and dad made it clear to all of us kids that we were always to do our best and have a go at everything in life. If we fucked up then just come home, reorganize and go off and try again. This implicit support and knowledge of their love has provided me with an incredible level of confidence on many levels. Like I mentioned above I was self-confident and self-aware. I wasn't conceited to think I didn't need the support of others but here again my Aussie upbringing and its approach to making good friends and connections with people far and wide was a natural resource that came easily to me as with many Aussies.

So I flew to the United Kingdom of Great Britain and Northern Ireland known as the UK. I arrived at Heathrow Airport and took 'The Drain' on the 'Waterloo & City Line' an overland/underground train from Heathrow to 'Bank' tube station in the City of London financial district. I waited by two large statues on the square adjacent to the Bank of England and waited for Debbie. Debbie was my sister Amy's Uni friend who I would be staying with in Stockwell. Debbie was dressed for her 'temp' job at one of the city stockbrokers in a pinstripe jacket and pencil skirt and sneakers! She looked amazing and oozed confidence. She had her high heels in a shoulder bag.

She had that fresh hair-tossing blonde Aussie girl attitude about her (unlike the stiff self-conscious wary Pommie girls I was to become familiar with) Although we'd never actually met there was an instant and long-lasting friendship created between us. Yeah we'd chatted over Skype a few times but there was little organization between us, just the date of my arrival, meet up and go to the flat to drop off my stuff and meet Janie her Aussie flat mate and then go to the pub!

I settled in very quickly taking up the tiny box room in the flat and began to explore London. I started this by buying 'The Stage' magazine and looking for opportunities to audition for shows. I'd also joined 'Spotlight' for professional performers and within a few weeks of being in London I had even secured an 'Agent' who would put me forward for auditions. I was under no illusions about finding performing arts work quickly but my savings and the money dad gave me provided me with a financial buffer for a couple of months at least. It was the month of May in London and therefore leading into summer there. The longer daylight hours plus the evening twilight seemed to offer and tempt me into exploring the artworks of this great city.

The overriding eagerness within me was to explore the art galleries of London, all of them, large and small, famous, and esoteric. As I explored them on almost a daily basis to begin with, I gathered information about art exhibitions, when and where they would be held and made detailed notes to attend, by fair means or foul! This is how I met Ellie who I mentioned earlier. Ellie was and is an established professional figurative impressionist artist with her own studio in north London as I was to discover.

As a budding West End performer or at this early stage as a West End wannabee I ended up grabbing cheap seat bargains on Tuesday evenings and matinees 'in the gods' at many West End theaters. The importance of this was making contact with people in the bar beforehand and during the intervals. I always seek to soak up an atmosphere wherever I am, and this often means I turn up really early and leave late. I try not to be part of crushes and rushes! By doing this I ended up chatting to bar staff and front of house staff at the theaters who were happy to engage before the rush started. I learned from them where they all went after the shows for a drink, and this meant that members of the cast also went along for after show drinks and a chin wag. Over a short period of time, I learned where actors and dancers would hang out during the day before shows and where they would gather when 'resting'.

'Resting' is that name performers give to the time when they aren't working! Although I enjoyed meeting up, I was and never have been much of a drinker! By that I mean that my taste for alcoholic drinks and their close links to social situations has never appealed to me. Quite why an Australian bloke doesn't like alcohol is beyond the comprehension of most people, especially other Aussie blokes. However, my parents were non-drinkers and socializing for men tended to be bingeing on weak beer after long periods of work on the cattle stations. In the climate I grew up in, the most memorable drinks for me were warm water out of bottles and canteens, and copious brews of tea! The long and short of this meant that I was never in tune with social gatherings in London with other performers because of their bias toward drinking alcohol. Parties for example are great places to meet people and dance to music but for me the alcohol played no part. A party without music and dancing for me is social purgatory! This had the added effect of encouraging me to concentrate my free time on the London art venues as opposed to sitting around in cafes, peoples' kitchens and bars boozing on alcohol!

Of course, I love theater buildings for what they promise but for me theaters only come alive when people are in them. They become magical places of smells, deadened sounds, colors, darkness, and light. Exciting places full of anticipation and expectation for visitors. However, when they are empty, they can feel cold and comatose! Just strange and attractive buildings waiting to be woken up by people rather like an anthill requires ants! Art galleries on the other hand are alive constantly, made so by the art. They do not need people. For me, a busy art gallery is not something I like! You can be completely on your own in an art gallery and it is alive. A busy art gallery suppresses the artistic atmosphere for me, and I prefer to be in a gallery at a quiet time, especially when there's a transport strike in London! Whereas I would rather be in a theater as a performer or as an audience member when it is a full house!

The art galleries of London were for me like Aladdin's Caves of wonder and exploration. So many of them, with established collections and regular exhibitions. The National Gallery, Tate Britain, Saatchi Gallery, The Courtauld Gallery, The V&A, Gagosian, The Tate Modern the list is endless as I spent whole days in them many times and I still do. I built my imagination from the artworks. Artworks I had seen and read about from being a child were there right in front of me and I was in creative heaven. A whole new world of artworks I never knew existed were hung alongside those I knew about and opened up a whole new world of costume, jewelry, ceramics, works of art in the genres of expressionism, impressionism, abstract but the works of art that attracted me and inspired me most were, figurative. This is still the case today!

The female artist Ellie happened to be in 'The Tanks' gallery at The Tate Modern one wet and windy midweek day at the same time as I was there, on my own as usual. She was with a small group of six friends and acquaintances, all art lovers. I hadn't noticed them. I can imagine that I was moving around in front of the art as is my habit. One reason I attend galleries when it is quiet is so that I can channel my thoughts into movement. I feel not only the flow of the art but also the art creates its own stories in my mind, especially figurative art and my body automatically begins to flow. I move and express the feelings and ideas in my mind, a kind of outward expression of an inner dance.

Feelings create ideas, creating action! The basic building block of my life. Unbeknown to me Ellie would later tell me that I was conspicuous to her and her group because I was slowly and expressively pacing in front of a work of art hanging there before me. Unfortunately, I cannot remember which work of art it was. It might have been an art installation. Ellie and her arty friends saw me and apparently were transfixed by my expressive movement as though dancing with the art that I was engrossed in. She approached me from where I couldn't see her, and she excused herself and spoke to me after gently tapping me on my shoulder!

Ellie was dressed in a loose smock top with an unfastened waistcoat on top of this. She had on skinny jeans and tattered black leather ankle boots with no laces. Her smock and boots were spattered with drops of paint. Her hair hung loose, and she wore no makeup. Smiling at me she looked to be about 50 years old with friendly eyes. She smelled of what I was to learn was a combination of 'patchouli oil' and oil paint. I learned this after spending many hours one-to-one modeling for Ellie in her own art studio.

"Hello, I hope you don't mind me disturbing you" she said immediately "but my friends and I noticed your unique method of studying art, you almost dance with it so we are intrigued. Can I introduce myself? My name's Ellie,"

"Crikey, er yes, I'm George, you made me jump!" I said matching her friendly confident tone.

I instinctively walked with her toward her small group of friends, and all appeared immediately friendly. Ellie introduced me and I shook hands with all of them in turn. All were female.

"Hello, nice to meet you all, I'm George," I replied. It was that simple, totally natural.

"Are you an artist because I'm pretty sure I have seen you before more than once?" Ellie questioned politely, slowly, and gently rubbing her chin.

It was at this point I noticed Ellie's hands were overly large in comparison to her skinny figure and her fingertips were flat like little spoons and her fingernails dark.

"Er no I'm not an artist as in a painter or anything, I'm a dancer!" I stumbled trying to find where I fit into this encounter.

There was a murmur of approval and Ellie clasped her hands together and said.

"Now that explains how you move! We were watching you immerse yourself in the art and it is certainly a unique style… to us anyway" she said smiling. "Would you like to join us for a wander here and perhaps coffee and cake later?"

"Er yes, of course, I'd love to, are you all artists?"

This caused the group to laugh and one of the other women in the group said,

"No, only Ellie is the artist, she's a pro, we are all just lovers of art in awe of her work!"

At this point I relaxed and enjoyed a wonderful appreciative and knowledgeable tour of the gallery with Ellie beautifully describing the works, from its probable construct to themes and expounding her in depth knowledge of the artists and artworks. We all spent a very relaxed hour before heading to the coffee shop where two of the women in the group scribbled down what each of us wanted and headed off to buy the drinks and cakes.

Over the course of the refreshments most of the talking involved me answering the questions from the group, starting with their noticing my accent, and talking about my background, my dancing, and ambitions. Fortunately for me my love of art created a strong bond with the group, and it was at this point Ellie touched my arm and surreptitiously said,

"I might have a useful proposition for you!" I was intrigued.

We segwayed nicely into her asking me if I had ever done any life modeling! I told her I hadn't and the whole group then confessed to being a life drawing group tutored by Ellie. The group were genuinely lovely creative people and thoroughly civilized and relaxed so we naturally explored in detail what it would entail for me to become an actual life model for them. It would be one afternoon and one evening every fortnight for which I would be paid handsomely! The group used the word 'sitting' as the term for a life model 'in action' which slightly alarmed me as I prefer to be on my feet! Ellie explained that was just a term of reference. The whole idea would be for me to model as a dancer and mostly in standing dance poses. She wanted me to take the initiative, to show them something new, challenging them and pushing them into discovery. Thank goodness! Ellie and I agreed to email each other to arrange a series of Wednesday mornings over the next month at her studio to model for her one-to-one!

We also penciled in an afternoon date for me to be a life model for the whole group at the home of a lady called Valerie the following month. Valerie was one of the ladies of Ellie's group of artist friends whose home was located in Pimlico, London. Valerie wasn't present that day, but she was mentioned often and therefore seemed to be an intrinsic part of this amazing group of diverse women artists. So it all began. My life modeling life began right there as well as a lifelong friendship and working relationship with the wonderful Ellie and an extension of this was an exciting 'collaboration' with the beautiful Valerie! #MOTL

Before I enter into my first time as a life model in front of a group, I think I should attempt to define what life modeling is for you. I don't want to get into an academic debate and explore it in minute detail so I will merely say this. It involves being completely naked and becoming completely still by adopting various poses for various lengths of time while artists of all calibers sketch, draw or paint you. You are paid good money as a model and for an out of work newcomer wannabee performer in the UK the money was excellent. As the book progresses, more detail will emerge where relevant rather than bore you here with details.

The venues for life drawing are numerous and in my experience this has entailed modeling in art galleries, museums, theaters, concert halls, church halls, community centers, stately homes, upstairs in pubs, as well as in private homes even outside in the fresh air! The sizes of the groups vary enormously from groups of up to studio theater size of 100 artists at one extreme although rare at this size, down to one-on-one modeling for artists. The usual size is between six and 20 artists. Poses taken up by the model also varies in length of time. Warm up poses can be anything between two to 10 minutes followed by longer poses of 15 to 60 minutes and in some cases much longer.

The longer poses are usually undertaken sitting or lying down but, in my case, my 'unique selling point' is the standing pose. This is because I am a trained dancer, and my muscular skeletal development means that I engage all the strong groups of muscles in the upright standing position which means I do not tire as most people would. In short, I am more comfortable and also more artistically creative as a model being on my feet. In a sitting or lying position I find that my joints, ligaments and tendons take the strain, and my muscles become so relaxed that my weight is transferred away from muscle groups into the ligaments and tendons and my joints begin to ache and become painful! Also, if I sit in a chair I become as interesting as a carrot in a cup!

Chapter Five

The Pimlico Set & Meeting Valerie

I emerged from Pimlico underground tube station with the directions to Valerie's home written on a scrap of paper. It was a warm fresh morning contrasting with the stale atmosphere of the Victoria Line underground. I was taken aback by the beautiful parallel lines of the white-walled three-story town houses with street side black railings and gates. Steps led up to elegant black front doors and each had steps down to converted coal cellars. I thought these houses looked 'Regency' and 'terribly posh' but left it at that. I was excited and a little nervous about my first life modeling gig. Some of these townhouses had been converted into apartments judging by the vertical rows of door intercom buttons. However, on finding Valerie's address it was clear it was still a complete house, all three floors and cellar. I did not know then that I would be spending many days and nights over the years at this wonderful London home and not just for life modeling!

The gate at the front of her home was open, inviting me to ascend the steps to the front door where I gave the ornate brass door knocker three firm but polite rattles. I'd arrived early as is my habit for any gig, meeting, audition or simple appointment. My reason for this is to familiarize myself with the location and importantly to absorb 'the feel' of the building outside and inside. This minimizes any chance of being surprised by anything that could affect my train of thought and spirit. I never have expectations in life because working in the performing arts, experience has shown me that expectations always lead to disappointments. Disappointments do occur regardless I suppose but it is best to reduce the surprise of them at least. Disappointments can seriously affect your creativity, and I've found out that arriving early even at places where I am familiar gives me that precious thing called time. Time allows me to interrupt any negative thoughts and readjust my mind into positivity and creativity. I'm constantly reminded in any situation that surprises me, the words of the great Sir Michael Caine…

"Use the difficulty!" but I digress!

The front door opened slowly and for a brief moment I imagined I'd see a butler or servant! Us Aussies still have a distinct image of posh upper-class Poms! After knocking I had retreated back down a step so as not to appear rude. However, right there standing slightly above me from my position was an extremely elegant woman I guessed to be in her early to mid-forties. She had dark auburn hair cut into a thick blunt cut bob, level with her sharp chin. Her eyes were a dazzling green and very friendly.

"Oh hello!" she said, sounding confident and sweet. I knew I had the right address. "You must be Georgie, our life model, I'm Valerie, come in, great to see you arrived looking fresh and so early too!" She added, laughing.

I think I had caught her by surprise!

"Hi, yes, I'm your model and at the right address obviously," I replied slightly nervously!

Valerie tilted her head playfully and raised her eyebrows and pursed her lips. I noticed she had little fine lines around her mouth when she did this. She then placed both hands on her hips and I instinctively thought that this older woman was flirting with me and confirmed that in my mind when she said.

"Hmmm, the right address for the right man I see!"

I didn't consciously flirt back with her as this was the first time I'd met her, and she was in the safety of her own home. I didn't want to appear cocky or nervous either.

"We haven't met, as in not with Ellie and her art group at 'The Tanks' but she has mentioned you. Glad to meet you" I replied.

"No, we haven't and no I wasn't, but she's mentioned you too" she continued in playful tones. "Actually, I've heard a lot about you from the others, quite perfect methinks," and she laughed a delightful tight-lipped 'huh huh huh' down her small pointed attractive nose in a low sexy tone!

Now I knew she was flirting with me, and I was still standing on the steps, and I hadn't even stepped inside yet! She stood there looking at me and now holding the open door with her left hand. Her left arm was bent at the elbow, hand at eye level, her right arm now hanging loosely by her side. Her body language was confident and inviting. She began to move backward and sideways slowly and then beckoned me courteously with a welcoming wave of her right hand. There was definitely a feeling of friendly informality between us, and I felt relaxed. 'Don't blow it,' I thought, 'Slowly slowly, now and use your silence, let her do the talking' and I continued to think 'in the moment'.

During the first couple of minutes, I had time to take in the intriguing vision of the lovely Valerie. She was dressed in slightly faded Levi 501s, well-fitting and they hugged rather than gripped her slim legs. They were faded in a natural way not 'distressed' giving her a cool look as opposed to juvenile. Her slim thighs were highlighted by what I have always appreciated as an instant sexual attraction for me; her 'thigh space'! It was two-fingers wide' and she was slim not skinny, she had trim curved inner thighs and strong defined quadriceps muscles. This woman obviously exercised on a regular basis. The faded creases of the 501s at her crotch angled deliciously diagonally upwards gesturing to that intoxicating thigh space!

In her belt loops was a wide brown simple leather belt highlighting more than a hint of deliciously toned skin above the waistband of the low-rise style of her jeans. The fishtails of a cream colored waistcoat (vest) rested atop just touching her belt buckle. It was cut away tailored in a feminine style at the shoulders to reveal her delicate square shoulders and deltoid muscles and neat lean collar bones. There was obviously not enough coverage to hide the shoulder straps of a bra, and the fashioned cut of the waistcoat contoured her breasts providing support there. It was in a traditional button-down style, and I noticed that the lowest button of the fishtail front was fastened but the cut curved upwards and away revealing two inches of her belly flesh and the tops of her pelvic bones. This band of flesh stirred my loins!

I remember thinking she had trodden a deliberate fine line between being brazenly sexual and demurely proud of her body. The healthy color of her skin, its tone and firmness highlighted her healthiness and quiet confidence. She was definitely 'gym-fit' and it was easy for me to imagine her defined abdominal midline. I discreetly glanced at her body at every opportunity, taking in her movements which in turn revealed gently undulating feminine oblique abdominal muscles above her belt.

I got the impression she intended me to look at her and she provided me, purposely, with many opportunities to do so by looking away from me in an exaggerated way for me so I could take in as much of her as I could without her 'catching me looking'! Her visible pelvic bones were alluring. The low-rise nature of her 501s had the effect of dragging my eyes there constantly. They were pronounced not jutting, sharp and covered with a serpent-like moving skin as she languidly walked.

This twin pairing of obliques and pelvic bones was the sign of a physically healthy woman with a healthy diet and exercise routine. The only 'excess' this classy, sexy middle-aged woman projected was the subtlety of her conscious, poignant aforethought to attract me to her. What made her behave this way? Or should I ask 'who made her behave this way' I thought? Yes of course, Ellie! What made her think she'd be attracted to me, a much younger man? She was obviously 20 years older than me, I thought! QED, Ellie, and Valerie were in cahoots most definitely! Valerie exuded natural self-confidence, and all added up to her having made preparations and plans. I remained quiet!

"Come on, come on, come in my friend," she said standing aside and gesturing again, and up I stepped and entered.

As I drew level with her, she popped out an arm as I cleared the doorway to stop me. I came to a slow stop, and she closed the door with an expert push which gave off a tight-fitting hiss and thump as it shut. The door latch clicked. She then stepped in front of me gently touching my arm with her outstretched hand and said,

"Follow me if you dare… wah ha ha!" mimicking a pantomime baddie and walked away leading me. I laughed and replied,

… "lady of the manor, I am but at your service," joining in the playful scene that she had set. She was creating the vibe, and I wasn't about to change it!

"By the way, you can call me Val. Val by name, value by nature?" she added laughing again.

Val had a wonderful skillful habit of informing and instructing by speaking in questioning sentences. This had the effect of creating a light mood, a hint of playfulness and a clarity of intent. Val knew exactly what she was doing. It wasn't rehearsed but she definitely had a 'loose script' to work from judging so far from her choice of clothing to her flexible humorous dialogue. So I played the same 'questioning' conversation starters…

"I hope I prove to be of creative value to you all?" I said, Val laughed out loud.

"If not the others, I can already see what a unique bargain you are going to be?" she answered with an Australian questioning intonation.

I learned later she spoke this way to rib me playfully about my Aussie accent. I was to inform her that such intonations were evocative of working-class

Australians, but even though she'd guessed the right class for me, she had no conception of the slow north Queensland accent where we tend to speak slowly and usually end a sentence with a downward intonation. It's always entertained us over the years.

This was all part of Val's playful personality, she never changed. At this stage, meeting her for the first time I was not about to say anything to alter her 'mood setting' and typically played my part and most definitely a heterosexual part at that! As she walked in front of me down that long well-lit deep hallway deep into the house it became obvious to me, she wanted to give me the opportunity to 'check out her ass'! She walked slowly and gracefully.

There was not a hint of arrogance about Val. She was genuinely interested in other people more than she was about herself. I digress! Indeed, her ass was worth showing off! Firm and small… wow! Her gait was that of a dancer, a slight turn out of her feet and a gentle sway of her hips. Light on her feet with a firm upright posture her 501s waistband rested effortlessly on her flesh not hugging or pinching and the litheness of her moving flesh above her belt, gently oscillated.

Looking at her from behind, the gap between her belt and the bottom horizontal seam of her waistcoat revealed enough flesh to tell me she had a delicate spinal recess and toned erector muscles, and it was also evident she had firm upper glutes! Her spinal recess made a finger-sized vertical space under the waistband of her 501s, an enticing little tunnel to her coccyx and further down to her ass cleavage. All of this movement and her carefully chosen clothes had the desired visual and erotic effect on me!

Val's ass was heart-shaped. You know 'a heart' the right way up! Not inverted like an upside-down heart, like the asses that modern 'booty' women create! At that moment, Val seemed to me to be a dancer, an athlete or something else which by default had given her a great foundation for her body. Val's body was a consequence of her lifestyle, like all bodies, good or bad. Every person's body is a result of what they do and what they eat but there's a subtle difference going on for some people. For example, for a woman to sculpt herself to resemble the body of a ballerina, or that of a female athlete she needs to devote the same huge amount of time to that end which is a full-time job. The body changes to adapt to the discipline, but the body shape is created by default.

As a professional dancer, body shape is not the primary objective, it's the love of your chosen discipline that creates it. Val certainly never had a body obsession; she had an underlying reason why she looked this good! #MOTL. Val and I both had bodies that had emerged from a discipline that was in no way driven by vanity!

I also took my visual opportunities while absorbing her body to ask Val about herself as we entered her huge naturally lit modern kitchen at the back of her house. It had a dining space and huge 'island' feature adding a modern touch to this homely townhouse.

"Are you a trained dancer by any chance?" I asked her while standing behind her looking at her.

"No, not trained, but I do love to dance, why'd you ask?" she said as she spun herself around with her arms out wide in a balletic 'demi seconde' position in tune with her humor.

It was her attempt to show me she knew I was a ballet dancer and that she knew a bit about ballet. By now I just could not stop smiling and I could feel my inner glow of sexual anticipation, exactly the same that I had had with Juliet and Alison and also with Issa, my current girlfriend! These were, and are still, special moments for me, the seeds of something special. This whole situation was set up by Val and it was left to me to fuck it up and I wasn't going to do that!

"Well, it's evident that you have the body of a dancer" I continued.

"What makes you say that?" Val asked with her green eyes sparkling.

I knew she was pleased I'd noticed her and that I'd brought up the subject.

"Just keep up the compliments please Mr. Harman!" she said laughing at the same time.

She knew my surname and continued flirting with me and I wondered how to reply,

"Because you have more than just a hot body…" I paused, "you have a dancer's poise and their playful chat." I said this knowing full well that not all dancers have a playful way of chatting!

Val was getting to me! I was starting to gabble. 'Resort to the power of silence' I thought, 'don't try to dig yourself out of this'!

"Well, Georgie, I've invited you into my lair, into my space so to speak, *where the living is eas*y" she said singing the five words from 'Summertime,' Porgy & Bess!

'Nice touch' I thought, smiling now, giving Val the lead, 'she must lead this vibe, it's her scene, don't steal it' I thought again! Val was a very cool lady, she'd be great on stage, she'd detected my growing awkwardness and came to my rescue. She instantly rebuilt the slow sexual momentum between us. She'd encouraged my confidence again by showing her continued attraction to me by soothing me. Her intelligent humor was meant for me to gain a rapid feel for her personality, she conveyed this restoring and encouraging my pace. It was like she had already accepted me, and she was saying 'you are good, Georgie, you are doing just fine!'

"And no, as I said I'm not a trained dancer, but I am a woman in a fortunate position to have a personal trainer…" Val continued.

I glanced playfully all over her body with professional approval. I really wanted to touch this amazing woman.

"Only two days a week, otherwise it's overkill for my spare time. Twice more each week I use a boutique gym not far from here, I have a key, and I can use it 24/7/365 if I want to, so it fits in with my busy ever-changing diary." Val looked around the kitchen as she said this, obviously aware of me gazing at her and I noticed her modest pride that I was.

"Well, whatever you are doing keep doing it" I replied very slowly hoping I didn't sound creepy! It did feel like a lame platitude, so I added.

"Genuinely, you look amazing."

"Not bad for 55, eh?" she added, smoothing her hands down her ribcage and hips wiggling them in a fun way.

She wasn't looking for compliments, more like she was assessing my reaction. I suddenly realized she wanted to be honest with me and find out whether I would still be attracted to a woman of her age! I repeat again, this woman had not a hint of vanity about her.

"55!" I quietly exclaimed in a soft tone.

I didn't want to go over the top, I just wanted to match Val's vibe.

"I'd put you at 45 absolute tops!" I added and meant it sincerely. I checked her expression as I said this to see if I'd disappointed her with my '10-year discount'!

Val just grinned at me and waved a hand at me in a downward motion playfully dismissing me.

"Well, I hit the dreaded perimenopause at 45 and I wasn't about to let my body go pear-shaped and watch my bum go south. I hadn't really paid much attention to exercise until then. My diet was always good but I read as much as I could about the mental and physical effects of menopause, so I started finding a routine at a gym, took lessons and instruction, had an evolving plan made to measure for me and began to see menopause as a new change of direction not 'the beginning of the end'."

Val smiled at me without any embarrassment, her confidence to be so revealing about herself actually turned me on. She then turned and walked over to the kettle to put water in it.

"Tea or coffee?" she asked, dangling the kettle with four fingers, her palm up.

"Oh, er tea please," I replied.

"Good choice, any preference?" she asked.

"Strong, very strong with lots of milk," I answered, "Two sugars, though, please."

Val laughed and said, "I was thinking about whether you wanted Assam, Darjeeling, Earl Grey, lapsang souchong" she giggled "aww I'm teasing your delicious Aussieness, very strong with lots of milk it is then and two sugars, do I have any!" She smiled and began to fill the kettle with water.

"Yeah, just a strong brew for me, Val," I said asserting my masculinity by using her name for the first time. I sensed that she liked that.

"I adore your lack of formality really you know" she said busying herself with tea caddies and a spoon and a teapot almost like a ritual she had forgotten, she looked in a bit of a tizz!

I had no idea why she said that or why she looked a little distracted, but I couldn't take my eyes off her, the way she moved and god, I desired her. After sorting the tea preparation and switching on the kettle some distance away from where I was standing, there was a natural silent pause between us. Then she started speaking again, the pause had had no effect on her revealing train of thought.

"At 55 my mum was diagnosed with early-stage dementia, so when I reached 50 I decided the time was right to do everything in my power to delay or even prevent that for me so I dropped alcohol and began serious training with my personal trainer. I cut out all obvious carbohydrates from my diet except organic brown rice when my body tells me it needs a boost and over the years… my body became this."

She let her hands rise and fall to present her body shape to me. She then did a polite imitation of a curtsy and we both laughed.

I wanted to take Valerie in my arms but stopped myself obviously. I understood now that she had a purpose in life and not unlike professional dancers her body was indeed the result of a dedication to a higher purpose rather than modern-day vanity. She was effectively living under a cloud of debilitating chronic neurological illness that could begin to strike at any time. Her life was about living it to the full and exercising and eating to enable that. Val was gentle and generous to herself and as I got to know her, she was the same with other significant people in her life. Val poured the tea for both of us in lovely white enameled mugs.

"So to cap it all off I took early retirement from my job at 50 and set out to expand my life ensuring I exercised my brain along with my body," she said, and smiled deeply into my eyes.

Her reference to mind and body had a clear message for me, she might have intended it. I sensed she was telling me she knew what she wanted, and she wasn't going to waste time getting it! Val clearly intended for me to know that I definitely had a place in her life if I so chose but I instinctively knew there was more to come in terms of explanation. So I adjusted to my default of 'anticipation junkie' mode! I nearly said that I'd love to be a part of her life but easily stopped myself from such a juvenile comment. I simply allowed the stillness and silence between us to remain until my smile revealed what I was thinking.

"I get it! I have the same approach." I replied, softly.

Valerie had brought my mug of tea over to me and then retreated a distance from me allowing me to see her full length while she sipped her tea with both hands. When she had entered my personal space to hand me my tea, there was a definite intimacy there between us. From where I stood looking at her now, I noticed her footwear for the first time. She was wearing white ankle-high tennis shoes, and I also noticed they were 'Stan Smith Adidas,' the Australian tennis player. Nice touch! The logo was green, and this subtly matched her green eyes! Everything about her attracted me. This lady had no need to stretch her legs in high heels at this time of day!

"You sound like there's some Scottish in your accent" I said, in keeping with the calm mood between us.

"Yes indeed, Dundee on the east coast, do you know it?" Val asked.

I shook my head, and we smiled at each other. I hoped my face said the one thing unrelated to Dundee! I didn't want to talk about Dundee! I wanted her to keep talking though, I felt so happy! Val hesitated for the first time, and I sensed she might be considering a change in direction in our conversation. Her eyes gave this away. Had she chosen to miss an opportunity to extend our familiarity at this stage or did she detect that we would descend into small talk? I didn't want small talk to take over one bit. This could have become an awkward moment for us. It was probably because soon we would be joined by Ellie and the art group which would interrupt our obvious flow. Maybe she thought it would be difficult to find it again. I decided to see how she would handle this. I wanted Valerie, I was now confident she wanted me too. If she couldn't find a way to reestablish our connection after the life drawing was over, then I would not just indicate my desire for her at every opportunity, if necessary, I would definitely take the initiative! Valerie continued speaking…

"But at around the time I was 13, my family moved to Middlesbrough in the northeast of England. My dad was big in the steel industry. You might be able to detect a slight accent from there too. In fact, there are many parts to me that you might find out" she said cleverly regaining the suggestive intimacy between us.

She was back on track talking more intimately combining it with the subject of her personal history. She started to laugh again, and she found her mojo once more.

"Well, I hope so… and I'm hoping to see your skills at life drawing" I replied.

We both began to laugh a lot together, standing about three feet from each other. I relaxed with her completely again. We talked in detail about our love for figurative art and Val suggested I hang around after the life drawing had finished so she could show me her art collection she had hanging in her home gallery. This excited and energized me. A collection, here, wow, what an amazing woman. Soon she suggested it was high time for me to see where I would be modeling. Jeepers this woman had mesmerized me and time was now pressing but she had managed to establish that more was to come later!

"The others will be arriving in about 30 minutes to set up," Val said, "Come see our usual set up and where you can get changed."

"Yeah thanks!" I said, "No worries" and I drained my rapidly cooling mug of tea.

Chapter Six

Group Life Modeling Begins

At the end of the long dining kitchen was a double sliding door on the left-hand side, leading into a broad purpose-built art studio space. Seven easels were set up in a circle with a table at the far end of the studio with stacks of different sizes of paper and drawing media including charcoal, graphite blocks and colored pastels. In the center of the easels was a large square of spongy yoga matting where I would be posing. Near the table to the right was a triple-hinged portable cloth panel screen. Val pointed out I'd be able to change behind it or as she put while grabbing my arm gently, winking "where you'll get your kit off!"

A lovely fluffy white toweling bathrobe was hanging over the screen. I motioned to Val that I would be going over to change and stretch. I thanked her. A good time for me to switch on my 'performance head'!

The studio was warm and superbly lit with Velux ceiling windows within the wide pitched roof as well as wall-mounted peripheral up lights to backlight the artists at their easels. The whole session was planned to last two hours with a 20-minute break for refreshments. Ellie had emailed all of the artists detailing the format and I'd confirmed my part verbally with Valerie as we continued to chat as I changed into the robe. The format was as follows; it is a very common format with few differences between groups.

- 2 x 5 minute warmup poses
- 2 x 10 minute poses
- 1 x 20 minute pose

Interval

- 1 x 50 minute final pose

Ellie had been adamant that I was to choose the poses. I had been given complete control. I'd confirmed with her that I preferred to remain on my feet in standing dance poses, rather than sit or lie down. This was met with complete approval. I am a dancer and wanted to project balletic expressive extensions and positional transitions. I was surprised to learn that this was completely novel compared with traditional life models who stand rarely and sit or lie down most of the time. Ellie had told me that she wanted to tutor the group as per usual to instruct how to capture my latent movement and expression which she explained as "an art in itself."

"We are a little weary of drawing the static human form, we need to capture 'life' not 'still life'!" she told me.

Totally inexperienced at life modeling I simply enjoyed the opportunity for creative freedom to adopt the dance poses which suited the length of the pose. I had worked out that the longer poses would necessitate fewer complex shapes and twists. In short, and very relevant for all life models is that holding a long pose with arms and hands above shoulder level is comfortable for me for up to ten minutes before the blood drains from my hands and the numbness begins to set in, followed by 'pins and needles'! I warn artists before I begin a pose that I will need to shake out my arms and reset from time to time.

The group gathered at their respective easels, and I emerged from behind the screen in the bathrobe only. The studio was silent as I took center stage! I introduced myself which is always polite if not introduced by someone else, and of course with this group everyone knew me by name already as we had all met at 'The Tanks'. I could still feel the connection with Valerie. We both felt it! Ellie welcomed everyone and spoke of her excitement that the group had the opportunity to draw a male dancer. She then set the timer for 5 minutes for the first warmup pose and I looked toward her for my cue.

As I mentioned previously my mindset was 'performance' and I knew not to speak nor make eye contact with the artists. In ballet, the eyes follow the extension of the extended arms and hands, so this was natural for me. This is from where movement originates and is conveyed. My eyeline is therefore above the heads of the artists so that eye contact is rare or accidental. Ellie nodded at me and started the timer and as she did so, I let the toweling bathrobe slip from each shoulder one at a time and catching it with my right hand I held it out at arm's length and let it fall to the floor after I had set my feet. At this distance from me the robe will not impede the view of my feet. I immediately assumed a pose that is a preparation for a *pirouette en dedans*. There was an immediate and audible murmur of approval and appreciation, and I heard a couple of the artists say softly to no one in particular,

"Oh… how beautiful, gosh!" And "We are so very lucky."

This resulted in further quiet and tasteful similar comments and put everyone at ease which was wonderful for me personally. I was actually for the first time ever, naked and motionless in front of talented artists and then that ineffable creative sound emerged; the sound of artists drawing and moving as they do so. The studio felt mesmeric as multiple pieces of charcoal swirled upon large A0 size paper accompanied by gentle shuffling feet. Ellie quietly and calmly began to tutor individual members of the group. Listening to her tutelage was eye-opening for me. When you are naked every human sense is heightened to every sound, movement of the air, sounds emerging from outside that would normally be unnoticed, and especially the temperature of the air.

If I am warm it is calming, energizing and intense. When I perform as a life model, I assume a character to portray usually a female ballet soloist from the classical ballets such as 'Manon', 'Giselle', and especially my personal favorites, 'Firebird' and 'La Bayadere'. I assume the female roles because they are more graceful and extended in outline compared to the male dancers. I mention this because this process of character portrayal came to me in a flash of inspiration after a recent visit to a figurative art exhibition. On this day I instinctively knew I was going to enjoy being a life model. As a lifelong art lover and dancer, life modeling with its performance intensity encapsulates the complete joy of being able to share my love for art surrounded by an audience who share the same love.

After completing the poses during the first half before the interval, Ellie thanked me, and the group broke into a relaxed babble and believing I'd mostly be unnoticed I bent over as elegantly as possible, feeling slightly self-conscious, to retrieve my robe and put it back on. I did this as elegantly as possible so as to remain in character and 'finish well'. This maintains the creative atmosphere, a theater habit and 'don't break the fourth wall'! #MOTL. I had rotated my standing poses so as to face in a different direction for each pose. This provides the artists with different points of view, variation in other words. For my final long pose before the interval, I had been full frontal with a sideways twist of my torso, and this just happened to be facing Valerie!

Tying the bathrobe around my waist, my eyes met with Valerie's. They were absolutely sparkling in that mixture of natural light and background uplights. Her fingers were blackened from the charcoal and there was a cute little smudge of it on her nose and left cheek. Her sexy waistcoat was completely clean though. Our gazing at each other remained locked long enough for both of us to be conscious that our obvious sexual tension would be noticed by some of the other artists! Until that dawned on me it seemed like time was standing still and it was Val who broke away from the gaze first, but she did it slowly, like peeling sellotape, keeping her eyes on mine until the last possible moment before she was forced to look away. She busied herself with her drawing, taking it down and laying it flat on the floor behind her. I then became conscious that others would see me staring at Val, so I pulled myself together, slipped on the flip flops that had been provided and went off to grab a quick drink and to mingle with the happy crowd.

Valerie and I purposely chatted to other artists in the studio rather than to each other. Coffee was poured and biscuits were nibbled but there was an unspoken understanding between Val and me not to make it obvious to the others that we had a special connection. The sexual tension for me was intensely wonderful. My 'anticipation junkie' mentality was at its peak and I'm pretty sure that the few discreet glances that Val and I received from the others proved that the sexual chemistry between us was palpable and that the others found it exciting too! I'm not naive enough to think that women do not pick up on each other's moods. It is instinctive I believe for women and very rare among men, or at least men that do have such an instinct react very differently. However, nothing was said or even hinted at by the other artists. Also, I was completely aware of where Val was in the room throughout the interval without having to look for her!

The studio was in a positive creative mood, and we commenced the second session. It was a 50-minute standing pose for me. I engaged every pair of my 'dance muscles' to prevent ligament and tendon aches and hence prevent joint pain. Using a ballet dancer's *turnout* has the effect of switching on and highlighting every muscle in the legs and glutes. These are the largest supporting and propelling muscles. I twisted slightly to my left and by dropping my left shoulder slightly I knew my back muscles would be defined asymmetrically. I'd purposely positioned my direction so that my back was toward Valerie's easel. I was in a slight quandary about this because it clashed with my professional approach to perform for the whole audience, not just for one person. I consoled myself by the fact that I had been facing Val before the interval so now facing away from her made rational sense. However, in my heart I wanted her to bore her eyes into me and all over me. I wanted to give her time to absorb me for as long as she wanted to reciprocate the obvious opportunities she had given to me earlier to devour her body visually when we were alone in her kitchen together. The thought of her looking at my naked body in detail for 50 minutes caused my head to swim.

So was this playing up to one member of 'the audience' a professional error? I don't think so because I had experience of working in a musical theater production with a brilliant director. She told us all as members of the dance chorus to pick out a member of the audience every night and focus on them, performing our songs and dancing powerfully just for them! The audience connection was transformed the following night when we did this judging by the increased applause and cheers. It seemed as if every member of the audience felt special and reacted in keeping with that. So even though I couldn't see Valerie, I was projecting my creative energies for her and the atmosphere in the room was electric.

After the 50 minute pose came to an end, as all the artists started to clear up gathering their stuff together and chattering loudly, Val spoke to me quietly saying that it was the worst long pose drawing she'd ever done because her brain was "in a complete tizzy!" She'd reconnected with me instantly! The sound of voices in the studio was like talking in tongues and the creative energy was now being channeled into verbal recollections and observations. I'd put on the robe again and I went around thanking everyone and receiving thanks in return and then I popped 'off stage' behind the screen to get dressed.

It was also time to allow the artists to have time to themselves. I heard Ellie's voice rise up and thank me from a distance away unseen and I shouted back that I'd email her about meeting up with her at her own studio the next day. It was all very informal and friendly. I felt part of that wonderful group. I began to feel a little tired, but I couldn't stop thinking about Valerie. How would this end today I wondered? As soon as I emerged from behind the screen dressed in jeans and a light gray vest top, I felt part of the creative vibe. An artist called Katie tapped me on the shoulder as she scurried around clearing up and purposely hoarsely whispered,

"Oh, hi there, I didn't recognize you with your clothes on!"

It was intended to be overheard, and everyone laughed. This was accompanied with mock 'tut tutting' and mock admonitions and the fun in the air gave me the chance to look around for Val. I saw her and she walked over to me very casually and said quietly, "I hope you'll be hanging around so we can have a quick healthy snack and for you to have a gander at my art collection… if you have time?"

I nodded and quickly smiled at her and I almost winked an eye too but held off. I became intrigued how she was going to play this out. Most of the artists left pretty quickly and Val made a great play of clearing up. She was trying to kill time. Others offered to help her, but she politely refused saying it was all under control and that she had a well-honed clearing up routine. I stood out of the way watching her glance around as though wishing the others to leave as quickly as possible! I checked out her cute ass and the flash of her skin below her sexy waistcoat as she bent down picking up paper and pastels and admiring her toned arms as she picked up easels and placed them closer to the walls out of the way.

Finally, it was just me, Val and Ellie left in the studio. I read the situation and immediately asked Val where the bathroom was. She gave me directions to go to the bathroom at the top of the first flight of stairs opposite the front door. I disappeared and purposely took my time finding the bathroom. There was a shower cubicle, a towel available and I thought I would just have a shower, so I did.

Chapter Seven

Valerie's Gallery and the Door on the Left

As I was dressing after my quick shower there was a quiet knock on the bathroom door and as I'd not locked it, I called out for Val to enter, assuming it was her! She walked in at ease, noted I'd showered and put her hands on her hips, as is her habit.

"I thought you'd gone and got lost and how clever of you to grab a shower, I'd left a towel out for you, glad you took advantage. I didn't want to say so in front of Ellie!"

"Thanks!" I said, "has everyone left?"

"Yes, most surely, phew, quite painlessly," she replied, running her fingers through her hair as I adjusted my clothes and put the towel to dry. Suddenly, she spoke very forcefully.

"Art or food first?"

"Art!" I said.

Turning right out of the bathroom was a long wide landing that led to two bedrooms both left and right alternately. At the end of the landing there was a 90-degree right turn continuing the landing toward the rear of the house. All along the landing walls individual framed paintings were hung each with a separate individual spotlight above. There was no other lighting along the landing as far I could see and no windows. The lit paintings gave the impression of a colorful tunnel of art. Val had obviously prepared this while I was showering.

"All yours to look at." Val said.

"Wow, yes thanks, I'd like to walk slowly to the end and back to take in the ambience and colors if that's okay? I do that to see what grabs my attention then go back to them again!" I replied, staring down the landing.

"Turn right at the end, there's more, the whole landing is my figurative art space," Val added.

She gently put her hand on my lower back as if to encourage me. I felt an electricity in that touch.

"Fill your boots ballet boy" she added in a sexy deep tone adding humor once again.

I slowly headed off into that 'tunnel' of color and atmospheric light and noted each painting as I slowly passed, oils, pastels, watercolors and I assume some acrylics based on the more modern looking artworks. I noted that all but two were of naked or partially naked studies of women, reposing, standing, sitting, alluringly captured by the individual artists. Two paintings, side by side, grabbed my attention especially. The first depicted two women, a watercolor, one female, naked lying on a chaise-longue with the other semi-naked woman looking at her. It was an evocatively secret liaison. The other was a self-portrait by Howard Somerville, with himself in the forefront and a naked female in the background smoking a cigarette, entitled 'Artist and Model', an extremely beautiful and erotic painting, especially for an early 20th century painter. I felt Val standing next to me as I stared into the Somerville painting. She had been following me quietly. I turned to look at her and she was looking deeply into the former painting of the two women.

Val spoke, "This is by Anna Airey, entitled 'Siesta', there's no sure date to it but it must be around 1930. The Somerville you are looking at is around 1912 and very daring for that time."

She paused, and then linked her left arm into my right arm and came close to me.

"These two are my favorites and you stopped here, wow!" she added.

We looked at each other. Her arm in mine was the gentlest of touches but there was an appeal in her closeness. I was exhilarated, so turned on. She turned her head again to look at the paintings and I looked at the outline of her breasts pressed lightly into her cream waistcoat. She smelled of sweet warm flowers, her neck below that shiny auburn hair looked edible. I noticed now that even though she was fair skinned she was lightly and healthily tanned, and the skin of her deltoid muscles was covered in tiny delicate freckles that I'd previously noticed on her delicate nose. She turned to look at me again and I slid my right arm behind her and placed my hand around her waist and accidentally found myself touching her gorgeous cool skin below the hemline of her waistcoat.

It was instantaneous, our lips met perfectly, the shape and width of our open mouths matched exquisitely and there was no hesitation in meeting our tongues.

Slow and gentle with deliberate searching movements our tongues caressed without eagerness. It was as if we both knew something had started between us and we could take our time. I pulled her close to me. With my left hand I held the back of her neck, and she wrapped both of her arms around my neck. I felt her rise onto tiptoe.

I was supporting her weight against me. I became very hard, and she responded with tiny involuntary pelvic thrusts against my hardness, pushing her pubic bone hard up against me. I slid both of my hands down to her waist and then placed my right hand slowly onto her firm left ass cheek, cupping it and pulling her in even closer. We continued to kiss. I pressed into her. Our lips parted for a split second as she took a short inward breath through her nose and mouth simultaneously then let out a tiny low-pitched sigh after she had filled her lungs as much as she could, but her sigh won the contest! Then we continued to kiss again. I felt her breathing into my mouth. Val became more eager, breathing deeply, I knew she was mine! I sensed clearly her mouth and body encouraging me for more. I didn't respond straight away, I wanted to savor this amazing sexy woman and her desire for me. The feeling was mutual. There was something illicit and yet so right about us being together.

I cupped her ass in both hands and with a slide of her right arm I felt her hand on the back of my head as she felt the shaven short stubble of my short haircut. She was still on tiptoes and her grip on me became tighter as she lifted her left thigh and hooked her leg around my right leg. I now supported most of her weight while still holding her ass. We continued to kiss but I don't have any clue how long this close connection took but it became clear to me it was my time to take the initiative again. I parted my lips from hers gently and reached down with my right arm and hooked it under her left thigh between my thigh and her knee joint.

"Hold tight around my neck," I said quietly.

"Yes!" was all she said instantly.

Then I reached for her right leg with my left hand in the same way and encouraged her to lift that thigh upwards too, and suddenly I had her legs in my arms wrapped around my back. I had all of her 110lbs in my control, she was straddling me as I stood there with her.

"Where to?" I asked.

"Behind you, toward the window at the far end," she replied. "The door on the left!"

I turned 180 degrees slowly and carried her toward the window, and we looked into each other's eyes, not speaking. I could feel her fingers interlocked at the back of my neck as she supported her upper body. The bedroom on the left came into view and I pushed the half open door wide open using her body. A double bed was straight ahead with natural afternoon light cascading onto it from a wall-to-ceiling window on my right. Stopping just short of the bed I slowly lowered her onto it, placing my knees one at a time onto the bed with her thighs still wrapped around me.

We kissed with our tongues rather than our lips. I was subconsciously demonstrating to her how I would eat her pussy! Her breathing was controlled but deep and sighing and I could taste the warmth of her minty breath that she exhaled without inhibition. I slowly put my weight onto my arms and engaging my abs, I raised myself into a kneeling position. Val's arms naturally dragged away from around my neck, and she let them flop and rest by her sides as she stared up at me looking very submissive. Her eyes were wide, and her lips slightly parted. She looked amazing. I pulled my vest top off over my head and unbuckled my belt flipping it open, then I loosened the three top buttons of my jeans. She reached up with her hands and with her fingers and palms she stroked and kneaded my chest. Looking her in the eyes I reached down and unbuttoned her sexy cream waistcoat button by button from top to bottom very slowly peeling the cloth back gently as each button slipped its buttonhole.

As I suspected she wasn't wearing a bra, and I was taken aback and sexually charged by how little movement her breasts made when released. They parted only slightly outwards and did not flatten. They stood proud, smooth, and beautiful. The skin of her breasts was lightly freckled too, and they were well-formed, so well-formed they were perfect in shape, size, projection, and elasticity! The idea of a perfect expensive 'boob job' entered my thoughts but glancing I saw no telltale scars below those deliciously freckled breasts. I hitched my right arm under her waist and took most of her weight in my arm and bracing us both with my left arm I wriggled us both further up to the center of the huge king size bed. As I did so her waistcoat began to curl off with the friction of the duvet. Stopping in the center of the bed she wriggled herself onto her elbows and alternately removed the waistcoat from each of her delicious shoulders in turn and it hung tightly against her toned slender biceps, so I said quietly.

"Put your arms around my neck again."

Without speaking she went still for a moment staring questioningly at me, but then she did as I told her. As she did so I put my arms around and under her waist and raised her until she was straddling me completely in my lap. She sensed what I was doing and dropped her arms in turn as I removed her waistcoat. I held it to one side with two fingers, shook it gently and she watched me as I flung it flat to the far-right side of the bed out of the way so as not to crease it.

"Just as elegant as you remove your robe before modeling," she commented.

"Huh huh!" I replied, quietly.

Val then put her arms firmly around my neck again and buried her face into it sucking gently, licking, sucking, sucking licking in a frenetic pattern of lust while making little eager pelvic thrusts against me. I could feel the warm firm pressure of her perfect tits squashing into my chest. She was saying 'now now' with her body, so I laid her gently back down onto the bed and pulled myself away from between her legs and moved back to the bottom edge of the bed on my knees. I then stood up, not taking my eyes off of hers as I finished unbuttoning the last two buttons of my flies.

I pulled my legs out of my jeans by bringing up each knee in turn and 'treading' out of them. I left them inside out at my feet with my socks removed in the same action. Val kept glancing at my stomach and groin area, I was wearing tight bottle green briefs. I then, without affectation, pulled my briefs down over my hard cock and felt it flap upwards as it was released. I then inched the briefs off completely until I was standing naked in front of her. A totally different feeling to how I feel when life modeling. It's amazing how each environment and attitude creates mood in different ways. I then began to crawl back onto the bed.

"Oh fuck!" Val said, "Oh fuck, oh fuck."

As I hovered over her, she gently touched my neck with her fingertips and nails saying, "Oh dear, I've left little love bites on your neck."

"Fuck it!" I said quietly, "they are mine now."

I knelt up again and reached down to her jeans and unbuckled her belt then unbuttoned her 501s. As I reached the last button, Val raised her hips slightly to allow me to take hold of the waistband and inch her 501s off. As they inched down, they revealed her wearing a very tiny black cotton G-string highlighting the pretty mound of her pussy. The tops of her thighs and groins were also delicately freckled. With her legs held high now and taking hold of her ankles in both hands I slowly put her legs together then I reached down and pulled off her jeans and flung them to the side of the bed.

I then slowly took hold of her ankles again and parted her legs until her legs naturally bent at her knees and she was spread before me. I left the G-string where it was for now because I knew it had her aromatic sexual essence soaked into it and I wasn't about to take it off and toss away this moist history of our day together so far!

Val raised herself onto her elbows looking down at herself and me. She then closed her knees together, pulled her knees back and then straightened her legs tightly together putting her feet and ankles in front of my face making me look around them. We were both smiling at this showy athleticism, and it turned me on even more. I suspected she might want to struggle, a bit of fun for me to force her legs apart, teasing me but she then spread her legs wide keeping them straight and extended and she pointed her toes like a ballerina! I could see the vertical engagement of her abdominal muscles as she maintained her raised legs.

I then reached down and using my index finger I hooked her G-string to one side to reveal her pussy. I took in the beautiful neatly trimmed dark blonde narrow rectangular strip of her pubic hair above the most delicate slit of a pussy I'd seen in my limited experience! 'Pure art' I thought. She lowered her feet to the bed by bending her knees again. I lowered myself slowly between her thighs pushing them further apart which interrupted her right hand reaching down to my cock! Her fingers momentarily touched it, but she had no choice but to remove her hand and flung her whole arm upwards and backward away behind her head in mock giggling frustration. It was then I noticed the little delicate white line of a scar in her right armpit. 'Ah ha' I thought, this is the proof of her amazing breast augmentation, it's where the incisions were made 'invisibly' under her arms to create her amazing youthful breasts.

She tried to raise her hips pushing against me but lowering herself uselessly against the weight of me she relaxed onto her back and let out another giggle of frustration.

"Oh god!" she said, "Grrr, teasing me."

I didn't want this to descend into a giggle fit, I needed to find her eager desire again, but I wasn't about to fuck her. I positioned my body so that my hard cock pressed against her pubic mound. I could feel the prickle of the short, trimmed hair of her 'landing strip' against the underside of my cock. I pressed more of my weight onto her, supporting the rest of me on my elbows. I was firmly between her thighs. Her breathing picked up again half through her nose half through her mouth. We began to kiss and lick tongues again eagerly. I put my right hand onto the top of her head and gently but tightly grabbed a handful of her hair and she hooked both of her legs around my back. Her chin rose up slightly as I pulled her hair a little more and to one side, baring the side of her neck to me.

I began to lick and gently suck her elegant neck without leaving marks. She moaned loudly as I slowly licked the full length of the side of her neck with the flat of my tongue! I did this up and down many times until I felt her neck desensitize and then pulled her hair moving her head the other way. I then attacked the other side of her neck in the same way with my tongue but more eagerly. She needed no extra encouragement and opened her neck up to me willingly, stretching the sinews of her little neck. At one point she lifted her left shoulder to cover her neck as she'd suddenly overstretched her neck muscles on that side in her passion, giving out a little whimper.

"It's okay, okay, carry on," she whispered.

Her shoulder went back down, and she turned her head sideways until the right side of her face pressed deeply into the duvet. Her mouth was wide open, and she became silent holding her breath with her lips tight over her teeth. She began to whisper repeatedly.

"Oh my god, oh my god, fuck, fuck, fuck, fucking hell, yes, oh my god!"

I removed my lips from her neck and hovered my mouth over her left ear and said slowly,

"You know where I'm going don't you?"

All Val said was…

"Fuck! Fuuuuuck!"

I kissed her neck again with little pecks just lingering there before I moved to each of her delicious, freckled collar bones one by one, dragging my tongue over them firmly so as not to tickle her and break her reverie. Reaching the nape of her neck I then dragged my tongue over her delicate corrugated breastbone to begin licking and sucking her perfect breasts. I circled each breast in full with my tongue without touching her swollen nipples. I spat gently onto them and spread my saliva with my tongue and lips and the moisture mixed with her body heat intensified the aroma of her skin.

For my own artistic pleasure, I began to lick the delicious area where each breast joined her ribcage tracing her beautiful toned diagonal pectoral muscles toward her armpits in turn. These places are another sign for me of a woman's health and fitness. I then licked each of her armpits with the firm flat area of my tongue and she let out a whoosh of pleasure and I tasted her delicate perspiration.

Her nipples were totally round and swollen and pronounced and as soon as I ran my tongue over each of them, they quickly shrank away to become tight firm points. Each nipple in turn I cupped with my mouth wide and sucked hard breathing through my nose heavily maintaining the suction until she grabbed my head. When she did this, I stopped sucking and used the flat of my tongue to press down on her nipple very firmly and pushed it into her breast tissue. I slowly rotated my tongue clockwise and anticlockwise alternating. All of this was second nature to me as it was exactly how Juliet liked her breasts sucked and she'd given me detailed instructions all those years ago! I looked up from Val's breasts still sucking and noticed that her chin was high, her neck taught, her mouth wide open, eyes closed, and the sounds she was making were making me ache to fill her neat pussy.

Val must have been reading my mind because she delicately put a hand on my head again and gripped the duvet tightly in her other hand. This I took for a signal to go lower. So I did! Still with my tongue I traced her abdominal midline to her navel quickly blew my warm breath into it and all this time her hips and pelvis were pumping up and down in tiny fast little movements. The smell of her warm skin was intoxicating for me, it was her aroma, part of her essence. I'm sure it is designed to drug me! My tongue reached her coarse narrow neat 'landing strip.' I was on my knees by now with my ass in the air and my thighs spread wide and I felt her lean thighs come together and squeeze my face for an instant before she spread them wide again.

I licked her short neat 'landing strip' until it was soaked and flat with my saliva. I combed it with my tongue upwards and downwards against the grain and with the grain and roughing it up completely repeatedly before smoothing it down again. A few times I spat saliva on it and made sure she heard me doing that! She put her hand on my head again and I slowly traced my tongue over her tantalizing neat little slit. Just the tip of my tongue at first. Her black G-string needed to be pulled firmly to one side into her groin with my fingers to clear the way for me to see this picturesque, sweet, neat, little oyster of a pussy. Her outer pussy was pink and swollen slightly with her excitement. Her pussy was super smooth, not a single hair follicle was visible.

Her moans of pleasure were electrifying for me. My nose was so close to the rolled up moist G-string in her groin, that I could smell the heat of her essence from it. I was uncontrollably drawn to smell it and suck at the black cotton with my lips. It was like an undefined roll of black cloth by now and I licked and kissed her groin area sucking her abductors each in turn. I returned to the G-string pulling it wide away from her now slightly gaping wet pussy. She was opening up! I hooked the G-string with a thumb, and she began again with little pelvic thrusts up and down encouraging me to eat her out.

I licked the neat parting slit of her pussy with the tip of my tongue, parting it open more and more using my tongue, deeper. I applied more and more pressure with my tongue and avoiding her clit for now I gently but deeply tongue-fucked her vaginal opening with as much tongue I could force out of my mouth. I adored her taste. She tasted of a warm summer day, a warm floral smell of pure feminine nature. Nothing could really describe it; Val's pussy was a sensation wrapped in an aroma! I can remember thinking for a second how delicately sweet she tasted compared with my hesitation to taste the unpredictable blatant hormonal heat and fleshiness of Issa's pussy; my current girlfriend! Val's pussy was like a warm semi-sweet warm wetness, totally delicious. Her pussy was practically fleshless! Her neat outer lips opened to reveal a clearly defined wet slit instantly! Her inner lips were cute, tiny almost non-existent, imperceptibly puckered, edged with an alternating color of her own flesh and little paler white sections #MOTL!

I swirled my tongue around her open slit feeling the delicacy of her vaginal flesh. I then alternated from this to her clitoris gradually building up the time spent on her clit until it received my full attention! Val was attempting to spread her thighs beyond her limits it seemed. She was like piano wire with erotic tension. I loved the whole visual and audible experience of her! Panting and moaning she slammed her straight arms up and down onto the bed in increasing intensity,

"Oh my god, I'm going to cum!" she squealed.

I'd learned from Alison how to edge a girl and as Val's excitement began to peak, I eased my tongue pressure away from her clit and raised my eyes to look at her. Sex for me has always been artistic and visual!

"Oh fuck, oh fuck, you bastard, you bastard!" she said knowing she was being teased, edged.

I pressed my mouth over as much of her inner pussy as possible and sucked her clit firmly. She had her mouth closed and gave out long loud humming sounds. She flat hand-slapped the bed many times. I eased off the clit sucking and very gently placed my forefinger into her wet cunt with the fingertip upwards and delicately rotated it against the little 'fish scales' of her g-spot. It was just off to one side, not central. Her moans slowed until she computed what I was doing and then she began making little tight-lipped yelps. I then inserted my upturned forefinger deeply into her cunt until the web of skin at the base of my finger became super-stretched. I then pressed my finger upwards using my whole finger, into the roof of her gently pulsing contracting cunt, again just as Alison had taught me! With my forefinger inside her as far as it would go, the knuckle of my ring finger pressed firmly onto Val's saliva-soaked asshole.

Val was so loud now! From where I knelt with my head between her thighs so close to her pussy I could see the detail of her swollen wetness, I reached under and around her right thigh with my left arm and placed my fingers onto her pubic bone and stretched the skin upwards putting a pulling tension on her clitoris. Not purposely denying her any longer I gave her what she craved and expected. I flicked my tongue from side to side very rapidly over her clit varying the speed and pressure until I found her natural rhythm and then maintained it, teasing her less and less until she started to speak in a rushed high-pitched voice,

"Don't stop, don't stop, oh god, that's me, that's me that's me, for fuck's sake, fuck, fuck, fuck, fuck!"

I could feel Val's pelvis pushing upwards again but slowly, once, twice a third time and up she went pushing her pelvis high, arching her spine! I tried to hold her down but no way! I had to remove my left hand from her landing strip very quickly and I had the sudden alarming thought that her upward thrust could easily dislocate my inverted forefinger which was still inside her! I revolved it suddenly and thank goodness I did! As Val thrust upwards in her prolonged climax her pubic bone punched me glancing blow to my upper lip! Ouch! I followed her as best I could, adjusting my kneeling position to chase her clit with my tongue. I found it, licked her rapidly and suddenly a small gush of warm neutral-tasting watery fluid shot into and around my mouth and she screamed, slapping the bed at the same time!

I could feel my top lip swelling! Val was in a world of her own. She'd dropped her weight back down onto the bed. My mouth was no longer on her lovely cunt. She raised her ass off the bed a little again and then slammed it down onto it again and shot her right hand down to cover her whole pussy! During a long couple of minutes neither of us spoke, I just knelt up between her legs looking at her deliciousness.

I could also see the beat of my heart faintly pulsing my hard cock. Val's body twitched delicately a few times, and her breathing became more controlled. Her hand was still covering her pussy, and her other arm had come across her breasts. I took this for 'leave me alone for a bit'! I smiled at her loveliness again. She opened her eyes wide and looked at me and removed her arm from across her breasts and said,

"Holy fuck!"

Then she raised herself up and rested her weight on her left elbow.

"Jesus, I've never cum like that before, holy cow!" she sighed.

I loved her casual confidence. Her eyes were wide and watery, just a hint of smudged mascara. A lovely sight. From my kneeling position I gently pushed her thighs open and reached down and removed her right hand from her pussy. Taking hold of my cock at the root and bending it horizontally toward her I edged myself forwards and located my cock just inside Val's soft, tight, wet, textured cunt. I went forwards onto my elbows so that I was above her looking into her face and just kept the tip of my cock positioned inside her pushing it in and out shallowly, savoring every second until I slowly pushed full length into her cunt with my weight hard onto Val's pubic mound.

I glanced down to look, and it was a vision of amazing dovetailed neatness. I then kissed her. Throughout this she stared at me through wide eyes and kept her eyes open as I did while she ate my mouth. We moved in a slow grinding rocking rhythm for a long time, neither of us talking. I remained relatively motionless inside her rather than fucking her. Val was still sensitive coming down from her orgasm, so I used the time to absorb every detail of her face. Staring at her I could see the 'girl' in her! Her delicate sandy freckles were mesmerizing.

I began to pick up my pace and began thrusting pulling and pushing the full length of my cock to the point it was almost out of her then thrusting hard and slowly back into her fully. Encouraged by her jutting chin I began to pound into her faster. I glanced at her perfect tits quivering with each slam into her as we fucked, she was perfection. Then I suddenly stopped and slowly pulled out of her and there was a look of mild shock on her face! I had to stop because I was on the edge of an exploding orgasm and one more thrust would have let that beast free and I didn't want to cum yet. I wanted more time to soak her up with all my senses. Without speaking I pressed both of her legs flat onto the bed then raised them vertically again.

Pressing her ankles together I reached down and slowly rolled her G-string up and over her thighs then up and over her calves and feet, freeing it. I could feel its warm dampness. Without unraveling it, I popped it back over her left foot and rolled it down her leg until it was relocated in her groin. Val watched me do this with no expression on her face, but her eyes were electric. I encouraged her legs flat onto the bed again and then flipped myself over it onto my back next to her, making sure I wasn't clumsy.

"Ride me cowgirl!" I said softly but firmly,

"Any fucking way you want baby," she said in a playful tone with a smile on her face. She was definitely in control now.

Val positioned herself very quickly to straddle me. Spreading her thighs wide it was my turn to look at her from below and the image of her tits in full, nipples swollen again and the gentle firm feminine roundness of her little belly, her neat wet landing strip dragging my eyes to the spread of flat thigh space and the beckoning spread of her swollen pussy. Her pussy was wet, swollen, pink and had spread open from me licking and fucking her. She reached down with her hand to my rock-hard cock, shiny with her girl juice. I noticed that she had little pale vertical stretch marks on her belly. In no way a turn off, they added to her alluring femininity. Together with her horizontal navel crease as opposed to a vertical one, it dawned on me that this athletic woman had previously been pregnant and borne children in her earlier life!

Val then brought up her left knee and hovered herself and located my cock into her cunt. Kneeling again she took only half of my shaft inside her. Was it my turn to be teased I thought? This slow change of pace and position decreased my chances of an uncontrolled orgasm which is what I wanted. She moved forwards and backward in a rocking motion with her weight taken on her straight arms and her face above mine. Then without warning she banged her pussy down hard onto me sitting up straight and placing her hands on her head.

She found her balance. I could see her abs kick in to support her upright position and she began to slam-piston up and down, smashing herself down on me taking my full length inside her. She let out a little winded breath with each slam which sounded so erotic. I could feel her cunt gripping my cock; she was squeezing that delicious cunt around it. She then placed her right hand on my chest and reached behind herself with her left hand and it was obvious she was playing with her own asshole. It was so erotic to see this. She didn't speak so I asked quietly,

"Are you playing with your asshole?"

"Oh yes, you bet!" and her face was blank, her mouth open breathing audibly.

I noted this for later! Then after quite a while she brought her hand back from her asshole and placed it flat on my chest and then reached down between her legs with the other hand taking hold of my cock which was still half inside her. Twisting her slender fingers around it, squeezing it and wanking me, I watched her. She then brought that same hand up to my face and pushed her fingers into my mouth! I didn't hesitate to suck them. I swirled my tongue around her fingers tasting her thickened juice and swallowed as my mouth watered. I wanted those fingers; it was a complete erotic moment for me!

She looked at me in a slightly pained way as though she couldn't believe what I was doing so willingly and eagerly. She was obviously really turned on and seemed to lose control in her enthusiasm! She took her fingers away straight after purposely pushing them for a second to the back of my throat to make me gag and then suddenly kissed me with complete abandonment. She'd become enthusiastically uninhibited and began kissing me and fucking me in a fast rhythm and the mixture of her saliva, hot breath and ecstatic sounds made me meet her enthusiasm.

I grabbed her ass with both hands to feel her movement through her taught flesh. I felt for her asshole with my fingers. I found it. It was soaking wet, slightly stretching, and contracting with her thrusts. Feeling me do this Val slowed her rhythm to keep my fingers on her asshole, helping me locate it. As she moved, her asshole undulated, and I massaged it with my fingertips pulling and stretching it gently at first but more aggressively as her movement and sounds encouraged me. It was elastic and giving, it had an extra eroticism for me because she was confident in her body, there was no hesitation in her. Her asshole was definitely an intense erogenous zone for her.

As I continued to massage it, I took away one hand and scooped saliva out of my mouth and then applied it to her asshole again to lubricate it. I was amazed how I did this instinctively and compulsively. I was surging, in tune with this woman's asshole! With the extra lube I found her asshole popped open and closed, she contracted and relaxed it as my fingers searched. I partly inserted a forefinger into it, and she contracted and gripped my finger. As she relaxed, I pressed and stretched the inner wall of that erotic hole with my finger pad, gently twisting and pulling.

Val expertly fucked me keeping my fingers there and my rock-hard cock was deep inside her eager cunt. I noticed how her anal contractions on my finger coincided with her cunt gripping my cock. Looking at her face, her eyes were closed and to be honest she looked like she was 'elsewhere', she was in her own deep reverie. I found this completely erotic. I knew she was completely submitting herself to me intimately and consensually and I loved it! She picked up her rhythm and speed.

Deep, deep, deep banging fucking! We'd found a new faster rhythm which suited me allowing me to observe her in every detail and without me prematurely cumming. I could see her twisted G-string still around the top of her left thigh; so erotic! I began a slow orgasmic buildup. I wanted it to be slow and controlled but that was going to be difficult now! Her perfect tits bobbed and quivered elegantly reaching a perfect resonance with her fucking.

"Cum in me Georgie, fucking cum in me, fill me up with your cum!" she suddenly half shouted half groaning, "mix with me, come on, cum for me!" she shouted.

So, I did! I had no choice, and so did she, for the second time! I lost myself in this dance of pure erotic sexual passion. She triggered every erotic cell in my body and brain to cum! We came together. I exploded inside her a split second before Val came! Our orgasms were intense, and I could hear myself moaning as Val yelped and shouted a long incoherent sound of pure beautiful ecstasy! Her nails dug into my pecs, she suddenly flung her head backward and she grabbed her own left breast with her left hand pulling and squeezing the breast tissue roughly through her fingers then pulling the nipple so incredibly hard it looked as though she would stretch it off! Almost simultaneously encouraged by the sight of her doing this to herself, I did the same with her right breast. My cum mixed with hers made her feel super smooth and incredibly wet and it slowly ran out of her and all around my tight balls, which became slightly itchy with the wetness! I expected my cock to go soft very quickly and slip out of her, but it didn't!

"Fucking Jesus!" she exclaimed.

After breathing hard through pursed lips and trying to control it she shook her head from side to side repeatedly for a few seconds and said in a deep quiet voice,

"That's a first, two massive orgasms minutes apart!" Then she looked totally puzzled.

"Oh god, there are more inside me, I know it, I feel it! Do you mind?" she gabbled!

She then suddenly reached down with her right hand to her clit, still straddling me, with me still inside her, she began furiously to play with herself and POW! She came again, slinging her head backward and forwards this time slamming my ever so slowly softening cock deep inside her.

"Fucking hell there's more, oh god!" she said wide-eyed and surprised.

She repeated her orgasmic tripping at least five more times very quickly but with each one she became more conscious and playfully connected with me. With each climax, nowhere near as intense as her first two but just as exciting for me as she looked at me and shook her head, grinning and laughing with me. She had a little young, puzzled look on her face like she couldn't believe what was happening within her body! At one point she stopped and squeezed my softening cock inside her cunt letting out a little giggle and giving me a playful apology just before another gush of wetness ran from her all over me! Amazing! I was also surprised at myself because I was still hard enough to remain inside her!

In retrospect, it was at this point I recognized in myself that my sexual desire for a woman was a mental connection before the physical; that my physical sexual stamina is inextricably linked to how my mind is connected with a woman. This is why I have had very few casual sexual partners in my life compared to some men. A physical fuck for me as in 'quantity over quality' is a mindset that prevents me from being promiscuous. Sure, sex for me can be impulsive and aggressive, visceral, and mind-blowing, but it is absolutely connected with all of my senses. In short, for me sex is artistically creative, not a numbers game!

I began to feel horny again and I started to harden, slowly but definitely becoming hard again while still inside her! She looked amazing! My sensitivity had died away mainly because Val had stopped being vigorous and her movements were gentle. I was inside her, but her pelvis and hips were still. We were soaking and this turned me on.

My own post-orgasm recovery didn't start from some regretful rock-bottom feeling of 'why did I just do that'! I felt completely connected with Val and wanted to repeat everything, I wanted more of her, not just that day but in the future! And there she was sitting on me straddling me, having given herself to me mind and body, totally uninhibited. Our cum juices had soaked my balls and ass cleavage and I was conscious of the wet patch on the soft white duvet cover. Looking at the lovely flushed-faced Val, I didn't give a damn about the delicious mess! I loved it. We had created it together! It was our collaborative art.

After she had orgasmed gently that last time, her playfulness with me increased. She looked amazingly joyful and happy. She continued to gently feel her clit with the flat of three fingers and it was now that I noticed for the first time her deep red painted short fingernails. Gorgeous and I couldn't stop watching this erotic vision of her.

Suddenly without any warning she said, "Oh wow, you are getting hard again!"

She had surprise written all over her face and her fingers became faster rubbing her clit from side to side. She began to become excited all over again and she spoke through stretched lips, little, short breathy sentences rather like someone trying to lift something that is very heavy!

"I'm cumming again, I'm cumming again, I'm cumming again, I'm coming again, I'm cumming again, I'm cumming again ohhhhhhhhhhhh I'm cumming again! Oh my god, what are you doing to me?!"

She became louder and in her normal voice like she was informing me and as though she was apologizing, "Oh god, I can't stop, oh god, oh god, you are gonna have to stop me!"

I just looked at her smiling broadly and put my hands behind my head entertained by her rich orgasmic tapestry.

"I'm not going to stop you, you eager slut! You are incredible!" I said laughing, "Just carry on!"

"Oh, shut up you're a bad boy" she replied, breathing hard and continuing to rub herself.

She wasn't offended, great, she just looked completely surprised at her own body behaving with a life of its own! What did stop her was that she moved her hips vigorously and suddenly, and my semi-hard cock suddenly popped out of her as she squeezed me!

"Oops, sorry baby!" she suddenly said, and she flopped down onto me squishing her breasts onto my chest. I felt their lack of 'give' remembering her breast augmentation.

The British have a habit of saying sorry for no reason and at irrelevant times! Very funny! Val kept her head next to mine and spoke gently near my ear, "Another fucking first," she said matter of factly. "I think that's what is called 'multiple orgasms', one after the other, Jesus, that last lot seemed like just one huge orgasm peaking and peaking, no troughs oh my god!"

I stroked my hands over Val's back, feeling and stroking the tone of flesh and over her ass. As I got to her thighs, I felt her G-string with my right hand. It was warm and damp and rolled up feeling even more like a strip of cloth. I playfully pulled it upwards and let it ping back onto her thigh.

"Ughhhhh!" she said into my ear and we both started laughing.

"Lie next to me." I said.

As she settled next to me in each other's arms with her leg cast over my thigh there was a silence between us for a few minutes. I was determined that she should speak first. She did.

"Do you believe that it can always be like this?" she asked.

The tone of her voice and the fact that she used the word 'believe' rather than 'think' made me realize that Val was attempting to protect her boundaries but without undermining our connection. She obviously wanted more from a 'type' of relationship, and I've never forgotten this. Over time I came to realize that men of her own age had put her on a pedestal. They adored her. By definition, putting her on a pedestal made men 'look up to her' and for her 'look down on the men'! Val didn't want to be adored, she wanted to be sexually desired and ravaged, sexually ripped away from her envied and busy leisure and social life from time to time.

She didn't want her lifestyle taken away from her by a doting man intruding on her time! I knew the age difference meant that we would never have a conventional relationship, but I definitely wanted to be 'lovers', 'fuck buddies' or 'friends with benefits' but with Val I instinctively knew we didn't really have a relationship definition. I knew we were going to connect sexually and emotionally on a really intimate level without end! Our lives were like the 'Olympic rings.' They are spread out but connected. All the rings can synchronize together but are connected whichever way they are pulled. Val was my 'Olympic woman'!

"What with a manky G-string stuck to your thigh!" I joked. I wasn't going to let this become a deep conversation.

Val slapped me playfully.

"It depends on how much time we have I suppose," I continued.

Val laughed lightly and then asked, "What do you mean?"

"Well, there are eight musical notes in music and limitless combinations of them to create symphonies and even more combinations of dance movement to unlimited music," I said lightheartedly.

"Go on!" she said.

"Well, I dance to music and I'm pretty good at it. My imagination is limitless and that's transferable to the bedroom or anywhere really!" I replied.

Was I making sense? Val raised herself up onto her right elbow and looked at me smiling. I winked at her and smiled back.

"So what you are saying is that we don't really have enough time to cover every aspect of sex together?" she asked.

"No, no, time is something we have lots of, it's going to be great fun creating" I said "I mean that I love dance and spontaneity and that's about as creative as a performer can be and when that performer is in tune with their audience anything is possible, so let's collaborate on 'sex symphonies' as and when the mood takes us huh?" I said.

This made her screw up her lips and half squint one eye in mock thoughtfulness. I love that little look she does, partly because it shows her little facial wrinkles and maturity, and I find that attractive. I was trying to say that I really want her but 'no pressure'!

"Shut up you cultured devil" she sniggered.

"That's a fine comment coming from the cultured Valerie who conspired and collaborated with her friend Ellie, her partner in crime, to include me in her life. Sounds like you could be trouble to me. That's the sort of trouble that gets me really interested," I joked rubbing my chin in mock thoughtfulness.

"Well, you've got me there mister," she laughed slightly embarrassed, "but in answer all I can say is I think we are definitely 'double trouble'!" and we laughed our heads off.

I turned onto my left side and Val lay on her right side and we looked at each other. She readjusted and nestled her left thigh between my legs now and we both looked down at that G-string and laughed again. Neither of us made a move to remove it! Val stayed propped up onto her right elbow. I reached for one of the pillows and rested my face on it. I was really chilled, and Val's green eyes were truly sparkling. We shared a long silent pause just looking at each other with ease. I wasn't really thinking of anything, just enjoying the feeling of absorbing this wonderful sexy woman. Val broke the silence with a big smile before she spoke.

"I squirted on you, twice that I'm aware of! What the hell was that all about!? I haven't done that before, not even with myself," she said, totally believing! "I've read about it in women's magazines, but I can't say I've discussed it with any of my friends! Why would we! It's one of those 15-minute reads to fill column inches for young women I thought," she continued.

"Crikey, whatever it is it's bloody amazing and hey is there anything you women don't do better than men!" I said rhetorically, laughing.

I wanted to put her at ease in case she was feeling I'd been put off by it.

"You can orgasm more, you can squirt, you feel energized post-orgasm, bloody hell let's make a list! Just take it from me, it's a great experience for me being squirted on, at, with…whatever," I said, and Val laughed. "And it's fantastic and I love it, please feel free!" I continued.

I phrased my words carefully because I didn't want to bring up the subject of Ali squirting on me when she was 17 and I was 15! Not the time or the place really!

"It wasn't pee, was it?" Val asked in a little voice looking for reassurance. "You know, did it smell like pee?" Val's face was gentle.

"Well, no it wasn't, and it doesn't… smell like pee!" I replied slowly. "If it did, we'd both be smelling it now, wouldn't we? We are covered with it and the duvet is soaked in it and I can't smell pee! It's well, err squirt!" I said grinning. "I loved it, please repeat whenever you want to, feel free," I added yet again.

I wasn't joking either. And Val squinted her eyes and laughed down her nose.

"Ok then, let's not analyze it eh?" she replied with a huge smile now. She obviously felt relieved.

"Let's just 'go with the flow' so speak, no pun intended!" I said and we laughed together again, Val slapping my arm playfully again.

She then placed her hand on my back gently keeping it there.

"Complete abandonment," she said softly, "In the moment always." she added.

"Precisely!" I spoke.

We lay there and chatted for a while. She began telling me about her upbringing. She told me her dad had moved the family to the northeast of England from Scotland in the very early days of the offshore oil industry taking off in the UK. He was a mechanical engineer and had begun to rise very high in the oil rig construction and maintenance division of a large multinational corporation. She also told me she had been married for over 20 years before her divorce. Her face looked distant as she told me this, so I didn't question her further.

Val had two daughters, 25 and 24 years old, the former working in Singapore in the financial markets there and the younger working here in London as a junior hospital doctor. Her younger daughter had her own flat and didn't live with Val in the very large Pimlico townhouse. Val also briefly mentioned the age difference between us of 29 years but without embarrassment and only in terms of me being one year older than her elder daughter! As she told me this Val had nibbled her bottom lip and raised her eyebrows so I knew she was playfully accepting of this, but I sensed she was thinking whether her daughters would approve! It didn't affect me at all that I was so much younger than Val, in any context.

However, I did say, "Do you think they'd approve, or is it worth telling them about me at all?"

"I've no plan to go out of my way to tell them but if we are seen together and someone tells either of them. I'll think on my feet at the time." Val replied.

Val was definitely relaxed about the whole matter, and I felt comfortable to joke with her.

"Well, if your daughter meets me, you can tell her I'm a gay friend!" I said.

"She's bright enough to know that wouldn't be truthful" Val laughed "but if you do meet my youngest it's hands off ok!"

"Well, you know women, women choose and besides if she's anything like her mum!" I joked.

Val put on a mock angry face and gave me a playful slap on my arm again,

"'Like mother, like daughter' and like you said, she's bright!" I continued joking.

"Don't worry, one look from me and she'll understand!" replied Val and we both laughed some more.

Val got onto the subject of her being single although she had a myriad of 'suitors'! I'd guessed she must have had. No woman of her age in her condition would fail to attract men of her age looking for that 'younger woman fantasy' wrapped in an amazing 50 something woman. Val was literally one in a million! I was flattered that she told me freely about them, knowing she had chosen me. She told me men of her age seemed to think they stood a chance with her by bragging about their wealth and cars and status. None of that impressed her. She mentioned again briefly about her mum and her life-changing decision to work on herself. Val added with sincerity that she didn't want a "conventional relationship" as she described it, especially with a beer-belly, skinny legged millionaire! Her idea of a relationship was a discreet one.

"I knew I'd develop a relationship with a man at some point who is the female version of myself!" she looked me straight in the eyes as she followed up saying, "and I think I've found him!"

I nodded smiling and in complete agreement and I kissed her before she spoke again thoughtfully.

"I believe that when you meet someone the first time, you meet the real person no matter how they change after that, and that you should maintain what created the relationship to happen in the first place, not destroy it with defaulting to possessiveness and jealousies which to me are signs of weakness and even personality disorders!"

Val paused a while thinking and it seemed she was about to speak from memory of a relationship or relationships with men, then looking straight at me by altering her position to affirm what she was about to say,

"I'm not keen at all on principled people either. It's a form of arrogance and is the sign of a hidden bully!"

Wow I thought and looking at her too I said,

"Your ex-husband? Or partners since your ex-husband?"

"Both!" she said softly, "the men who desire me are like carbon copies of each other and I've always wondered where these men have been 'made' to be like that!"

We both paused and I found myself nodding in complete agreement. I had experience of some fine friends who had personality changes when they either wanted a woman or when they were with their partners, so much so I didn't recognize them! I didn't tell this to Val before I said.

"I get it," and we both came to an easy bonded understanding.

I did get it, and I did 'get' Valerie, and she knew I did! Val looked at me again and her face said that she knew I understood everything she had said to me. Val then lightened her mood and added.

"I don't like being controlled, unless…" she paused looking coyly at me, "it's like the control you've had over me today. So, I would like, I want, for us, you, and me, to carry on just as we are today, we started this way, so we carry on this way" she said quietly.

I tingled inside and tried not to look too much like an over-excited kid in a sweet shop!

"I know you have a girlfriend, Ellie told me, and it doesn't bother me or affect how I think of you one jot" Val said.

This kind of took me by surprise but I suddenly realized that I'd mentioned my girlfriend, Issa, to Ellie when I'd modeled at her studio the previous week. Ellie and Val were extremely close, so it was hardly surprising that this fact had cropped up in their 'plans' for me! I nodded to Val and decided it would affirm me 'getting her' if I didn't try to validate my relationship with Issa, so I simply said,

"Quality not quantity."

Val nodded quickly and smiled her beautiful smile.

"Yup, there are no flies on you, Georgie ballet boy!" she said laughing again.

Val then looked very intellectual as she continued speaking,

"We have started to create an intensely intoxicating bubble together, for us to play in and expand and transport each other anywhere we want to, mind and body."

Another reference to the link between the mental and physical 'relationship template'! I agreed with this, and it excited me in my soul. I've always been excited by situations that are uncertain and unpredictable and to have this wrapped up in a bubble with Val was completely thrilling for me.

Valerie then continued to tell me she was financially independent but not super rich and that she had created a life full of her interests and passions in the art and fashion worlds. She then told me something I have never forgotten.

"Like me you have a well-defended sexual soul that intertwines and weaves through the life that you lead. Sex is particularly important to you I can tell, but it's not what inspires you. It's not your pursuit. Your seeking-soul inspires you. You follow it. I learned that about myself much later in life; or rather I knew it but allowed life and relationships to squash it into submission!" she said sincerely, suddenly adding "I believe we are soul mates!"

I paused thinking about what she had said.

"That is the first time I've had the term 'soul mate' defined exactly in terms of how I instinctively understand it for me, so bloody glad we met," I replied.

I knew we'd connected on the deepest of levels.

"The men I've met since my divorce have been like bees around a honeypot for me! Men have increasingly become more and more daft and silly toward me the more I've worked on myself. They're stereotypically conventional and dare I say live completely boring conventional lifestyles and their slowly degrading bodies literally makes me feel sick! Such men, most men repel me! That's harsh I know, but I look at you and I'm actually thinking 'thank you god' for sending you to me and all the way from the other side of the globe!"

Here was a woman who wanted me in her life but didn't want to change me! Wow!

Val then asked me about my upbringing in Australia, my passions and suggested all the arty things we could do together with the added thrill of complete discretion!

"People will guess, obviously, but who wouldn't and who cares! We'll never give them clarity; we'll just leave them to their own conclusions" Val said conspiratorially.

Val confirmed that Ellie was the only person she could really trust having known her for 30 years, and here was Val trusting in me. I knew I could trust Val and in turn she would receive my trust and respect. By talking with Ellie about me it was obvious that they had conspired to introduce me to Val. Apparently Ellie had told Val not to jump to conclusions but that the life drawing group had discovered a great life model and 'the perfect man to fit the missing piece' for Val! Bloody hell, I thought! Women control us implicitly! The twice weekly modeling I'd done with Ellie since that fateful day meeting at The Tate, had enabled her not only to capture my dance movement and expression in her art, but she had slowly ensnared me to 'show me off' to her great friend, Valerie!

"I want what you want, Val" I said, "and none of it involves materialistic vanity."

It was my turn to become 'intellectually thoughtful'! I continued.

"My dad had told me he always knew from my early years as a kid that I would follow my own passions, in my own time, treading my own path, not unlike he did against the odds! He also told me that material benefits follow by default in a life of creative challenges, by 'doing things' not just by 'thinking about things'. He did say though, that financial security is the only thing that keeps us safe and allows us to follow our passions but the single pursuit of money shouldn't be the objective in life."

"Wise man your dad," Val replied, "and you are obviously wise too for listening and remembering."

"He just seemed to understand me, always. He knew my thoughts when I was silent! He encouraged me rather than trying to mold me," I said thoughtfully.

"Georgie you are focused and yet so flexible in every way," Val said smiling "something guides you; you have a 'guardian angel'," she said touching my back softly. "Knowing you will also keep me on my toes too," she added in a fun but honest reflection.

"What on demi-pointe or pointe? You will need a lot of training" I said, teasing her.

I was pleased she understood what I meant regarding my ballet terminology.

"You never know I might get myself some pointe shoes, but you will definitely be extra inspiration for me, mind and body and that delicious expectancy in my everyday life." she said.

"Make that anticipation," I added.

"Yes, exactly, yeah, with you in my head I won't let things slip, I'll go the extra mile for myself and us, not selfish body vanity." she added to acknowledge my own point of view.

"Because, that sums me up completely, I'm an anticipation junkie without any expectations!" I added.

It was at this point I remembered the telltale signs of her breast augmentation and I remained silent because I didn't want to suggest any hypocrisy on her part talking about not being vain but having had a 'boob job'! This didn't affect my mood with her at all. I loved the way she spoke her thoughts to me so freely and honestly. She was gently mulling over what was on her mind by carefully suggesting rather than planning ahead for our 'permanent alternative relationship'.

I was then completely in tune with her. I understood her boob job was not vanity but to repair her body from the effects of childbirth and restoring her body confidence after her divorce, or for whatever reason she had undergone the corrective surgery. That is what it was, corrective. I had also observed the extreme neatness of her inner labia. It was almost non-existent and looked incredibly neat and pretty. The neatness of it was a huge turn-on for me and left me with no hesitation about eating her out. My experiences with eating pussy before Valerie had not always met with my visual appreciation and took a little personal effort and self-motivation to go for it, but not with Val!

"Nothing strikes me as selfish about you, Val, fuck no! Only the envious and the jealous and the delusional men who can't own you would call you vain! Or women who resent you! You obviously love nice things for sure, including yourself for all the right reasons." I said.

"I'm a typical Libran," she replied smiling again and she sounded lovely, sincere, and naturally modest.

"Hey, I'm a Libran too" I replied.

"O-M-G!" she said "Librans, you know, are the only two matching star signs who get on well together in a relationship because we share the love of space, art and balance." she added.

I've never forgotten that either, or I always now try to find out if someone is a Libran! There was a long restful pause between us, and we cuddled up together skin on skin, a meeting of minds, entwined mind, and body, warm in that natural light still cascading through the iridescent net curtains of the window.

Chapter Eight

Uninhibited Compulsions

We automatically began to kiss again. It became passionate and I was aware that I'd become hard again. I rose to my knees slowly and half encouraging her, half gently pulling her, she lay flat on her front compliantly. Quietly she said in surprise to herself,
"Fucking hell!"
Val looked exquisite. I kissed her freckled shoulders and kissed each individual delicate mole on her back. There were about a dozen in a wonderful asymmetric pattern. Kissing her ass, I felt her tighten her glutes and then relax them again. I gently parted her thighs by pushing one then two of my knees into the expanding space between them. I then took her waist in two hands as I knelt behind her and silently encouraged her to kneel up with gentle pressure. Val did so and automatically spread her thighs much wider. She was obviously making herself comfortable for what she knew was coming!
Her back arched down deeply, and she popped her ass up as high as it would go and it spread open before my eyes, beckoning me. I could see the detail of every part of her most intimate spaces. I was so turned on looking at her light brown pigmented neat asshole with its attractive uneven delicate anal ridges and compressions. Below this amazing moist prettiness her pussy was pinkish-toned and still slightly swollen, wide open and very liquid wet with our cum. I was fascinated to see how wet her pussy, perineum and asshole were! The inner lips of her pussy were almost non-existent revealing the entrance to her cunt so vividly.
As I guided my hard cock into her, she reached behind herself with her right hand, turning her head slightly that way too as though to speak but she didn't. She was attempting to watch me. She then spread her fingers over her firm ass cheek and placed her third and fourth fingers on top of her asshole and pulled at it spreading it before me! I was completely transfixed by her precise uninhibited

actions; an unspoken acceptance of her submission to me. I positioned my mouth directly above her asshole and began to summon up saliva, letting it slowly drip from my mouth onto it. As it hit its mark, I began to massage it in with my thumb and Valerie quietly moaned with pleasure. I'd learned how Val's asshole was an erotic erogenous zone for her previously. I applied more pressure with my thumb and partially pressed it into her anus, in and out gently many times adding more saliva as I did so. I adored the flex of her anal muscle. She was purposely relaxing and contracting it for her own pleasure.

I took my left hand from her waist and used it to position my cock into her cunt and then placed the same hand under and around her sharp pelvic bone. I could smell the warm poignant aroma of our sex as I slid my cock full length slowly and firmly into her gaping but tight wet cunt. I watched that sexual art with pure erotic desire for her. Val continued to moan her approval, and I began to increase the speed and strength of my thrusts and began pounding into her holding onto both of her pelvic bones. She was extremely wet and shiny smooth inside her cunt, and I couldn't now feel the pressure and tight texture of her vaginal rugae. I began fucking her and controlled her backward thrusts with my hands to quell her eagerness, which left unchecked, would have made me cum very quickly!

Val removed her right hand from her ass cheek lowering her head to the bed and placed her arms straight out beyond her head. Her fingers of both hands clenched and unclenched repeatedly. The downward arch in her back was extreme and erotic! I continued to pound into her as she spoke slowly, stuttering against my thrusts,

"I find it… hard… to cum… in this… position! I love it but… after cumming so much I…" and her voice trailed off!

I began to ease off my pounding of her as I computed what she was saying. I completely eased off into a very slow penetration of her enjoying the slick wetness of our creamy mixture on the shaft of my cock. Val suddenly said very quietly,

"My asshole isn't out of bounds for you… if you hadn't noticed!"

I slowly pulled my cock from her cunt and placed it at the concave entrance of her asshole. Her words to me were completely clear for me, they were more than an acceptance that she wanted her ass fucked, she desired it! I began to think how much I wanted to fuck her ass but in no way did I want to do it naively and hurt her! Looking at the erotic sight of her asshole I felt a complete and sudden overwhelming compulsion to use my mouth and tongue on her. I wanted to rim her, I really wanted to push my tongue into her ass and tongue fuck that delicious ring.

I moved away from her and positioned my head to rim her. I could see that her hamstring muscles were extremely taught with her thighs spread to her limit. Her defined abductors acted like a signpost toward the gaping of her cunt. I pushed my tongue into her cunt and then slowly dragged it over her perineum until I reached her asshole. The aroma of her sex was suddenly piquant. Her initial freshness was now replaced with a hot wet oakiness and a powerful pollen-like smell of my own cum. It wasn't unpleasant, it was commanding!

Val was glistening with wetness and little folds of creamy white girl juice! I began to lick it all up eagerly and our sudden instant strong taste began to ebb into a mental sensation for me! Val moaned deliciously as I licked firmly at her, contorting my tongue everywhere. I put my elbows beneath her pelvis and propped her up using my hands on her pelvic bones to stop her moving and she moaned even louder at the surprise of this. I was completely abandoned and began to push my tongue hard into her asshole.

It was so erotic and felt natural and I couldn't stop, encouraged even more by Val saying, "Oh god don't stop, lube me, lube my ass you filthy fucker!"

These words immediately distracted me, but Val was growing in her eagerness, moaning, and saying slowly in a whisper over and over,

"Yeah, yeah, yes, yeah, yeah, yeah!" repeatedly.

I knew we were still in sync! I started circling her anus like it was her clit. I then took my hands away from propping her into position and placed each of my hands onto her ass cheeks and spread her like she had demonstrated earlier. Her pale saliva-soaked asshole popped open easily enough for me to pop my little finger into it, but I chose to bury my tongue into it as far as I could push it.

Every so often as Val pulsed herself against me gently, I would occasionally stop rimming her and spit on the cleavage of her ass just above her asshole allowing the weight of saliva to run to her asshole where I coaxed it into her with my tongue! I loved my abandonment to indulge in this taboo activity. Val's asshole became completely relaxed. Her breathing had become gentle like she was being massaged. She became almost completely still as I rimmed her ass out! My tongue had become a willing small cock, tongue-fucking her. I was producing so much saliva it was running either side of, and into her pussy. Completely soaked with my saliva I slowly stopped and got to my knees.

I'd never rimmed a woman before this day, and I understood that Val's confidence was matched by her own cleanliness. She had clearly prepared herself! I used my right hand to position my hard cock and applied gentle pressure against her lubed slightly open asshole. Suddenly but gently, I saw the end of my cock almost climb into the delicious flexible ring of her anus as though being sucked in. It stretched and the color of it lightened and contrasted with the dark swollen head of my cock. The glans of my cock then snugly popped beyond her anal ring and felt snug and tight just beyond it. Val gave out a little long sigh mixed with a very slow little rocking of her ass. I remained completely still soaking up the incredible vision of this erotic act and listened to Val's growing comfort through her erotic moans.

"So wrong but so perfect" she said.

My head went dizzy and because I'd kept still, I felt the muscles in Val's ass loosen with her comfort and she seemed to be encouraging me to go deeper. I marveled at how this slender woman accepted my cock going slowly deeper and deeper into her ass. It felt like a really tight vagina and with all the saliva lube I'd fed into her there was no hesitant friction. I didn't stop my slow push into her until I could see the whole length of my cock was inside her ass. The sight of it blew my mind. I squeezed my cock harder, and she let out a long slow,

"Oh…. my… god… yes. Fuck, fuck, fuck"

I knelt behind her for quite a while without thrusting and caressing her back, her ass, the outside of her thighs, tracing my fingers down the exquisite recess of her spine.

"Are you ok baby?" I asked softly. Val's reply was soft and seemed far away as she rested her chin on the bed and she spoke in the direction away from us,

"Ohhhh yes, oh god yes, feels amazing. Stay still, I'll do the moving, god I SO LOVE IT!" she suddenly shouted out loud, surprising me and I felt her ass squeeze my cock tightly.

I was even more turned on; this woman blew my mind so many times. I gently held her around her waist and remained still not thrusting as she made little movements forwards and backward, rocking us rather than pulling herself from me and pushing herself onto me. We pivoted on our knees in unison.

"Mmmmmmm Mmmmmmm." Val constantly repeated.

Her rocking increased in pace slightly, I sensed this and stayed with it. Then slowly she changed her rhythm. My cock was still hard inside her ass, and her ass was completely relaxed. I took my hands away from her waist and looked at that erotic vision of us joined together, my cock in her ass! Fuck! She pulled away from me strongly and my cock emerged about an inch, and she slowly pushed herself back to take it all again. She began doing this slowly at first and then picked up her rhythm until she was using half of my saliva-lubed cock to fuck her ass. I watched with amazement and the feeling and sensation for me was intensely stimulating and I could feel the beginning of another slow growing orgasm. I wasn't going to suppress it, and the sensual pace of Val's exquisite ass fucking edged me out naturally.

As Val became completely in control balancing her pleasure as she picked up the pace, she became even more vocal,

"Yeah… yeah…YEAH… Yes… YES… fuck this is amazing, oh fuck, fucking amazing…"

The tone of her voice and her words turned me on totally. I took hold of her waist again, as much to distract myself but I couldn't take my eyes off her. The black G-string was around her left knee I noticed, adding to my growing excitement. As my hands gripped her waist, we began a vigorous pushing and pulling rocking motion in unison together. I was squeezing my cock harder inside her ass not fucking her. I was pushing my pelvis at her and she drove her ass into my groins. Val raised her head from the bed, using her hands to support herself with straight arms to give herself more traction to push against me and we began a small circling motion, our hips, and pelvises together still in unison as though we were drilling into each other! We created an erotic anal sex dance totally abandoned and amazing!

My cock began to pulse, and my head swam with an irresistible orgasmic buildup. It was more than physical; all the triggers were visual and mentally simulating because Val had entered my head! I suddenly came, a long slow drawn-out climax more mental than physical as I had unloaded most of my cum inside Val previously. The realization of what we were doing and the erotic sounds coming from Val were intoxicating! Val felt me cumming and then automatically began playing with her clit using her hand between her legs in a frantic motion, selfishly abandoned! I occasionally felt her fingers against my balls as she played with herself. I had no idea if she orgasmed or not, but I had, and suddenly it was extremely hard for me to balance and stay upright on my knees with my head swimming! I hung on to Val's waist to keep my balance and she slowly sank her head back down onto the bed. Her back was so arched her ass looked disconnected from her spine, it was there erotically presented to me, and I was still deep inside her.

I began to feel myself softening rapidly and I was extremely sensitive. Val sensed this also. We were both really still and I was simply staring at her body.

"Withdraw really, really, really super slow when you are ready, baby," Val said clearly and quietly.

I followed her instructions. I began to withdraw my cock from her ass almost imperceptibly at first and as the tip of my cock reached her stretched anal ring, I felt the flutter of this erotic muscle and I popped out of her extremely quickly with one final involuntary anal contraction. My sensitivity hit the roof as her asshole released the end of my cock. I watched how Val's asshole reassembled itself very slowly as it contracted but not completely nor as tightly as it had been before I'd entered her.

I flopped down onto the bed next to her and we spooned together, with me behind her. And we rested silently together. I kissed her hair a few times and stroked it gently. Val spoke first as I caressed her and what she said was 'off topic' not specifically about what we had just experienced but an overall expression of what she was feeling.

"There's something about the tone of your voice when you speak to me that triggers me to cum. Do you know that? You are a…." Val paused, "… you are a girl whisperer!" Val said almost matter of factly.

"I only tell you that, just this once, so you don't ever forget what you do to me ok! Clear?" she said playfully now but with meaning.

"Clear." I replied.

Considering our closeness, skin on skin, she was complimenting me beyond the physical, the sex. I sensed she felt vulnerable after she had revealed this, as though giving too much away because she followed up with, "and your happy trail is sooooo sexy!" making a big sigh and then giggling.

To be honest I had no idea what a 'happy trail' was and didn't ask her. I was content to just lie there with her thinking what a lucky man I was to have been chosen by this amazing woman. Val was an emotionally intelligent, extremely feminine woman. I realized that I'd only known girls previously!

I was smiling away behind her, she couldn't see my face, and I kissed her shoulder. I was like a 'shag on a rock'.

After a short and totally chilled few minutes, I spoke to her when I realized she was also chilled because she kept taking in audible breaths and sighing contentedly and I could just see the right side of her face and she was grinning. She rested there in my arms, and I was the one who referred directly to what had just happened.

"The anal took me by surprise but I was so turned on by you. And the rimming oh my word, I felt completely compelled. There was no way I wasn't going to do it!" I said softly.

Val laughed quietly and sighed again with contentment.

"You know I think I have a place in my ass that triggers my g-spot! Or I've got a g-spot in my ass!" Val said, laughing at herself now.

She sounded completely like she believed what she was saying though and so did I!

"It's going to be amazing and fun exploring that phenomenon," I said without sounding like I was joking.

"Mmmmmm" Val replied "There you go again that girl whisperer voice of yours! I can find that special g-spot on my own in my own way but that's the first time I was relaxed and turned on enough to just lose myself like that with someone," she said in a little high-pitched girl voice. "I hope you enjoyed the view too! You know I took advantage of you don't you!" she added rhetorically and playfully.

I answered her anyway.

"Fuck yes, you are completely amazing," I said a little too quickly, so I added slowly how I really felt. "Everything you are and what you do compelled me! The rimming, the anal fucking OMG I could do that for hours."

"Er… maybe not for hours, very very often, like *EVERY* time, but not for hours!" she said with a giggle, and I joined in. "but I do love it as you now know!"

"You have THE neatest pussy too" I added.

Val slowly stopped giggling.

"Nothing like a couple of thousand pounds didn't sort out plus weeks of pain when walking! Taking a pee was no fun either!" she said slowly, giggling again.

She slowly went very still as though holding her breath waiting for me to respond. I didn't know what she meant, and I didn't know what specific question to ask to find out what she meant!

"Can you elaborate?" I asked, trying to sound intelligent!

Val paused a little and then said, "Some homework for you, Georgie… look up labiaplasty sometime and then it'll be fun watching your face next time I see you! That's L A B I A P L A S T Y," she said gently, spelling it out.

What she said sounded final in that moment and also intriguing so I decided I would find out!

"Okay, I'll be a very private investigator and find out and report back" I added, stroking her shoulder with my fingertips.

I was filled with a feeling of something and everything long-term and discoverable about her. She trusted me implicitly. It was obvious by the ease with which she spoke so openly and intimately.

"I'm gonna tease you with the odd text message and sneaky peek pics of my prep for next time, play up to your anticipation addiction" she said, with complete excited playfulness, sounding like an excited girl!

It wasn't lost on me that she'd remembered that I said that I'm an 'anticipation junkie'. She was going to stretch that out enough to make me rampant! I guessed she'd wait to get me going when I was least expecting it as well as baiting the hook to be with her! I also knew what she meant by her "prep time". Val would be absolutely pristine in every way for me, and I got to know how erotically exciting it was for her to prepare herself. She eventually called it her 'adventure park ritual'!

At this I glanced down at my now very soft cock and there was no embarrassing sign of what we had done, my cock bore no evidence that we just had anal sex. She'd prepared herself for today and she was reassuring me of her intended cleanliness for next time, every time! What a woman!

Val's everyday attitude and casual mood when talking about kinky sex was such a turn-on. The whole day was about pulling away the folds of hesitation, peeling away inhibitions relentlessly and sensuously. It was a delicious process. This was the inevitability of being mutually 100 percent at ease with each other. Subconsciously from the moment we set eyes on each other we slowly but surely pursued our lust for each other. Oh my word, we had broken down hurdles continually with each other all day to end up right where we were. Most people would have fallen at the first fence! Val took a risk with me, but her confidence as a result of working on herself and not needing a man to validate her, made her quite like no other woman I've ever met!

I think we both fell asleep at that point. I know I did, and when I woke up Val stretched herself for a long time with a big accompanying satisfied yawning sigh and she told me I was the best 'spooner' in the world! I kissed her neck and then she said.

"That isn't a 'I've got to go now kiss' is it? Cos you don't have to rush off on my account. If you want a shower, you can have one in my bedroom en suite because that's where I'll be heading at some point, you'll find it next floor up, straight ahead. Feel free. I'm going to make us another pot of tea," she said delightfully.

"Earl Grey no sugar" I shouted to her as she absentmindedly looked around for something to wear as she slid off the bed! "Oh, and you can slip into my vest top if you are desperate!" I added joking.

We both laughed. Val looked amazingly relaxed. She walked like Bambi across the bedroom and with her back to me she deftly bent down and peeled the pesky 'parasite' black G-string from her left leg and then she turned around and threw it at me!

"Here you can wash this for your new collection, Aussie," she said joking "Don't worry I've got dozens of them!"

She then very quickly and elegantly skipped out of the room picking up my light gray vest top as she did so and sliding it over her head. She disappeared out of sight and within seconds she came back in, wearing my vest top in the style of a very short mini dress! She looked so fucking sexy. Her nipples were erect and only just inside the neck loop revealing a shiny defined youthful cleavage and the bottom of it just covered her thigh space. I still have this image of her in my head. Without speaking she turned on her toes deftly and slowly walked out of the bedroom again. The vest top highlighted the contours of her cute ass clearly clinging to her butt cleavage. She looked like a delicious little young slut!

"WOW!" I shouted out, then loudly adding a playful,

"YOU KNOW, VAL, YOU ARE DISGUSTING!"

I heard her giggling and then she shouted back.

"YES, I AM AND DON'T YOU JUST LOVE IT!"

I lay there for no more than five minutes, got up and put on my green briefs. Remembering the sight of Val in my vest top I decided to follow her to the kitchen while she made us that pot of tea. The shower could wait. I wanted to be with Val. I walked back along the 'tunnel of art' to the top of the stairs and walked silently down them and turned toward the kitchen. As I approached it along the hallway, I could see Val wearing the white toweling robe I had used during my modeling. Val had her back to me and didn't see or hear me approaching. Wearing it but with it untied, she was using the folds of it to vigorously wipe herself between her legs front and back! She was really digging in there! She had her legs spread really wide and she was really concentrating! I could hear the kettle becoming louder during the boil, and I used this sound to cover any noise of myself moving back out of sight toward the bottom of the stairs again. Basically, I didn't want to surprise her and embarrass her during her private moment as she made herself dry and comfortable. I called out from where I'd retreated.

"Where are you baby girl?"

"In here, in the kitchen, gorgeous man," she answered, and I went back to join her.

Valerie and I became exactly what she told me she wanted. We did indeed visit many galleries, art exhibitions, and fashion shows together and of course I've modeled for her with the other artists in 'The Pimlico Set' countless times. We never arranged to meet others when we went out though, but we were comfortable when we bumped into people she knew. Val only introduced me as "Georgie, dancer and life model" which I loved. She also educated me so much about female artists and women in general!

I dearly love her to bits and everything we have is built on the foundation of sex first and sex last and everything else in between! Essentially it was left to me to fuck it up and I nearly did! Does Valerie play any part in the rest of my adventures? #MOTL

Chapter Nine

Artist Tom and Issa

The visual arts, especially figurative art is my connective creative tissue on every level in my life. Whether this is private inspirational ideas or my outwardly visual activities, art is the fuel. Was I always consciously aware of this I ask myself? No, it wasn't until my early 20s. At that time the concept of this was embryonic but the more artists I met and worked with, the more artworks I absorbed in the amazing art galleries and museums I visited, I became increasingly conscious that art was the fabric of my creativity, my whole life in fact!

Looking back over more than 20 years, I realize that artists play a pivotal role in my life. Artists of all genres influence the way I think, why I change my mind, opening my eyes to art that previously made little impression on me. Most importantly they inspire me to mix artistic genres creating new trains and patterns of thought. I love and admire how artists see the world. Fundamentally though, figurative art is what I look for. Art is also the reason I travel. I don't go on holiday to sit still on a beach, I go in search of art. Art links up how I discover life, living in the moment rather than just existing. Without art and artists in my life, my life would not expand. My creative life would never have started and if I was taken away from art, my life would be insular and dull. I would probably end up overindulging in alcohol, tobacco and recreational drugs!

All forms of art represent risk. Artists continually take risks; the best artists take risks continually. Art has encouraged me to take risks, conceptually and demonstrably in the performing arts. This also means that I am prepared to make mistakes, even to fail. I fail a lot! I accept the risks and all the imperfections that risks generate and are represented in my life. The actor Brian Cranston, for many years sabotaged his acting career by trying to perfect his characters and by his own admission he became a victim of his own nervousness. In his own words he grew to discover his own amazing creative style.

"Letting the imperfections of the work be okay. The imperfect is your paradise. You don't want to drill away every shred of spontaneity and freshness. You have to leave room for discovery."

I also adapt the wise words of my dad for my work, for me the imperfections and asymmetry of figurative art generates feelings within me for ideas, then the ideas become actions, and it is in actions where risk resides. My dad of course gave me advice on how not to let emotions form the basis of my actions. He was attempting to, and successfully imbuing in me how to deal with negative situations in life. I merely extended this advice into how to deal with positive situations in my life. Either way, there must be a formative idea in between emotions and actions.

For me, art and artists are absorbed into my soul, they are the chemical and biological catalysts for how I create my own life. 'I balance my life by standing on the shoulders of giants'! I have always completely been drawn into the unfathomable wonders of creativity, how it transforms every aspect of my life. To the onlooker or listener, they must think I grab my ideas out of thin air!

Being involved in artistic processes too, is not work for me, even though I receive payment. Payment or monetary reward is a byproduct of the work I am involved in. Artistic processes, whatever they are or wherever they are, is a way of life for me. So what happens when the stresses of life and other influences upset this creative way of life for me? Some stress is necessary to boost the creative solutions, imperfections lead to new solutions. Solutions to problems, because all problems have a solution, are personally esoteric for me and not easily nor readily transferable to help others because many people lack the inspired imagination to solve their own problems in most cases. For me stress is a signal to become more creative in new and different directions not 'more of the same'.

My own stresses in life tell me to 'get out there' rather than becoming insular. It takes a lot of effort. Most people with all their often-self-imposed stress, usually hope that things will get better! 'Hope' for me means 'waiting for as long as a piece of string'. When my life faces stresses often out of my control, I learned to work on myself in detail, resorting back to what I love in life, including exercise, reading, absorbing art and meeting new people by doing what mum told me many times when she saw me looking too thoughtful,

"George Rufus, go out, get outside and go create some happy coincidences!"

Even today, I often repeat to myself what mum would tell me. I am lucky, because of art I have been able to find outlets and solutions for stresses in life. Things go wrong for example and when they do, I also always think of Sir Michael Caine saying, "Use the difficulty!"

My friend and Pilates instructor Katy of 'Uplift Pilates' pointed out in her social media posts that when things go wrong, we need to have personal systems to fall back on for us to bounce back. Katy should know having been a professional ballerina and bouncing back from a debilitating injury. It was her own character and Pilates that inspired her to find good systems. However, without major stresses we are not inspired to develop good systems. We either develop them or we sink!

So what happens when stresses are so perniciously sneaky that you are not aware of them and what happens when you are unaware of the effect they are having on your creative life? I was 27 years old, and life was good! Or was it? I'd been enjoying London and the arts for six years. An early seven-year itch? No, not really. An itch is obvious and needs scratching. Was I becoming bored? No way. My life had been full of auditions, performances, art, dance, and life modeling but I found myself a little out of kilter, out of control, but underwhelmed.

I was fortunate to be busy but unfortunate to find myself 'never alone'! Being alone, for me, isn't loneliness. Being alone is a temporary place, a foundation, a beginning for my personal recovery systems for creative rejuvenation. I have only experienced loneliness in the presence of other people or in social groups. These are the places where I feel hemmed in and eventually imprisoned. The only way out is for me to work on my own 'self' alone! Sometimes though, we need a helping hand!

The beautiful and wonderful, Valerie messaged me in that pre-smart phone non-predictive text style, to tell me that an artist she knew was exhibiting some of his art at a small gallery on Gower Street in London.

"His name's Tom intro yrslf, mention me iv filled him in abt u, not hw u fill me in tho! Keep me posted on outcomes n cu soon or shud tht b c2me soon!!! the address is… prev night is …xxxxxxxx"

On that lovely spring evening I went along to see Tom's exhibition. I had no indication of his interest in me, offers of work or even what his artistic genre was. Valerie had networked me as usual, entirely unselfishly, she hadn't even conjured up an evening opportunity to be seen out together just instructions to go and meet 'Tom'! Besides, even if I had more information, I would not have had any expectations as I like the excitement that comes out of uncertainty and unpredictability. I saw Tom almost immediately as I entered the gallery.

I'd arrived early as usual and there was perhaps a dozen people present already, and Tom was talking to three women. I took an orange juice in a champagne glass from the hostess and half glanced around the exhibition and discreetly inspected Tom. Tom was jocular, slender, flamboyant, and full of demonstrative character with a low sonorous voice. I've since heard people say he is "full of himself" but that is far from the truth. Tom wants everyone to feel the love of art as he does and tells all who will listen, and those who won't, about what he is thinking.

I slowly wandered over to Tom and I could hear his conversation with the three women was introductory in style and I wouldn't therefore be butting in and appearing rude. I'd merely be listening in. He carried on speaking and looked at me as I approached. The three women turned and looked at me and smiled, they all looked wealthy and arty, not a usual combination! I briefly introduced myself and offered my hand, but he pushed it away in a friendly fashion and proceeded to give me a huge bear hug! He slightly lifted me off my feet and I felt my lower spine 'click'! It has always done that but when I choose to do it! I cannot paraphrase here what we talked about in any order as Tom never stopped talking and included everyone in it who stood around him.

People naturally gravitated to him. An amazing man and artist. However, we managed a few quiet minutes later on after he'd approached me. I saw others watching him as he walked toward me, swigging his bubbly. People moved aside and clapped their eyes on us both. I noticed that when Tom went to talk to a specific person, others stood a polite distance away.

Tom began by professing his love and admiration for Val and spoke of his pride to have two of his figurative artworks hanging in her 'Tunnel of Art' collection. As I had already briefly looked around the exhibition, I had recognized that his distinctive style was represented along Val's gallery. Tom's art is dreamy, almost liquid, including some cityscapes as well as figurative art.

The gallery had filled up and was very busy and quite noisy. Tom was in obvious demand, so he passed me a small card with his name and address and contact details as he intended. I felt very special, and this connection made others in the gallery look curiously at me leading to some interesting conversations. I read the card briefly and noted that his studio was in Margate on the southeast coast of England. This excited me because Margate is the location where the British artist J.M.W. Turner created some of his most iconic masterpieces, all bequeathed to the British nation. Tom's current exhibition included some seascapes, and his latest figurative artworks were full of scenes hinting at pre and post erotic encounters. I could imagine the atmospheric inspiration of his studio's location in his art. Tom had invited me to contact him for me to travel over to Margate to spend a day with him and I couldn't wait!

We were coming to the end of spring with that variable weather in the UK, when I traveled over by train from London to visit Tom. I'm not going to leave you guessing here. Tom was obviously gay and as you know I am straight. Tom's motives for inviting me over to his studio were in no way predatory and in all my years of knowing him, this great man has never shown any obvious sexual interest in me. His passion is his art, and his figurative art is predominantly of the female form and extremely feminine. Meeting Tom in his studio for the first time that sunny day was instrumental for me as a young man. I was as Tom would reveal, a young man of many pieces but slightly coming apart!

I'd been in a relationship with my girlfriend Issa, for nearly two years and during the previous six months she had moved into my apartment to live with me. Issa was a Ukrainian ballet dancer, working in London. I'd begun to feel that my life wasn't going too well. I was very busy and in demand but somehow my focus was upset, and I began to feel that too many people wanted a piece of me!

Tom greeted me at his studio, again with a big hug, but I was prepared this time and kept my spine in place! If you want a picture of Tom in your mind, think of Liam Neeson, that incredible Irishman and actor of the big screen. The place was filled with natural light and a bit chilly for my liking as well as drafty! It was located on the very top floor of an old building with the sea in full view along one side of the studio. A history of his art, practice and processes lay around festooning the space.

Easels, canvases stretched on frames, some partially painted others blank, most of them propped up together around the walls at floor level. They were a concertina of color catching the light. A huge carpenter's workbench stood proudly in the center of the large square studio. It had many draws, and a huge steel vice fixed to it. Two large, battered steel black filing cabinets were set against the far wall below a small window there. I found out the cabinets were used for keeping canvases, paper, and other pieces of artist gear. Atop the cabinets and the bench were masses of pots containing paint brushes of all sizes, tubes of paint of every color and pallets of incredible size and shape covered in a kaleidoscope of old paint.

What struck me most was that paint was everywhere, drips, splashes, splatters, spatters, and speckles all over the ancient dark parquet floor, the walls, the aforementioned bench and cabinets, bloody well everywhere! It looked wonderful and incredibly atmospheric. Not just accidental but doodles and swirls of old hardened paint of every color of the rainbow and more! He obviously tested colors in various light and shadows around his studio. Tom saw me staring around smiling. I was also taking in that familiar smell of an artist's studio similarly redolent of Ellie's in north London, solvents, turpentine and oil paints and tobacco. Tom spoke enthusiastically of his painting mainly with oils but also acrylics for his rapid figurative artworks. To sketch he mainly used combinations of charcoal, graphite blocks, pencil, conte pencil, and sometimes pastels if he felt "reckless", which always made me laugh! Only at the completion of a sketch or drawing would he add a touch or hint of pastel or chalk to those he actually liked and only to highlight specific muscular areas of movement and expression in the figure. If he didn't add this, he wasn't happy with the finished drawing.

I did a lot of modeling for Tom over many years but I rarely stood still for him. He wanted to capture my movement. I would literally dance as I chose to, and Tom would sketch at high speed. He also did many balletic studies many of which I still have in my possession. He loved my reference to my dancing as 'walking with style' and that stuck with us. We never mentioned dancing or moving, we always called it 'walking with style'.

"Alright Georgie…," he would boom rolling his tongue, "you git walkin' with style and I'll git sketchin," I loved the man.

I always wore a ballet dancer's dance belt when modeling for Tom because without it, dancing naked is bloody painful! It is a supportive flesh-colored 'jockstrap-like' flexible thong that male dancers wear to pull everything out of the way! In short, your balls are pulled nowhere near between your legs where bad things can happen! I have always called mine my 'harvest festival pants'… all nicely gathered in! Oh, my word, to attempt to dance ballet or contemporary without one would require a medevac within minutes! A dance belt is what gives a male ballet dancer the traditional 'bulge between the legs' so obviously highlighted under dance tights! Sometimes I wore complete ballet gear, a low-cut back and front vest top and tights and dance pumps because of Tom's uneven and splintered studio floor! I also wore dance gear when Tom's studio was really chilly, especially when there was a cold breeze coming in off the sea.

Tom encouraged me to dance brief repetitive repertoires from various classical ballets. I confess here that I made most of them up! Tom sketched and drew furiously like the best artists do. Lots of long-armed sweeps spending 80 percent of his easel time looking at me, studying my movement while he drew. He particularly loved to capture the lines and extensions of my limbs especially capturing my eyeline and transitions between movements and dance positions. His eye for detail of movement combined with my knowledge of physiology led to many incredibly interesting conversations about figurative artists throughout the history of art. To me 'dance modeling' for Tom was a wonderful creative door opening into areas of modeling beyond life modeling such as digital TV commercials and underwear modeling. I learned so much about the many similarities between choreography and painting. There were commonalities with character and developing the minutiae of ideas to define detailing.

The most formative long-term and important personal conversation I had with Tom was during that very first time meeting him at his studio. He understood and brought together all the stressful issues and disconnections I felt in my life that I didn't understand. Tom not only encapsulated the problems I was facing professionally and personally but came up with a simple long-term solution. Tom had a way with words as he had with a paint brush. He brought things alive and three-dimensionally! I mentioned above that Tom and I had a conversation, but he did most of the talking. I did most of the listening, nodding occasionally, taking in all of his words of wisdom in a language I understood. He coincidentally brought together much of the casual chats I'd heard as a boy between my sisters about boyfriends! I'd absorbed my sisters' views about men specifically and in general by osmosis! Tom's own personalized knowledge and learning, his experience eased into my brain!

"I hear from our 'flame-haired beauty' that you believe everyone wants a piece of you!" He said, catching my attention.

The 'flame-haired beauty' was our reference to Valerie, sometimes shortened to FHB!

"… but dear boy it's not that everyone wants a piece of you, it's simply that someone has you in pieces!!" Tom continued. "Your energy flow is disturbed," he added, looking at me and pausing.

"Too right" I said eventually thinking where Tom was going with this.

My mind was turning over to find some perspective with Tom's sudden avuncular approach and subject matter. I thought about Val and his mentioning her grabbed my attention. I felt the urgent need to tell Tom that Val was in no way to be considered as a reason for my current state of flux. I quickly told him that in fact that my creative spirit wasn't lacking, it just felt blocked. I was busy, I was easily covering my living expenses with plenty to spare. I just couldn't put my finger on the cause, or the reason and I didn't know how to put it right! Tom put up his hand in a soothing manner.

"Let me assure you I know that FHB is not the cause, to be honest with you she is concerned about you and asked me for my help" he said.

I was all ears!

"Your personal life is definitely eating up your creative life and I know how inspiring your relationship is with Valerie, for both of you, this isn't about you and her" Tom continued, "it has everything to do with your current girlfriend! Could it be that you are like a thirsty man giving away your water to someone else perhaps?"

"Who, with Issa, my girlfriend?" I asked, guessing.

"Yes," Tom said softly without confrontation.

Issa was currently in major rehearsals six days a week as a member of the corps de ballet in a production of 'Giselle'.

"How much in love are you with Issa?" he asked.

I didn't really understand the question, in fact I definitely wasn't in love with Issa.

"I'm not in love with her, there's nothing irrational about how I feel about her" I replied.

"And you've been together for how long?" Tom asked.

"Er, two years I suppose," I answered thoughtfully "and she moved in with me six months ago" I added wondering whether that was significant.

"Hmmmm, who's paying the bills?" Tom said with his tone darkening slightly squinting his left eye.

"We share them but TBH my income is pretty steady whereas she's constantly penniless. She lives basically hand to mouth, smokes too much and auditioning for greatness seems to be her great purpose in life!" I said, trying to lighten the tone.

There's a sudden revealing truth in humor sometimes! I was attempting to sound laid back about it, I surprised myself by the sheer clarity of my relationship with Issa! I was actually listening to myself! I'd described it in one short sentence. It was true and it made me think 'why am I with Issa?' I was kidding myself that the diminishing connection between us was due to her workload. However, it is one thing knowing that and then understanding the can of worms that would open up if I were to confront her with my simple analysis!

"Tell me more!" Tom said, rhetorically, "I'm going to apply some S.W.A.G."

"Huh?" I mumbled furrowing my brow, "what's that mean?"

"A Scientific Wild Ass Guess" he answered, smiling at me, and putting me at ease. "Now listen carefully to me and tell me I'm not wrong!"

I always loved Tom's use of double negatives to emphasize the positive!

"You are what is known as 'cunt struck', Georgie." Tom continued wobbling his stretched fingers in front of him in a gentle gesture, "you are in a relationship with Issa which should seem like a fair business transaction. You see, men give up financial resources for access to pussy! Issa is giving you access to pussy for access to resources, your resources my lovely boy! And now, and I'd bet my pallets, she is giving you less and less access to pussy now than six months ago and you are paying an incremental increase in resources for less pussy. I'd also say that you are paying far more in emotional resources for less access too! What do you get in return for your time, money, and creative energy? Think about it! How about assessing what you are receiving in return then? Certainly not contentment and happiness!"

I was hooked by what Tom was saying. It confirmed that Val had been speaking to Tom about me. Thinking of the amazing and inspiring Valerie suddenly put Issa into perspective. Val was my lover, and I'd continued to see Val but less so since living with Issa. Val made no bones about me having a girlfriend, she never mentioned her, never asked any questions and to be honest nothing had changed between us. Val had dated other men, and I asked her no questions. Val and I were more connected than ever. I might not be in touch with her for weeks and then when we reconnected, we reconnected instantly and intensely. I now realized that by talking to Tom, Val was genuinely concerned about me. She had noticed a change in my creative edge.

Tom continued after watching me think. My face must have been a picture deep in thought!

"Now young fella, we've now established that you are giving up your time, money and creative energy for access to a certain pussy, a pussy becoming more and more scarce! This is actually robbing you of contentment and happiness which you need in order to propagate your creative world. You are now living together which is worse because you are sharing the same space unequally!"

I opened my mouth to speak but Tom held up a hand to stop me. He continued,

"You are an extremely attractive, sexy, and desirable man. You should never, ever, never need to be obsessed with one woman. You can have as much pussy as you want as and when it comes to you, concurrently if you want it. By using that as your mindset whether you go for it or not, you will refocus on your passion and love for the creative arts."

I was standing listening to Tom amazed at how his words resonated with me. I've never forgotten a word! I had turned down and even ignored a number of sexual encounters while being in my relationship with Issa. Worse, I hadn't been to a gallery or any art exhibitions for nearly six months. I'd even canceled a fucking life modeling gig twice, to help Issa prepare for her auditions.

"Also," Tom continued, "Issa is a Ukrainian woman, I've been told! And my man, women from that part of the world especially are materialistic and financially acquisitive! Believe me, the rule of hypergamy will kick in sooner or later with her…"

I looked around and found a stool to sit on and must have looked puzzled and he raised his hand again to stop me speaking and continued,

"Let me explain… she'll soon be fucking and fleecing some cunt-struck 'City Slicker' financier, some millionaire hedge fund manager, yep soon enough who will provide her with even more of what she wants and at that point she will drop you. Believe me she has probably already finished with you but has not said so yet because she won't leave you until she's 'monkey-branched' into a relationship with another man. She won't jump ship until she's firmed everything up! Then she will drop you like a hot potato!"

I nodded at what Tom was saying, in the sense that I was trying to cover up that I was feeling a little upset. Tom carried on with his analysis of my reality.

"I would also bet that Issa is extremely beautiful without doubt but right now I would say that when you are both together at your apartment she's going to be makeup free, greasy hair tied up onto her head, wearing knackered old joggers and stuffing her face with Doritos while sitting on your sofa watching your TV and stinking your place out with fags! She will call it chilling but you and I know she's taking the piss!"

Tom's 'litany of truths' wasn't far off the mark! How did he know? Valerie had gathered the data from comments I'd made obviously! I looked at Tom and he took a deep breath and gently pointed a long slender finger at me as he continued to speak some more…

"You now smell her sweat, her farts, the smell of her shit in your bathroom, your laundry basket is full of her stinking gussets, and I bet you put that crap into your washing machine for her!"

Tom was serious now! He knew from my expression that he had hit the 'realization bullseye' with me. Suddenly I knew I had a genuine ally in Tom. I felt no anger toward him, none, zero, zilch! He had no ulterior motives. He was absolutely correct in describing my current relationship status with Issa. I pictured my sisters in my mind eavesdropping on Tom telling me how it is and all of them would be having what we called a 'mirth ball of a time' at my expense. If I ever wanted a mental benchmark to measure where I was at, that should be enough! My sisters would be stacking the shits with me! Tom had paused to allow me to take all of this in and looking into his kind eyes he smiled genuinely at me. We slowly began to laugh quietly and then we laughed louder and louder, laughing constantly. Tom continued,

"I'm right when I say your priority isn't pussy aren't I!" he said half-rhetorically with a grin.

I knew it wasn't a serious question, he was being funny, but I sensed he wanted clarity in any case.

"True it just comes along but Issa came along, and she became my 'official' girlfriend," I replied and then quoted Peter O'Toole's understanding of women.

I'd not seen Val as much at all recently, but we'd had a few afternoons and some evenings together just socially. However, I did see a growing monogamous future with Issa. Tom had latterly been preparing a pot of tea while we were talking.

"Absolutely dear boy, I can understand that" Tom said in response to Peter O'Toole's theory. "Inter alia that's exactly what you were doing and should be doing constantly, by default, you shouldn't be acting like a moon around someone else's planet!" Tom continued. "I hope my words have put you back on track?"

"Yeah, they have," I replied, smiling "but I definitely think I'm a quality over quantity sort of man though" I added.

"Oh yes, you mean you shop in Harrods rather than Tesco" he added joking again "but remember shopping in Harrods could be a high maintenance problem so you'd be back in the pussy trap… you get my gist?" Tom said suddenly, looking straight at me!

I wanted Tom to know I'd listened to him, so I gave him a visual analogy to confirm that and hopefully humor him too. I continued using his 'shopping analogy'.

"Yes, I understand where the traps lie, Tom" I said laughing "Harrods is very expensive, and the customers are conspicuous consumers and I cannot be bought as a playmate but I might do some 'shoplifting' to try out one or two goodies! But I'd say that TK Max is my sweet spot! A lot of quality items that pop out at you without draining the bank account plus I can often wander around TK without spending anything even if I can afford to. If there is a business relationship between men and women, I'd say my own definition is just as I shop; do I want it, do I need it, can I afford it? And if the answer is no to any of those questions I don't bother! I need three yeses!"

"Very good! I like your style," Tom said, nodding and he came over with a mug of tea and he ruffled my hair.

"And…," he began again laughing and looking jokingly conspiratorial "ballet girls are a tad prone to yeast infections are they not!" I began to laugh and looked embarrassed, "and I bet that your current, once sugar pussy, is now redolent of fish these days and she's a bit parsimonious with the old ladyshave too, yes?!"

We both roared with laughter. I knew he was joking but it did pop into my mind how there was zero comparison between Issa and Valerie when it came to which of these two women's playtime preparation I preferred!

"So, what's the solution?" I asked.

Tom spoke softly still with tears of mirth in his eyes.

"I've no particular advice about Issa, never met the girl, but your big solution is most definitely 'abundance'. Go out there as you've always done, open your eyes, reestablish your artistic soul, work on yourself and lo-and-behold you will not only find your creative mojo again but you will notice that you are prowled by and preyed upon by all those women who want to sink their nails and teeth into your very cute ass I shouldn't wonder! It's high time you realized that you are a 'sigma male'. Look it up, find out about it. You'll understand yourself far better when you do."

Tom went over to his kettle again giving it a shake to check it had water in it. He clicked it on and looked around for my empty mug and swilled out his huge blue enameled 'Falcon' teapot he'd used earlier. He began to make a fresh pot of tea again as he spoke thoughtfully, occasionally looking around at his artworks all over the studio.

"Abundance, abundance, abundance in all things concurrently. Never pay a high price for one thing… or one pussy! Like I said, get back to working on yourself again and the drag of Issa will fall away. Treat her like she treats you and she will either try to recapture your value for herself again or she will just bugger off. Either way just politely ignore her, and she will show her true colors. In fact, dear boy, if I were you, I'd just get the whole thing sorted ASAP and ditch her!"

Tom turned to face me. And his voice rose into a 'performance crescendo' waving his arms around like the conductor of an orchestra. He then impersonated Louis Armstrong's voice and final words at the end of the film 'High Society', "END OF STORY!"

We giggled like schoolboys and I knew Tom and I would know each other for years and years.

Tom and I then spent a wonderful arty chatty early evening in Margate by going off to a little restaurant near to his studio. The staff welcomed him like a celebrity. In fact, in the art world, he is a celebrity. Not another word was said between us about Issa but I knew she was 'toast' as far as I was concerned. Tom had done the caring work that Val had wanted him to do plus he got a male life model to draw. Importantly we became lifelong friends. I also knew I would not be allowed to fall into a 'pussy trap' ever again! Before I left that evening Tom took the time to speak to me quietly before I left. He told me the five simple tests for any man to assess whether he is in a successful long-term monogamous relationship.

"My dear boy…" I always knew he was about to tell me something profound when he started with that phrase, "these are the five tests… Is she useful to you? Is she a slut in bed? Is she verbally respectful with you? Is she emotionally intelligent? Does she have obvious mental health? If the answer to any of those questions is 'no' then look elsewhere! You have created your life subconsciously, consciously, and instinctively. You learn but create from what you continually learn, my boy your life is like John Singer Sergeant's body of work. It's contentious, enigmatic and sexually charged but unlike him scandal has evaded you because you don't seek it. That's why I say you live your life in the moment. If you become distracted you will develop a scarcity mindset; you will be submerged into mediocrity that will cause you intense mental confusion. Remember, 'abundance at all times' and I mean 'concurrent abundance at all times'."

My relationship with Valerie was cemented yet again right there! She both owned me, and she had set me free! In return I owned her, and I'd set her free too.

Catching the last train home to London that evening, leaving Tom 'holding court' at the restaurant I made my way slowly back to my flat. I even stopped off at a local pub near Stockwell tube station for a shandy. As I sat sipping the sweet weak beer I did a mental inventory. The tenancy agreement on my flat was solely in my name and I worked out my income and outgoings. I had been thinking of treating myself to an arty trip to Edinburgh and Glasgow in Scotland and Belfast in Ulster. When I eventually returned to my lovely flat there was no Issa. I'd made up my mind about her and made sure the 'Banham' door lock was latched to prevent her coming in and surprising me. I'd need time to prepare myself for her return. It was late but I expected her back but to be honest I didn't want her to come back. She always turned up whenever she wanted to at 'Hotel Chez George'! Her absence would make things so much easier!

I looked around my spacious one-bedroom apartment and realized Issa's 'shit' was everywhere. It had previously seemed like part of her personality but now it was just shit! I grabbed her huge cheap cavernous hold-all from under my bed and stuffed it full of her cheap clothes. Clothes that made her look chavvy! I really enjoyed stuffing in her ridiculous 'puffer jackets' with their ridiculous over large hoods and styled so short that they barely covered her naked midriff in cold weather! What a fashion victim she was! I recalled how much time she spent arranging her clothes in my full length mirror every time she went out, even for a quick trip to the local Tesco Express. She spent a lot of time exaggerating every detail to make herself look cool and casual.

She would always turn her back to my full-length mirror to ensure a hint of G-string was showing above the waistband of her low-cut jeans! I waded through my laundry basket, tipping the unwashed clothes onto my bed and sorted out Issa's stuff from my own and put hers into a bin bag. Tom was right about her stinking gussets! Her copious shoes I also double-bagged. In her largest handbag I dumped her knackered cosmetics and everything that cluttered up my bathroom and bagged up the rest of her ludicrous handbags! Why so many handbags! All this crap looked like a mess next to the main door, so I put it all outside on the landing. Issa had keys and would be able to gain access through the street door. My flat door had three locks, as well as the Banham it also had two Chubb locks, for which she didn't have keys. I knew I could lock her out especially as I had no idea how she would react. I was completely calm, but I could feel the passion for devilment inside me!

At about 3am I was woken by my mobile phone. It was Issa's personalized ringing tone. As I went to answer it, I noticed that there were at least six unread text messages I'd not heard. As my phone rang, I could also hear a banging on my flat door. I correctly assumed it was Issa! The banging on the door was loud and incessant. In fact, that little gal was kicking it! The door was solid wood with no give in it so bless her little ballet feet I thought. I decided to text her rather than let her in. Cruel, yes, and I take responsibility for my actions, past, present, and future but Issa never contributed a bloody thing to our relationship, and it was my fault asking her if she wanted to move in.

'Kick the door all night if you want. We are done. Take your stuff and bog off.'

I followed up with,

'Email me a list of your stuff I haven't bagged up and I'll make sure you get it all back.'

Issa replied.

'IL SU U 4 THIS'

Yeah right, I thought. I made myself a brew and listened to her voice mails after she had obviously buggered off. They were venomous and full of bile and her accent made her sound like an east European gangster's whore! I deleted them all after concluding that they were evidence enough of that bloodsucker.

Despite Issa's understandable rants I received a lot of conciliatory text messages from her over the next few days. Some of her friends too acted as 'character witnesses' by text, but I wasn't taken in. She even made sure she bumped into me a few times at various places to confront me with her 'crocodile tears'. She wanted to talk to sort things out and get back together again. I even went round one evening to the place she was staying with friends near Borough Market, and we ended up having what I can only describe as a very lengthy 'closure fuck'! Alas, for Issa she saw it as a 'new beginning fuck' and yes, she did smell of fish!

I didn't waste any more time, energy and resources on Issa. Tom had effectively rebooted me and reset my head and my heart in the right directions. Unfortunately, my cock had got the better of them both with Issa! Never again! Whenever I have become aware of the 'pussy trap' and the inevitable 'cunt struck' stage that follows, as all men are fallible, I've recognized it and not fallen for it since. Always abundance remember!

In fact, I now know that the collective term for 'pussy' is 'an abundance of pussies'! In all seriousness, by concentrating on myself and improving myself by tiny margins on a regular basis without selfishly neglecting the people I love and respect, I have found that I have enough emotional energy to help people without draining my own. I have never treated a woman as a business transaction but I'm afraid by definition that is exactly what it is for both parties. I am in love with my work in the arts, but I have also learned how and when to burn my bridges and just walk away at times. In fact, if you do not use the power of walking away when a creative atmosphere becomes negative you have more to lose as a performer by the attrition of your creativity over a prolonged period of time, compared with just ending the whole energy draining palaver instantly!

Chapter Ten

Loretta the Painter… Red flags, expletives, and alliterations, run Georgie, run!

I'd been approached by a large well-known publicly funded art gallery by their newly appointed exciting and ambitious curator. Her name was Angela. She had an artist background, a master's degree in fine art and she wanted to attract more people into the gallery spaces. Numerous artistic events were planned as a rolling program and me and another life model, Cara were slated for a six-month contract as the appointed life models to the gallery. We were both excited. I'd never met Cara previously, but this is typical for life models. Models rarely meet except coincidentally. I once met a group of male life models in London for a social and it was just the once! It was like a scene from 'Brideshead Revisited'! I have modeled as a duo twice with female life models, but as for socializing, it doesn't happen. I call these pairings a 'pose de deux'! Basically, life models are like ships passing in the night. I can state here also that I have never had a sexual relationship with another life model.

I met at the gallery with Cara, Angela and the appointed tutor for the life drawing, an artist called Maggie, to go through the life drawing calendar of events. We discussed the allocation of dates and times, we signed the paperwork and got to know one another. The complete program was to be tutored by the entertaining Maggie and judging by the size of the huge well-lit side gallery we were to use, the events were going to be very well-attended. Maggie went through her 2 ½ hour format for the life drawing. There were to be two sessions each week for four weeks then a break for four weeks and then repeat over the remainder of the year, sixteen sessions in total. A nice source of income for a model. I took the Tuesday morning slot between 10am–12:30pm and Cara took the equivalent Friday slot.

Cara was about 35 years old and stereotypical of the female life model. Very curvy and most definitely a 'sitter' and a 'recliner', whereas I would be on my feet in dance poses for 80 percent of the time. Both Angela and Maggie liked this contrast of modeling presentation. This then formed the background for me to meet Loretta!

Loretta, I was to learn, had booked onto the Friday life drawing class with Cara as the model. However, after the very first week of drawing, Loretta, a quiet elfin professional artist and a very knowledgeable academic suggested that each model should alternate from week to week, meaning I would model on a Tuesday and the following week I would model on the Friday. This would she said, provide each group to experience more variation. This made sense and was agreed. Cara and I had no problem adapting to this.

The following Friday, I went along to model. As is the custom, Maggie the tutor introduced me and reiterated the format for the session. The first hour would involve 4 x 5 minute warmup sketches followed by 4 x 10 minute fast drawings all tutored by Maggie. After the interval there would be 2 x 30 minute poses to practice the detail from the techniques learned during the first hour. Maggie had her own easel from which she would demonstrate techniques to the artists. Each of the 24 attendees had an easel from which to draw from. Maggie had had a word with me before the session and agreed the poses I would do, and she relayed these to the artists. She informed them that as well as ballet positions, I would be using Yoga and Pilates positions for poses too. There was a fluttering of applause and verbal excitement which took me by surprise. All the easels were arranged in a large circle which I personally preferred.

The gallery was Georgian in style and the side gallery we were in had a very high ceiling with a long rectangular glass 'lantern' fixture which shed masses of morning light into the gallery. The gallery was extremely well-maintained, but it was quite cool and as a result I had brought along my own silent fan heater with an electrical extension cord. I would be able to model in a pocket of warm air. Maggie brought everyone to order after they had arranged their easels with boards and drawing papers. I flicked on my heater and dropped my robe to begin my first 5-minute pose.

When I life model I actually perform. I am not 'playing myself naked', I am 'in character'. Personally, I could not stand naked as myself in front of people anywhere! Also, by posing in character I am able to be more expressive and represent movement. This day I adapted the dance poses from the ballet 'Firebird'. Also, by being in character I create a theatrical 'fourth wall' whereby the audience of artists draw the character and not me personally and they follow a storyline. As I mentioned before, I do not speak unless spoken to by the tutor and I do not make conscious eye contact with the artists.

As all the classes were tutored, Maggie spoke regularly and quietly 'tout le monde' and also individually with artists as she moved around or when dealing with individual artist's questions. I changed the direction of my poses each time as usual to provide different points of view for the artists. During one of the initial ten-minute poses I happened to be front-facing with Loretta. Maggie at this point was talking with Loretta and she had greeted her by name, and it was obvious that they knew each other quite well judging by their brief friendly chat. Listening in I heard Maggie use Loretta's name and reading between the lines it was evident that Loretta was a highly accomplished professional artist. She was attending the life drawing to improve her own drawing techniques whereas the rest of the group were essentially beginners and there to be tutored using various drawing media.

After their chat, Maggie moved away from Loretta and my eyes followed the back of Maggie's head and then as I flicked my eyes back to the front they met with Loretta's eyes. It was an unconscious thing and unprofessional, but it does happen occasionally and is instantly corrected. However, I found my eyes locked with Loretta's and I was so shocked I couldn't tear them away! I wanted to look away, but Loretta was deeply staring at me to make a connection and then very slowly she licked her lips with the tip of her tongue in what was an unmistakable sexual act! She then slightly opened her mouth and subtly pouted her lips and tilted her head down to stare at me from under her eyebrows!

After she assumed I'd gotten the message her face returned to neutral, and she began drawing again at arm's length very freely. I struggled to stay in character and to be honest I was shocked and had no idea whether she intended to look at me like that, whether she was teasing me or whether it was just her subconscious drawing attitude! As all but four of the artists that day were women, I had the sudden feeling that the other women would have noticed what Loretta had done. However the way the drawing boards were arranged, the angles and size of them provided her with a lot of 'cover' so she obviously felt quite confident. Of course, Loretta's 'stare' at me seemed much longer than it would have seemed to the casual observer but as artists are absorbed in their own drawings, they rarely consciously look at each other.

Over the years of actual life modeling to that point, it was the first openly visual sexual advance toward me I had experienced. As I mentioned before, when you are naked, every one of your senses is extremely heightened, even exaggerated and Loretta had completely scrambled my concentration. Let me make it clear I was not remotely turned on by her actions! My mind went into overdrive. I had to rely on all of my professional theater and performance experience to hold character and to settle myself down. I did not react to Loretta in any way except to return my eyeline above the head height of the artists. I felt for the first time as a life model a 'naked nakedness'. In that moment it equated to bloody fear! She should not have done it and had it been a male artist consciously doing that with a female model there would have been hell to pay but I'm a man and to be honest it's like 'so fucking what, move on'!

Things happen on stage, things go wrong, usually from the sublime to the ridiculous so I heard Michael Caine in my head saying, "Use the difficulty." For my final ten-minute pose before the interval I went for complete characterization of a highly extended ballet position derived from a ballet 'arabesque in first' but with my right big toe 'à terre' for extended balance. Only ten minutes for the artists to draw but for me every supporting muscle ached like a bastard! My eyeline alone as part of the position for the pose was a 'stress position' but it had the effect of resetting my concentration. The artists benefited from something out of the ordinary. Adrenaline had kicked in!

"One minute to go" Maggie said.

One minute passed. I actually counted the seconds.

"Okay that's it for this pose and now the break. Please leave all your drawings accessible and we'll start the next session with the 'show and tell.'"

There was a muted mirthful groan and giggles from the artists due to the fact that many of them were beginners and felt a little embarrassed by being asked to show their efforts.

"Thank you, George, we've all really appreciated your graceful long lines," Maggie continued, and I received words of thanks and a smattering of applause. "Let's go for tea and coffee, juice, there are biscuits and cake, yum" added Maggie.

"Let's have a mingle."

While Maggie was speaking, I put on my robe and quickly grabbed a brew before the rush. I bloody needed it! It's rare for me to talk at length during intervals unless it is with a private group I am familiar with, so I sipped my tea to one side away from the throng. With tutored groups, the tutor is Queen or King, so I stay out of the way, and I do not mingle. This is my approach and is a habit that is true of theater. Again, I try to maintain the 'fourth wall' but if I am approached, I will of course engage. Afterall, life drawing is an artistic experience for those paying for the pleasure to draw. I'd put Loretta out of my mind. I smiled and nodded freely to those who looked my way where I stood sipping my tea and I spoke briefly to a couple of the artists. Suddenly I felt a gentle touch on my shoulder from behind me. It was Loretta! I turned to look at her feeling incredibly vulnerable!

Loretta was about 5 feet tall and extremely dainty. She immediately struck me as a six-foot-tall supermodel in miniature! All of her proportions were perfect but tiny! In no way could you describe her as skinny. She was wearing a tight black stretch vest top making her look even smaller. I could see her tiny collar bones and her arms were narrow and her belly was flat. Her right arm had a full length celtic black ink tattoo from wrist to deltoid. The hem of her black vest touched the elasticated waistband of a pair of mid-gray very baggy joggers with elasticated ankle bands. The bagginess of them accentuated her tiny waist and yet highlighted her elfin figure beneath them.

A faint hint of pale flesh was visible between her vest top and the joggers and reminded me that I'm a sucker for flat abs! She wore no makeup whatsoever and the most striking thing about her was her hair. It was dark brown straight and extremely long and thick reaching to her waist. It was blunt cut at the back with a very straight thick fringe, very high on her forehead revealing her pretty face and highlighting her large brown eyes. Her image was made more striking by her solid very thick, unkempt dark brown eyebrows. The most incredible fascinating and attractive thing about her healthy hair was that from scalp downwards there were extremely shiny silver individual hairs evenly spread throughout her locks every centimeter or so, set against the shiny dark brown of the rest of her hair.

They looked so even and equally spaced that you could be mistaken for thinking that an expert hairdresser had created the whole look by braiding them in. Her thick hair was super shiny and iridescent and shimmered as she moved. I put her age as late 30s early 40s but my success rate at guessing a woman's age is pathetic!

The sudden image of her completely distracted me from the initial shock of her previous sexually provocative stare as I took in the whole image of her. I found myself speaking first.

"Wow I love your hair, it looks amazing," hoping I'd conservatively complimented her without encouraging her as I began to remember 'that stare'!

"Thank you, George, I'm Loretta. Gotta be quick as I want to catch Maggie, but here's my card. I work out of a shared studio on Holborn. Drop me a line. I'd love to paint you" she said, in a clear low voice, an octave lower than you would expect from someone so dainty.

Her voice was rich and level and naturally sultry. This also took me by surprise. I took the proffered card from her tiny hand, scanned it politely and put it in the pocket of my robe.

"Er yeah, thanks" I said… "er I'll drop you a line tomorrow, fix something up."

"Great. Quickly, of course I'll pay good rates for your time, thinking a couple of loose hours of sketching next week and then a full day the week after next to paint you. The Thursday week after for the full day if you could confirm asap" she said. "I saw you on stage in 'South Pacific' recently" she added quietly and touched my arm "you have great stage presence!"

She turned immediately and walked away gracefully with her tiny hips swaying before I could reply. I was speechless. Not because I was standing there alone but because the way she had 'booked' me was like she was giving me no choice and expected my compliance! Or at least she was attempting to show her enthusiasm to book me. She'd seen me on stage; was that a coincidence? I watched her as she walked directly away in front of me for quite a distance with her head turning right and left as though scanning the room for Maggie, when we both knew that Maggie was directly behind me not more than ten feet away! I checked out her posture and gait as any dancer would but also checked out her cute tiny ass. It dawned on me that walking in front of me was intentional. The rear seam of her joggers was pulled up tightly between her butt cheeks!

"Oh, my word," I said to myself under my breath.

The second hour of the life drawing began with the 'show and tell' followed by my two 30-minute standing dance poses. Maggie had kindly put on the music from the ballet 'Firebird' very softly. All went well and time passed very quickly as I zoned out into the music. I ran through the choreography of the ballet in my head. Maggie wrapped up the session with a few comments detailing the following week and I received claps and thanks from everyone present. I was not aware of Loretta at all. Maggie then quickly approached me and said,

"I draw with a group of artist friends on Sundays, let Angela know to allow me to have your contact details if you'd like to model for us. I know you are about to get changed so I don't want to disturb your routine now" she said.

"I'd love to, yeah no worries" I replied, "er how well do you know Loretta? She's just booked me for next week and the week after at her studio."

"Has she now!?" Maggie replied, touching her chin with her right index finger.

I thought she was about to say something funny, but she paused for quite a while and said,

"Hmmm interesting, she's not known for her figurative art! I know her as an artist but not personally. Let me know how it goes. Very interesting."

Just as I was about to wander off to the private changing area designated for the model, I absentmindedly looked around the bustling gallery as the artists cleared up and chatted away. Loretta was already leaving with her extremely large rectangular portfolio case strapped diagonally across her shoulders and her artist's box of drawing media in her hand. She was wearing oversized big black army boots that gave her a very interesting artie look. Suddenly she stopped and slowly turned around and our eyes met! I flinched inside myself, and she gave me a little casual wave with her free hand. She then left. Holy cow we had a connection, but I can say with all honesty it was a connection I didn't really want. I consoled myself with the prospect of paid work with an extremely good artist.

The following morning, I drank my morning brew and munched on vegemite on toast and thought of Loretta's card. I just took the 'improv approach' and said to myself "yes and…" out loud. I emailed her but did not add my mobile phone number. I thought that if she responds too quickly, too enthusiastically it would be a bad sign! I kept my email wording friendly and businesslike. I then focused on preparing my body with stretches as I do most mornings for the supernumerary role I was playing with a leading opera company over the next two weeks. Seven performances both weeks including two matinees on both Fridays and Saturdays. These background character parts are totally unstressful, improvised easily at rehearsals, pay very well and in this show, I got to dress up in period costume. Well, in this production a baggy canvas shirt, made-to-look dirty jodhpurs, rough looking gators and my arms, chest, and hair sprayed with dilute 'baby oil' to make me look sweaty and greasy. Bloody bonzer fun plus I love the un-mic'd power of opera singers on stage, they make my spine tingle.

I then chatted with mum over Skype and made plans to be at The Royal Opera House early to soak up the atmosphere of the front of house, the auditorium briefly where partial pre-show rehearsals would be taking place with the orchestra and then venturing into the back stage buzz before going on to the friendliness and excitement of the dressing rooms. Sitting in one of the dressing rooms at around 5pm my Blackberry pinged telling me I'd received an email, and this also reminded me to silence my cellphone! I checked the email, and it was from Loretta. Briefly and without fuss she asked whether I could make it to her shared studio in Holborn at 11am the following Thursday for "a couple of loose hours" for sketching me and she signed off the email with "L xxx." That's not OTT I remember thinking. I emailed her back quickly as it was time to change into costume, with,

'Righto, see you there' with no 'kisses'.

Suddenly another email came through…

'… silly me the address is… etc.

I read this quickly and smiled. I thought she's just like all artists, a bit scatty. I sent her a laughing face in reply.

'… :))'

This had the effect of making me feel a lot easier about the enigmatic Loretta and put me back on an even keel.

Thursday morning arrived for me to travel to Loretta's studio by the underground, 'the tube'. I felt good. All was right with my world. I took the Stockwell tube changing at Green Park and onwards to Holborn. I carried a small hold-all containing my robe and a few toiletries and stuff I needed for the RoH performance that evening. Under my arm I carried a yoga roll. I easily found the address. A street level door between two shops and a staircase that led upwards that doubled-backed on itself leading to a closed door on the first floor. I knocked and entered simultaneously. The space was a typical artist's studio similar in most ways to Tom's. However, this floor space stretched left and right from the doorway and covered at least two shops below either side. In effect it was long and fairly narrow.

I was met by a bloke who introduced himself as Carl. I told him who I was and why I was there. He was friendly in a nondescript way, and he pointed to his right, my left, telling me that Loretta's part of the studio was located at the far end. I thanked him and he offered me a coffee which I accepted. I wandered over to find Loretta while taking in all the artworks of that well-lit studio. There were even partially completed figurative sculptures, some with wire frames jutting from them partially molded in clay. It was a warm day and some of the angled windows were open. The smell was pungently evocative of a busy artist studio, and I could hear the familiar rising and falling clatter of London black cabs in the street below. There was also a gentle background music which I knew was traditional Cambodian music. Very relaxing and I liked the place instantly. It felt right.

Loretta greeted me by kissing me on both cheeks and again she wasn't wearing any makeup. She wore flip flops on her bare feet and her toenails were painted shiny black with not a sign of a chip. Freshly done the previous night was my quick conclusion. I then realized I was constantly on my guard in every detail with Loretta. I didn't feel threatened but there was something, just something to keep me on my toes, or so I thought. She was wearing extremely baggy oversized 'Oxford bag' jeans pulled up high over her navel level and fastened extremely tightly around her waist with a very broad black leather belt. The folds of the oversized waistband under the belt were gathered together and it fluted outwards above the belt; she looked like a Christmas cracker!

Above this she wore a skintight white crop top covering her small proportionate breasts and revealing flesh and the edges of her ribcage. Under the crop top was a needless delicate light blue pastel colored bra and the shoulder straps were visible. This was obviously a fashion statement and well thought out and added a touch of cool color to her outfit. She looked extremely dainty especially as her delicate head was highlighted by her thick silvery-stranded hair which she'd tied back in a loose flowing long swishing ponytail. The natural light flickered around her silver hair strands. She looked really sexy but a contrived sexiness as though she was trying to find a balance between looking like a working artist and being overly fashionable. The sudden thought of banging her senseless naked, over one of her free-standing tables shot through my mind and then disappeared!

The coffee arrived delivered by Carl who then left instantly without saying much to either of us. I analyzed him but there was nothing about him that made me feel uneasy. Loretta must have noticed and told me Carl had his part of the studio at the far end and that he was extremely busy making theater props. I could go over and meet him and have a look later if I felt like it, she casually told me. She then made it clear we wouldn't be disturbed, and she put down her mug of coffee and began to unfold a long vertical cloth screen at least six feet high and placed it between us and the rest of the studio space. I offered to help her to break any residual ice, but she declined it pleasantly.

"You'll need your strength!" she commented teasingly in her natural low dulcet toned voice,

And then she 'cackled'! A really loud incongruous cackle. It sounded demented! It was completely at odds with her natural voice and much higher in tone and far too loud! I thought it was her joke comedy laugh not unlike the wicked witch in a pantomime but no! She cackled again. I was unsettled by this!

Holy fuck! I thought and my natural 'spider senses' jumped up two notches! I sipped my disgusting coffee which didn't make me feel any better leaving a really bad taste in my mouth to go with the metaphorical one I now had! I wandered around the space a little while, that had clearly been set up for my modeling and I tried to find my creative mojo. I was starting to paddle like a bloody duck to be honest! Loretta finished positioning the screen and I suddenly realized that she was quiet whenever she did anything.

Usually, most people would talk and chat a bit while they pottered around doing stuff in their familiar environment but not Loretta. It made me feel uneasy and the 'power of silence' was backfiring on me! The saving grace was the light tinkle of the Cambodian music in the background but that often became swamped by street noises. Then she walked toward me and stood just that little bit too close and asked out of the blue, what I was performing in currently. I told her and expected a supplementary question or a comment of some sort, but she said diddly squat! So I asked her awkwardly about the artworks around her studio but with no bloody interest and interlaced that with comments here and there that I made up on the spot rather than being inspired.

With the screen in place to her satisfaction, having needlessly popped back a couple of times to adjust it, I felt a little hemmed in! The sounds also seemed to be dampened by it but that could have been my growing uneasiness pumping energy into my eyes. I was very watchful of her! I began to feel like she was a she-spider spinning a web around me. Fucking 'Shelob's Lair' I thought, holy shit! The sooner this "loose couple of hours" begins and ends and hopefully in silence, with her visible at all times, the better, I thought!

There was no obvious place to change. When I say change, I mean strip fucking naked in front of Shelob... I mean Loretta! I also scrambled around in my head for a character from a ballet to use to get into performance mode as quickly as possible. 'Use the difficulty, George', I kept thinking to myself. Maybe my uneasiness was just me over-thinking, but I have very good instincts, and I trust them! I needed to take control and decided it was 'prep time'. I therefore stood to one side opening my hold-all and started to prepare to model. I took out my thick white cotton bathrobe and it gave me comfort as Valerie had given it to me. I laid it carefully over a chair and took off my Levi jacket and vest top and put the robe on. I then unrolled my yoga mat and spent precious time to calm down by making it flat, so it didn't curl up at the ends. I flipped it over eventually, so the curls were pressed flat against the floor. Under my bathrobe I was still dressed from the waist down in Slazenger trackies and tennis shoes that Val had also bought for me. Standing on my mat, I proceeded to remove my tennis shoes, socks, and trackies but I left on my underwear.

Loretta watched me as I did all of this. I could see her peripherally and sense her gaze and eventually she spoke… thank fuck!

"Ready for business," she asked rhetorically.

I answered anyway trying to feel at ease,

"Yeah, no worries, what would you like to start with?"

"I'm thinking maybe ten two-minute poses dance style followed by a bunch of five-minute ones. Then take it from there."

I nodded and said "Righto", trying to force a smile. I thought why she hadn't said all of this earlier rather than watching me in silence, while I stripped off! I suppose I could have said something, but I'd have sounded lame and nervous. How could this tiny little elf of a woman have me in such a state? I dug down into my thoughts and there it was! It was that hideous witch-like cackle of a laugh she had. It had totally spooked me!

"I work quickly," she said. Typical of pro artists. "I'll be using charcoal as my medium both large scale at my easel and on A4 on a board while wandering around you, to detail your physique," she added with her hands deep inside her Oxford bag jeans.

Holy shit I thought, she's going to be where I can't see her and my sense of hearing suddenly boosted as if by magic!

"Yeah, that's good," I lied! "Whatever suits you."

No wonder female life models I have met from time to time do not like modeling alone one-to-one with male artists preferring, if necessary, female artists. Me too, but not Loretta!

I'd at least managed to find my character in my head to begin modeling and let Loretta know that I'd be using the ballet 'Spartacus' for inspiration. I mentioned earlier I like to use female ballet dancers to inspire my life modeling because of their grace and expression but today with Loretta I wanted to be very, extremely masculine! It was a form of self-defense! She popped over to her phone fiddled with it and the orchestral music from the ballet Spartacus came from it, sounding like it was being performed in a biscuit tin! At least it wouldn't cover up any sound of her getting too close to me and would distract my overactive mind! I told myself to calm down and remain in character. She was hardly a virago ogress!

"Thanks" I said, attempting to sound, if not feel, more relaxed.

I stood on my yoga mat and politely turned my back to her because I suddenly didn't want to start 'full frontal', I needed to build up to that. My bathrobe was hanging loose. I'd kept it from flapping open by keeping my hands in the pouch pockets at the front of it. It was time to strip off. I pulled my bathrobe slightly apart and slipped out of my underwear. I was wearing a pure white cotton and lycra men's thong, my favorite Homme brand. I bent down to remove it and stood up with it in my hand and for a second, I couldn't think what to do with it. I didn't want to lob it to the chair where my tracksuit and jacket were hanging, risking it landing on the dirty floor. Then I decided to scrunch it up and pop it into one of my bathrobe pockets. Loretta had approached me as I did all this and suddenly, she was standing next to me with her hand out.

"We'll put that baby somewhere safe, eh?" she said, sounding playful.

'What the fuck' I thought! She didn't sound creepy, and she was grinning in a fun way and before I could think of an alternative, I submissively passed her my thong! I instantly thought that if I'd refused, she would have detected my growing sense of unease so to disguise that I essentially made myself feel worse!

"Oh, it's still warm," she said gently, looking at it.

She folded it quickly and shoved it with aplomb into one of the front pockets of her baggy jeans, turned around and walked to her easel. I tensed thinking she'd 'cackle'. I swear if she had I'd have run out of that studio like my ass was on fire! She didn't thank god!

"My process is that I am both a visual and physical artist in the sense that I like to be tactile…" she began.

I had no problem with that, I knew many artists who used their fingers as part of their artistic method, but she went on to make me feel even more nervous!

"So with your permission I will occasionally feel your musculature and connective tissue like your tendons occasionally with my hands as I sketch. I like to feel the latent energy in the object of the form, not that you are an object of course, I want to capture the life in you in my sketching so that when I come to paint you, I will capture your energy."

My mood was such that I felt like saying 'bullshit, I'm off'! However, the music was keeping a lid on my mood and again I just thought 'just go for it' let's get this over with'!

"No worries" I heard myself say,

and then attempting to lighten my mood if not the reality of my situation I said,

"I feel safe in your hands."

What a ridiculous platitude and it was incorrect, I didn't feel safe. Not that I thought anything bad was going to happen. In my mind I was looking for an opportunity to escape without overreacting and causing a fuss. I certainly didn't want to hurt her feelings and neither did I want her telling the art world I was a bad life model! That was the reality of my situation. Neither did I want Loretta to sense my negative vibes. As she'd moved quite a distance from me to where her easel was standing, I quickly removed my robe and took up my first two-minute pose. I started with my back to her and decided to rotate for each two-minute pose in the direction that would delay me being full frontal with her!

Thankfully, I started to get into it, and I could hear Loretta scratching away at her easel. Loretta was timing the poses and after each two minutes there was a little ding from the mechanical timer she was using.

"I don't suppose either of us is keeping count of your poses, so I'll just keep my eye on the clock, and you change your pose when you want to" she said in her lovely normal dulcet voice.

"Okay, sounds good," I replied feeling more in control.

Loretta's artistic style was demonstrative at her easel and after about six poses she took up her small drawing board that would support a piece of A4 paper. I knew she would be coming closer to me to sketch the 'detail' she spoke of!

"Your body is a creative masterpiece," she spoke, as if to herself.

She was out of sight behind me close to my left shoulder. I could hear her sketching. She moved to where I could see her at my next pose and after a short flurry of the charcoal she dropped her hands by her sides. The leaves of paper attached to the board fluttered as she dropped her arms. She popped the charcoal into her pocket. She then reached out and felt each of my extended arms. Her hands were cool and delicate, she wore no nail varnish, but her fingers were dirty from the charcoal. I had the impression she was actually shading me in with it!

This process went on for at least four more poses for over 20 minutes during which she felt my back, rib cage, shoulders, upper thighs, and calf muscles. It wasn't sexual in my mind; she came across as extremely professional with her concentration and the amount of sketching she was doing. Loretta was a talented artist, and she wasn't a chatty person. I decided I'd been overreacting, and I felt more positive and creative with her.

"You are going to need a shower after this I think" she said sincerely,

"Ah no worries, I can grab one before I change for tonight's performance," I replied.

"We don't want that lovely white underwear getting dirty do we," she suddenly said!

Oh, my goodness! I expected her to cackle but she didn't thank god, but my previous uneasiness sprang back into the present again! She then moved back toward me with a larger drawing board and knelt down behind me and explained she was going to draw my legs and gluteal muscles as they were, right then, in situ. Occasionally I felt her touch me, but she warned me beforehand, so she didn't surprise me, and this process went on for perhaps 15 minutes. Then I felt her fingers lingering and tracing out my lower back, sacrum, and coccyx area and then she put a finger into my butt crack and traced my glutes! This is an erogenous zone for me, and I felt a sexual flutter within me! It was purely the reaction to her physical touch, not sexual attraction for Loretta. However, I felt the stirrings of a potential hardon! Just the beginning of a slight swelling! I immediately resorted to thinking about my collection of vintage cigarette cards featuring interwar Australian and English cricketers between 1920 and 1938! They were in a frame on my bedroom wall as a boy. By thinking of this I could easily dismantle any physical arousal and sexual feelings! I have used this method on quite a few occasions when required!

Then I felt Loretta feel my ass with the flat of her hands! I thought of those charcoal fingers and what a mess they'd make of me and cover my white underwear later on! I don't have OCD, but I do like my nice things!

"I adore the indents at the sides of your butt cheeks" she said, not drawing me!

She lingered there a little too long and then, still behind me I felt her hands come around to my chest and she felt my pectoral muscles. She lowered her hands, and they reached my stomach area, and she traced out my oblique abdominals very gently. Unfortunately, I am extremely ticklish on my lower left stomach and even the image of Sir Donald Bradman with his bat raised in the air, could not distract me! My pose at the time was essentially a preparation for a pirouette and just as I heard her say,

"Wow, you are trickling with sweat."

my muscle memory kicked in along with my shock at her obvious sexual advance and a feeling that I'd had enough! So I immediately went into an actual pirouette! I saw Loretta stagger backward as I turned. She was okay and after I had completed a stumbling half turn, I dashed for my bathrobe that was on the floor about three feet away! I put it on quickly as I heard Loretta laughing… not cackling!

She recovered the situation as though nothing had happened and again asked about the role I was playing that evening, while she recovered her drawing board and walked back to her easel. We began to force a chat. She indicated it was time to take a rest and suggested we have a coffee, and I noted that the time was past 12:00 and I intended to leave by 1pm at the latest.

"…and we can leave it there if you like, shall we?" she said, completely happy and laughing a little. "Thank you so much, this has been surreal, and I'm so charged to transfer my sketches to paint you!"

"Okay!" I said, trying to look cool.

I relaxed a little as she hadn't reacted badly to my sudden 'get out of jail' reaction! She didn't even mention it, so I wasn't going to. No apologies were made, and I started to busy myself getting dressed.

"Are you sure you don't want a shower?" she asked me, "what with the charcoal mixed with all your lovely sweat…" she then paused and continued "I'm not sweaty but I'm definitely wet!"

Oh my god I didn't know where to look so I laughed without commenting! She took the hint without any obvious reaction and started yet again to ask about the role I was playing in the opera. This was obviously her default tactic when she felt she'd spoken inappropriately! We began to chat as she cleared her stuff away.

"Another coffee?" she asked,

I didn't want a coffee, but I was relieved to see her skip off without waiting for my reply. The music from Spartacus was still tingling away from her iPhone and I'm pretty sure in my mind it was exactly at the point of the 'death scene'!

"Fucking Shelob's had a taste of me," I whispered to myself.

I then shouted out into the studio aiming at Loretta's dainty retreating figure, "MAKE MINE STRONG, LOTS OF MILK, TWO SUGARS!"

I'm not sure she heard but it had the effect of returning my mood to normal at least. I bustled to get dressed before Loretta returned and suddenly I realized she still had my favorite shreddies in her bloody pocket! I thought to 'go commando' and bring up the subject when she was back with the coffee. I put my socks on first, then my trackies, then vest top and lastly my Levi jacket. I literally walked into my tennis shoes and laced them up. As I did so I thought of Valerie, and it calmed me. I felt the sudden urge to see her. I missed her. We hadn't met up for over a fortnight. We'd both been busy and understood that. As I thought of her, I began to feel genuinely turned on. It didn't take long with that amazing woman on my mind! This situation with Loretta was a reminder of how other women's sexual attraction for me fed my lust for Valerie! It always did. I always told Val about the attention I received from other women, and she always did the same with me describing the men who fawned all over her! Within seconds we'd be tearing off each other's clothes and we'd fuck like steam trains!

I heard two voices approaching and it was Loretta with Carl. He had a mug in his hand and Loretta had two and passed me one. I tasted it and it was delicious! I felt relieved that Carl had come along with her, except of course, I couldn't ask Loretta to return my underwear! Carl wandered over to look at Loretta's sketches and she stood quite close to me, and as I sipped my coffee she whispered,

"… enjoying your coffee, Mr. commando?"

I decided that now I was dressed, and the atmosphere had changed that I should play along with all of this. So I laughed a little and made out I was perfectly happy. I was, but I defo wanted my fucking shreddies back! Carl began talking and he was a very nice guy and spoke eloquently of the work he'd done as a theater props maker. Loretta was actually bubbly and chatty which surprised me! She was totally different around Carl. She'd let out her hair from the ponytail and it looked amazing, and she frequently swished it around as she remained close to me. The conversation between the three of us turned to her drawings but she made no reference at all to her 'touching and feeling' technique! Carl was obviously in no way romantically involved with Loretta, which became evident, and the suspicion that they might be 'in league' together completely left me.

"You finished early," Carl noted.

"Yes, we got to a point where I'm ready to prep to paint" replied Loretta.

I said nothing, just smiling and sipping my coffee.

"Oh, are you painting this afternoon?" Carl asked.

"Noooo," she replied, "next week, are you available next Thursday, George?" she asked, turning to face me squarely.

She had her coffee mug in both hands close to her mouth as she asked me and her eyes and indeed her whole posture made her look like a little girl asking for a favor. I noticed her previously dirty fingers were now clean. 'Not all actors are on the stage' I heard my dad say in my memory, but she looked cute, and I replied,

"Yeah, righto, no worries, I'd already made a note in my diary."

"If you could come from 9:30 to 12:30 that would be great. I might not need you that long, but I will pay you for the whole day."

"Yeah, it sounds good," I said, sounding a little monosyllabic.

For some reason, probably because Loretta was so close to me, and not engaging with Carl, he politely excused himself and left us alone together. With an eye on the clock and wanting to take the initiative I looked Loretta straight in her eyes,

"Are you keeping my underwear for any reason?" I asked politely, raising my eyebrows. I was beginning to feel like a right galah!

"I suppose if I hang on to it, you'll be sure to turn up on Thursday" she giggled.

"Well, it's my fave but if you insist, I suppose I could search you and take it back right now," I replied, smiling too, and trying to make light of it!

"Oh, hadn't thought of that" she added, laughing coyly.

And then she reached into her pocket, and I thought she was going to fish out my thong, but she brought out a roll of banknotes and handed the money to me.

"Here's £150 to cover today and next Thursday" she said.

"Hey thanks" I replied, "but I'll turn up anyway, eagerly accepted, and thanks again."

As I took the money from her, Loretta cocked her head to one side accentuating her diminutive childlike physique. She was definitely a very sexy and attractive woman and had a mystique about her.

"It must definitely be next Thursday," she said in all seriousness, "If we have to rearrange for any reason, it won't be until next month!" she really emphasized, this still tilting her head, eyes wide and appealing.

"Okay, I'll be here, I can't think of anything that might cause a problem," I replied, reassuringly.

"If we do have to rearrange, it will in fact have to be exactly 28 days later from next Thursday." Loretta said looking concerned.

"28 days sounds significant, is it?" I asked,

"Oh yes, I'm very err… lunar" she replied smiling again. "The transit of the lunar cycle is important to how I feel creatively, it gives me greater purposefulness."

I hadn't got a fucking clue what she was talking about, and I was conscious of the time yet again. I didn't think to question her further and gave it no more thought. Artists can be very superstitious, like actors. She then put her hand into her other pocket, here comes the return of my underwear, I thought! She pulled her hand out and opened her fingers. Nothing there!

"Huh?" I said looking surprised.

"I'm wearing it," she said, with a straight serious face!

"Wearing what?" I asked, fearing the worst!

"Your thong, silly!" she answered, trying to feign embarrassment after looking at my facial expression!

Thank goodness she didn't 'cackle'! Silence was my response. I've learned to keep silent for example when listening to choreographers and theater directors. I prefer not to interrupt them or at least not to reply when they reveal something they think is profound. This way they follow up with more information or insight than they intended. It puts them back on the spot. It's for them to explain rather than elicit a spontaneous reply from me! Often, they respond and offer more additional information than they intended or planned, often coming out with revelations of their true thinking. Once they do this, I find that I know them better and usually this builds a better connection and sometimes a bond of trust. This is especially the case when they reveal something confidential and suddenly, they realize they need me to be discreet and be able to trust me. I go on to prove their trust in me thereby building a long-lasting connection. This also has the effect of them remembering me in the future.

Loretta just stood there staring at me and her face softened. All she could say was,

"Do you mind?"

She was at my mercy, and she knew it. She instantly knew she'd gone too far, and this evened things up between us, in fact it gave me the initiative. I decided to play it down with humor. Maybe she'd learned her lesson and she would be more open, genuine and at ease with me, so I replied.

"Well, you've definitely put them somewhere safe... don't tell me you put mine over the top of yours?" I said with genuine humor.

Her shoulders lost their growing stiffness, and she came closer to me smiling appealing to me. She put her arms around my neck in an undefined way, not friendly, not sexy, somewhere in between. I'm only 5′ 8″ tall but she had to crane her neck to look up at me. I put my hands on her waist to keep her distant from me, not to draw her closer. She got the message; I wasn't going to kiss her. She felt birdlike and looked very vulnerable.

"I'm really sorry" she said again, meekly,

"Let's just not mix business with pleasure and see how things go between us" I said.

I lied really because I wanted to keep it businesslike and in no way wanted anything else from Loretta. Yes, she was gorgeous and sexy but there was something odd about her that I couldn't put my finger on and it kept cropping up making me feel uncomfortable.

"In some situations, my business is my pleasure," she replied slowly and thoughtfully "and sometimes pleasure is my business, but I'm my most creative when I don't compartmentalize and mix everything together."

To be honest I thought I understood her. She was socially awkward, and I've found many of the most talented people to be like that. I gave her the benefit of my doubt. She was being honest but euphemistic, but it was her euphemisms that left me with the idea not to let down my guard. What she said had some similarities with my own creative life. I couldn't argue with her, without being a complete hypocrite. But I drew a line when it came to work. Fucking while working was not something I felt comfortable with, afterwards yes! I personally have loose boundaries, but I adapt them to the situation I find myself in. If I am not comfortable with a situation I definitely compartmentalize. And I prefer to keep my private life private until I am completely sure about someone.

I sensed this was a good time to leave and head off to the RoH. She sensed me pulling away and quickly tensed her hands at the back of my neck and held tight,

"Hey, you need to reach into the back pocket of my jeans" she said in her lovely low dulcet voice.

I was curious. I slid both of my hands down over her cute little ass and pushed my fingers into both of her back pockets simultaneously.

"Hmm take your time," she said, giggling nicely.

With my left hand I found some soft material in the pocket there. I grabbed it between my fingers and pulled it out and held it up behind her. As I did so the soft material unfolded and revealed what it was. My brain took time to compute, there in my fingers hung an extremely large, huge pair of faded black knickers! It dawned on me these were Loretta's knickers she'd taken off to put on mine! They were extra-large by any standard of measurement. I mean massive! 'Period pants' is what I've heard them called. Definitely not sexy, unless you are idiosyncratically turned on by such things! They could not be her size; two Loretta's could technically fit into them.! They would be far too big for her surely, I kept thinking and then I felt a sense of repulsion! As I moved them around in my hand with my fingers I was confronted by the horrifying evidence of a smeary gusset! I was horrified. Why would she even think to show me these dirty knackered old knickers? My doubts about her came flooding back in spades!

"Keep them, I'll keep yours, bring them back next Thursday if you want to exchange them" she said, in complete seriousness!

She was upping the ante as I saw it, but what a way to do it! There was definitely more urgency about her now she sensed I was leaving.

Loretta was completely 'in the moment', a completely different one compared to my own! I felt like I had been' short-changed' at best and totally disgusted. I twizzled them around in my fingers so I could hide the creamy mess and crumpled them up into a tight cloth ball before ramming them into the side pocket of my Levi jacket. I had more luck with this maneuver than I have when dropping toast which always lands butter side down! In this case I was happy none of her mess had ended up on my hand! Why didn't I just chuck them away, cut my losses and fuck off! I don't know! As a bloke I have a possible explanation, she was so fucking gorgeous! It's amazing how much a man will put up with when in the presence of a sexy woman. I remembered Tom's words; I was not going to pay any price for access to Loretta's pussy, which was for certain! My obvious failure wasn't 'access', it was failing to exit!

I forced a smile and took my other hand from her waist and motioned backward to suggest she released her hold behind my neck. She did that slowly while staring at my lips. I knew she wanted me to kiss her but to be honest all I could think about was that she was crudding up my favorite underwear and I wanted to get out of there! I turned and reached for my mug of coffee that was lukewarm by then, and I drained it ceremoniously to draw a line under the morning.

"Want another coffee?" Loretta asked.
"Er not right now, I need to get going."
She stood with her hands in her pockets looking tiny and vulnerable and chewing her bottom lip. I responded by going over to my hold-all, zipping it up and rolling up my yoga mat. We exchanged a few pleasantries, and I made to leave with a euphemistic…
"See you next Thursday!" emphasizing this to test her true feelings! She was oblivious!
Really, I thought. Am I really going to come along again, but then I remembered the cash in my pocket. Already paid for! I made my way back through the studio and felt a lot more cheerful. I couldn't see or hear Carl to wave a cheerio to him, so I looked around at the place trying to enjoy it to distract myself. As I approached the door to make for the stairs, fuck me sideways, I heard Loretta cackle!!
At the first available public litter bin I reached into my jacket, tentatively pulled out her grotesque knickers and without looking around, chucked the fuckers away!

Thursday the following week.

As planned, I made my way to Loretta's studio by tube for our prearranged Thursday appointment, to be painted by her. I was in a fine mood. Much had happened creatively to focus me during the intervening week, and I hadn't given Loretta much thought. She was an appointment in my diary, and I hadn't mentioned the shenanigans to Val when we'd met for Sunday lunch by the Thames and an afternoon of kinky sex at her house. The street door was closed when I arrived but unlocked. It was 9:30am. I was early by one hour but this being my second visit being too early didn't seem like a problem. I decided to go in rather than kill a few minutes buying a coffee or a sandwich for lunch later. Also, by being early, it would put Loretta out of kilter if she was planning any more 'artistic adventures' that might not pass muster with most life models, if you get my gist!

I entered the studio quietly so as not to interrupt any other artists there, but the space was empty of people. This was not a surprise to me because artists by and large, start late and finish late. I walked toward Loretta's studio area at the far end on the left and I could see the portable screen had been put in place creating the private space in which we would be working together.

What was it about that 'Loretta cackle' that put me on edge so much. I began to recall it as I approached the screen. I'd tried to put it out of my mind during my tube journey to Holborn but being back in 'Shelob's Lair' uneasy thoughts came back and echoed in my head! Not a good start! 'Never make decisions based on feelings or emotions' I thought as I remembered my dad's wise words. These guiding words had never let me down and I needed to apply them here. I now knew I should have formulated enough ideas to have gotten myself out of this potential mess I could sense approaching. I was there now so I decided to give Loretta my full professional creative attention. She knew Maggie the artist and tutor, we'd both worked with Maggie, she was a professional artist with a studio in London, but those niggling doubts were based on that fucking incongruous, unnerving cackle that came out of the most unlikely body! I walked quietly around the screen and there was Loretta busying herself in preparation. I startled her.

"Hi" was all I said, smiling.

"Oh my gosh, you made me jump," she exclaimed, putting her hands to her face, "good to see you, great, fine, oh… er!" she continued, slightly flustered gesturing around her studio with straight arms and open hands. "Grab a drink, water, juice it's all out, over there on the drawers, help yourself" she continued to gabble.

I was smiling at her trying to put her at ease out of pity really, and on guard for red flags, I began to see the first one! She was dressed in what I could only call a bloody rough brown sack with sleeves! It was full length only occasionally revealing her bare feet when she walked. Bare feet in an artist's studio are not a good idea. The sleeves of her 'sack dress' were so long she irritated me with her constant pulling at them and attempting to hitch them up. The neckline was so wide one of her tiny shoulders was visible, no bra strap. She looked like a 19th century Victorian workhouse urchin! I walked over to the drinks and placed my hold-all and yoga mat on the floor.

I looked around sipping some disgusting vegan juice she'd put out and watched Loretta scurrying around busy doing nothing in particular. My creative vibes had taken a hit! All around the studio were copious sketches presumably of me, stuck to easels, walls, the portable screen and cupboards. They were there for her reference, I hoped, what else! In the middle of the studio Loretta had prepared a pristine white sheet over what looked like a futon mattress. This pleased me as that's where I would be adopting a reclining pose, I assumed. No worries. Loretta noticed me looking around and seemed to have gathered herself and started speaking into the studio space rather than to me directly.

"Right, hi, sorry, I was a bit late getting here," she lied "and my plans to arrange the studio for us are a bit rushed…"

"No worries" I replied, and we looked at each other. "Is there anything I can help you with?"

I felt relieved in a way that Loretta was coming across as distracted rather than calculating like the last time I was here but also being with her alone again was an emotional rollercoaster for me. She ignored my offer of help because basically she hadn't listened to me!

"Okay" she said, forcing a nice smile and taking a big breath, "As you can see, I've put out my sketches of you from last time and set out the bed for you. I've positioned it in line with the angle and proportions I would like to paint you from my easel."

I tried not to make anything of her referring to my reclining support as a bed! I went off to one side where there was clear floor space and got changed. I'd brought along some flip flops to protect my feet before posing. Dancers are literally paranoid about their feet as you can imagine, 'poorly feet, don't eat'! I then slowly walked over to the covered futon and flicked off the flip flops and stood on it dressed in my white toweling robe.

I'd only been in the studio for about 15 minutes or so and things were moving along which was fine by me. I wasn't slated to start until 10:30, the 'witching hour'! Here we were approaching 9:45 am judging by the huge ornate clock that hung from two wires attached to a high beam. Loretta just went along with it and seemed at a loss how to fill in the time until 10:30 so I was pleased she was just getting on with it. I felt I was in control of myself, and Loretta could please herself. I was pleased that there was no continuation of the way we had parted the previous week with her hanging onto my neck. No mention was made of the 'knicker swap'!

"I was thinking of a reclining pose, on your back, top of your head pointing to the screen over there, feet angled to my left here at the easel, one arm of your choice above your head with the other outwards at 90 degrees. One leg straight and the other raised bent at the knee." she said, looking at and tilting her head at the futon. "The important thing is for you to feel comfortable."

I lay down still in my robe to 'block' the pose, a kind of rehearsal. She liked what she saw but added that she would like it if I could tilt my head to look away to my right, away from her at her easel, because as she explained modestly, that she wasn't very good at painting faces. I was happy and things were trotting along and very professionally without fuss. I knelt up and removed my robe and spread it out flat next to me where it wouldn't get dirty, then assumed the pose that Loretta had directed, and I wriggled myself into a comfortable position. Before I positioned my head, I looked at Loretta as she approached me looking like 'Radagast the Brown' ostensibly to take a close-up view. She then walked herself backward slowly to her easel again. I was happy and comfortable and ready for her to start her process.

"I'm ready when you are, Loretta," I volunteered taking the professional initiative, "Let me know if you want any adjustments."

"Thank you, you look fine, lovely in fact, perfect, let me know if you need to stretch at some point" she replied.

I was conscious of being completely naked in a prone face up position on the floor, but I was able to 'zone out' and I would try not to fall asleep!

Tilting my head away from her as agreed I could just about see where Loretta 'the sack cloth doll' was and able to detect her movements as she worked at her canvas by using my peripheral vision. I could hear her clinking, and clicking, scraping, and scratching at her work and then I detected her dragging her easel across the floor for a short distance. No worries I thought, she's adjusting her position. Then all went quiet. Then I understood what the 'clicking' noises were all about. She'd put on music. Fucking whale music! I bloody hate that shit. It's like brain torture for me! If I were to be tortured that crap would have me confessing all my secrets within five minutes! Red flag, she's a fucking 'save the planet leftie' I concluded feeling ratty!

A few more minutes passed, and I should have asked her to change the music, but I was suddenly aware of Loretta standing at my feet. I kept my head in place as every good life model would do but I could easily detect her standing there very still for longer than felt comfortable for me. She didn't say a word. I started to feel a little wary and felt compelled to move my head to look at her because she obviously wasn't painting. She looked at me looking at her and then she slowly lifted that disgusting brown sack cloth dress up over her head and she was completely naked! Her thick brown silvery streaked hair looked disheveled and statically charged, and she looked ghoulish! Her big eyes under her high square fringe looked friendly though with a half-smile on her face. However, it was a red flag!

My initial surprise and wariness and unease at her probable intentions were then completely distracted by what my eyes were drawn to, grabbing my full attention. Her pubic hair! I really don't mind a well-tended thatch (a WTT my sisters used to call it) but Loretta's was like a massive nest of flattened bird-eating spiders! Fuck me! A huge thick black mass with wispy frayed edges! I thought the only flattering description for her disgusting fourth-generation feminist black minge wig was 'au naturale'! Fuck that description I thought, Loretta's pubes were 'au what a mess'! Urk! I knew some female dancers who have a genuine WTT to prevent what Tom the artist had referred to as 'yeast infections' and for BV prevention! I'd heard some of them lightheartedly chatting about such choices. Loretta's wild bush looked like it could smother a bush fire! In fact it looked like the embers of a huge bush fire!

Looking at her for far too long, transfixed by her unkempt Amazonian wild rain forest of jet-black pubes, made me think that there would not be anywhere near enough room in my white thong she'd nicked to cover up that disaster of a minge! Then I thought that if she ever did give it back to me it would end up in the same public waste bin as her knickers! I could not help but examine her in detail from where I lay. I was too amazed quite frankly to say a word to her. The width, depth, thickness and overall spread of her pubes must have been a 'Guinness Book of World Records' entry! They were halfway up to her navel and outwards into her groins. No razor, scissors, waxing or clippers had ever been anywhere near it! Jeeeezers, she'd need a machete and an angle grinder! This sight of her was made more ridiculously surreal by her having a navel piercing where a large twinkling diamond dangled from a silver chain! It twinkled away innocently like a forgotten bauble on a discarded Christmas tree in mid-January! Fuck, it was like putting a pig in a tutu, it's still a pig. From where she stood my view between her slender thighs, her hairy bush gathered in a swirling thick nebulous black cloud! The chorus of the rugby song *Mayor of Bayswater* sprang into my head…

"And the hairs on her dicky-di-doe,
Hang down to her knees…!"

Nowhere to be seen was any evidence of her pussy. It was lost in there, somewhere! Lost to die in the deepest darkest jungle of planet woman; my Australian 'pull no punches' humor had now kicked in, thankfully. My complete astonishment was only just suppressing a combination of disgust and hilarity for me. I did want to laugh but I suppose that would have made things worse. I didn't want to embarrass Loretta, but I did want to escape from her! Every Australian knows that a sense of humor kicks in in the face of adversity! Worse though, the visual impact of her was made more intensely distorted because Loretta's thick tangled mass of pubes dwarfed the proportions of her dainty body.

Fuck 'vagina feminism', I thought! Then I thought with complete clarity that there was no way on god's earth was my cock going anywhere near that snail-trail forest of a crud factory, and wild horses couldn't drag me to eat her out! Despite this I simply could not stop staring at it, 'no way Jose' would I ever be getting a smidgeon of a hardon!

Why didn't I just stop there and get dressed. It struck me that by staring between her legs for so long looking mostly fascinated, that she might have thought I approved! In the back of my mind though, I now began to consider that the lovely Loretta was some kind of wacko! I knew it would be better to be patient and let her think that she controlled the situation and wait for something to go wrong, like someone disturbing us, to put an end to it all. I did know that she would be easier to handle and easier for me to make my escape if she remained calm and rational. If I'd upset her, it could have had convoluted complicated consequences for want of a better alliteration!

I also had the underlying feeling that if Loretta wasn't the one to end this farce, she could well turn out to be a stalker! Or she could easily blame me because how would I explain my fear of her minge as an excuse to leave her in the lurch? Fuck, I instantly understood the reason for John Ruskin's asexuality even impotency! I felt both sympathy and empathy with him, myth or not! Ruskin's 'The Political Economy of Art' also took on a new meaning for me being confronted by Loretta's politically inspired pubic hair 'manifesto'. She exhibited a very poor 'economic management' of the most quintessentially beautiful embodiment of feminine art, the vagina, for the sake of using it to represent an ugly and persistently unhappy negative ideology!

If you treated a work of art like she maintained her pussy it would be reckless incompetence. Staying rational and acting kind was the best approach and therefore I was going to have to play this out carefully before making a break for freedom, or should that be escaping femdom… I'm not sure which!

If Loretta had not cackled like a demented soul yet again at that very next moment, I reckon I could have remained rational and improvised a polite extrication of myself! My mood changed instantly to one of almost blind panic as she continued that insane cackling! George the Aussie began to lose his sense of humor! I was fucking terrified. I was naked, on my back, looking up at the 'wicked witch of the West'! I lost my focus and froze. Irrationally I pondered whether there had been any recent evidence of male life models being murdered in London by a serial killer! I suppose this was a remnant of my sense of humor reminding me some of it was still available if I needed it.

Then Loretta cackled yet again like an impaled hyena for fuck's sake as she knelt down on all fours. She started crawling toward me with my left leg between both of hers as she did so. I lowered my right leg and raised myself up onto my elbows but then I became completely frozen as I watched this crazed apparition! She was to her credit trying to look sultry and seductive, but her dark brown silvery-threaded hair hung down in front of her like a thick curtain of snakes and her short high fringe made her eyes look genuinely demented! I suddenly realized too that her thick jet-black untended eyebrows should previously have given me more of an indication about her lack of attention regarding her pubic proclivities!

She was quite literally a very attractive woman without doubt but not right now. She looked like she was staring out of the mouth of a brown hairy monster that had swallowed her feet first! I felt a growing sense of paranoia because she actually looked at that moment like the creature from the evil pussy lagoon! Oh, my word, they say that in every fat woman there's a pretty woman trying to get out! Maybe then, with Loretta there's a gorgeous neat little pussy lost in there trying to get out! However, without doubt, there was no escape from the 'Fangorn Forest' of 'looney leftie Loretta the lost labia lover' when she's the one who threw away the key to the chainsaw cabin!

My sense of humor was now definitely swamped by a rising catatonic state of panic! Crawling toward me with her hair brushing my chest she positioned that explosion in a black mattress factory of a minge, directly over my left thigh and knelt there. She flicked her thick hair over her shoulders kneeling suddenly upright looking down at her tits. She started to squeeze and massage them with her right hand and her full-length arm tattoo looked like a crazed snake writhing away with its fangs stuck in her nipple! She then looked me straight in the eyes. I looked away; I didn't know where to look. I was thinking I should slide out from under her and get away! I looked between her legs drawn back to that hideous black mass that was now even closer to my face. I could see the detail of wispy hairs curling at their ends, never once trimmed, very long and I have to say, really repulsive!

Loretta must have noticed me staring at her minge and began to frig herself with her left hand! Her fingers searched through her mass of pubes searching for her clit and to be honest I looked back at her face, I couldn't bear to watch! I should have kept on looking at her fingering herself though because I might have had warning of what was about to happen. She spread her legs wider and nestled her minge squarely and firmly onto the top of my left thigh using it to rub herself against, using my thigh to masturbate with! She came forwards onto her arms and her hair covered my face and it tickled like fuck! I had no choice but to move my head left and right and use a hand to keep it out of my eyes and my mouth. My cock does not need a mention other than I think he had played dead in terror!

As Loretta seemed to sense some non-existent enthusiasm from me, she continued to rub herself harder and faster on my thigh. I didn't feel her mass of pubic hair, I just imagined it because the overriding feeling on my thigh was wetness! I managed to part the curtain of her hair that hung down all over my chest and shoulders now, and discovered the middle third of my thigh was covered in blood! She was bleeding on me!

"I'm painting you, George," she said, in a silly voice and then she cackled again.

It was so loud and close to my face that I literally panicked in my head, made worse by her using my name like we were amazing lovers! Lines from John Proctor in 'The Crucible' jumped into my head "do what you like but give me my name!." The subconscious thought of her being a witch and remembering those words basically boiled down to me thinking 'fuck off and leave me out of this you pervert'! But I didn't say a thing. Then it hit me! Loony Lunar Loretta the tree hugger vegan had mentioned the week before about her "lunar cycle". Her fucking 'mental menstrual cycle' more like! I got it, if I had missed today, it would have needed to be '28 days later' (now there's something for you to conjure with) when she would be gushing like a slaughtered beaver again! At least she knew she had the advantage of predictable periods, jeezuss christus! And there was my defenseless, disinterested, debilitated dick playing his part, continuing to play dead! I knew I could rely on him when needed either way. Definitely the right decision in the case of Loretta!

Did Loretta take my silence for sexual interest? Surely, she couldn't be that delusional, but I take full responsibility for my own actions, and they were not actions at all. I was stupidly letting her do this crap to me! Surely, she must have had some inkling of my horror. I started to think probably correctly that she was a deranged pervert! Married couples don't do this shit! Do they? She then raised her left leg stopping her smooth slow rubbing on my thigh, revealing the various tones and textures of her dissipated glutenous runny uterine wall all over it! She then proceeded to straddle me around my waist and plonked that now bloody hairy mass onto where my non-existent hardon should have been! Before she did this, I saw blood drip from her onto my stomach! Holy shit, fucking mad woman I kept thinking! The horrific thought of her eventually positioning that blood dripping slaughtered black goat with its throat cut over my face both scared the life out of me and made me want to gag! How did I get into this position with her, what the fuck! I automatically placed both my hands firmly just below her breasts to stop her forward progress and turned my head away to one side. Good George, action, keep it up, get out of here my brain was screaming as she rubbed herself against my lower stomach.

Loretta though just shuffled her knees further forward toward my head, despite me holding her back and she coated more of my stomach from that blood-soaked black mop! My legs by now were squeezed together and stretched straight out from me. I usually adopt this position when I am being painted with period blood by a deranged menstruating artist! Seriously, I was consciously readying myself for extraction, extrication, evacuation, and exit! I looked up and she was looking down at me fucking smiling like it was a summer's day!

"That's far enough" I said slowly but firmly.

"Don't worry" she replied smiling crazily, like a lotto winner!

'Don't worry, don't fucking worry' I thought! By now she must have seen the disgust on my face! Surely? Then it hit me! How much worse could this get!? I'd begun to wonder what the occasional wafts of a strange odor were. You never can tell with art studios, but this smell wasn't solvents, paints or the like. It grew into a pure rancid almost gut-wrenching stink that assailed my nostrils! It was without doubt the smell of blood and rotten flesh, even shit! I'd grown up on a cattle station and I was familiar with some bad smells but not in a closed environment like this one and not stuck underneath the stinking carcass! I knew all about this less-than-fresh blood stench! Why the fuck couldn't Loretta smell it? Why the fuck didn't she react like any normal person to such a stench?

There was a warm fetid thickness to it that I could definitely taste at the back of my throat. The blood rot and whatever else was leaking out of her was so bad. There was a mixture of an iron metal smell mixed with something decomposing. The smell was a fog, a smog! I knew what dead livestock smelled like in a hot climate at various stages of decomposition working on the cattle stations in Queensland. To be honest this was worse because it was on my skin! Loretta leaned forwards against my defensive arms and reached out to her side,

"Excuse me!" she said.

'Excuse me!' what the fuck, I thought! What the hell is she doing now, my mind was screaming? From under the futon mattress, she searched with her left hand in a determined way and pulled something out from under it. As my eyes made sense of this I suddenly realized she'd pulled out the biggest fucking vibrator I'm ever likely to see! At least 30 cm long, bright purple, textured and the girth of it was so thick there was no way my fingers and thumb would touch around it! What a circumference!

"You aren't going to use that thing on me!" I blurted out,

You'd have thought my tone would have shattered any moment in any situation, but it was like water off a duck's back with the looney Loretta!

"I said don't worry" she replied calmly sitting astride me examining that brute! "I'm always horniest during my period."

I was done and helpless against her lack of rational thinking! She then switched it on with a contrary twist with both of her hands and then fiddled with it, and squinting with concentration she pressed her thumb on a button which scrolled that monster through a series of pulses, buzzes and rhythms of varying speeds and loudness! Damn it she cackled again like 'Eucalyptus the Witch' and I definitely felt like I was the imprisoned 'Paulus the Woodland Gnome'!

She decided on one of the buzzing-grinding 'options' and started to squeeze the vibe horizontally between my stomach and her messy black crotch! I remained totally speechless! She was so tiny there was hardly room to create space for it, but she pushed at it and located it I suppose, where she wanted it to go. I could feel it thudding in a buzzing rhythm against my belly and I could see the top of it, the 'non-business end'. It was close enough to me that I could read the small writing on the end of it, 'Made in the PRC'! The pulsing throb of it made the sound that reminded me of a small two-stroke Japanese moped with a hole in its silencer. It also had an intermittent grinding sound, and a varying rhythm like some invisible throttle was being turned at irregular intervals revving it up and down! What a ridiculous spectacle it was, and Loretta became enthused by it!

Wide-eyed, she pressed her weight down onto 'Purple Pete' which in turn pressed it into my stomach. I assumed she'd found the location of her clitoris within that frayed wet black rug! I had to tense my abs to stop the pressure of the vibe doing me an injury! Was this the end of it? No way! She straightened her back, wafted her hair behind her shoulders again, held the vibe in place with the blood-covered fingers of her right hand and began squeezing her tits with her other hand yet again! This time her tattooed arm looked like the snake was trying to return to hide in the jungle! The breast squeezing wasn't unfamiliar to me, women do this but now my ears were assailed by the noise that came out of her mouth. A unique, unrelenting, unselfconscious insane noise like a little girl imitating the sound of a police car siren! I kid you not!

"Woo, woo, woo, woo, woo, woo, woo…." ad fucking nauseam!

It rose higher and lower and higher again in intensity in a crazy synchronicity with the huge vibrator as she approached some weird orgasm 'zone'! There was no clue from her how long it was going to take! I then hoped Carl wasn't around now to hear this crap but then I thought if only he was, so he could disturb her and help me bring this catastrophe to a halt! Finally, after an inordinate length of self-absorption, I assumed she'd cum with one last long note like the police car had pulled up at the scene of the crime with its siren still on at full tilt…

"Wooooooooooooooooooooooooooooo"! She woo'd!

"That was exceptional!" she squeaked with glaring eyes!

Too fucking right, it was! I was now convinced Loretta was many things but best described in a polite way as definitively delusional! I really had to take the blame though. Why hadn't I gone walkabout before this ridiculous scene? I could have given her hard earned cash back to her. Had I been the female and Loretta a man it would definitely have ended way before it got to this stage, that's for sure! The double standards modern blokes have to contend with is ridiculous, but we really don't care to be honest unless you're one of those modern blokes who've given over to thinking like a woman. Loretta was still and silent basking in her own pervy oxytocin hit with her eyes now closed. I hadn't moved from my position propped up on my elbows with my knees locked together. I decided to lie flat as my neck was aching and it would hopefully give her the impression of a contented black labrador having had his ribs tickled! I was done.

During her afterglow or whatever name, you could give to this drongo's current state, I tentatively felt my way down to that bloody buzzing purple 'python' and pulled it away gingerly from between us with a finger and thumb. I tried my best not to look at it and I held my breath not out of shock but to help me restrict the stink assailing me constantly. It was obvious it did not assail Loretta! It swung vertically and precariously in my fingers, but I managed to keep hold of it and I moved it out to my right side as far as my arm would reach and I dropped it with a thud onto the floor. I then, finally, began to ease myself out from between Loretta's thighs using my elbows to lever myself out. Of course, I could not stop my legs dragging across her now free-flowing bloody vagina from within her blood-plastered pubic hair 'blanket'! I couldn't help but look as my legs were smeared with the stinking gunk. She watched me as I did this, still silent.

I stood up on the edge of the mattress in front of Loretta. She remained kneeling and unsurprisingly there was not much of a mess on the white sheet where my body had been until I saw her drip blood onto it! At least it didn't resemble the 'Turin Shroud'! The vast majority of her mess was on me though. I stank of a 'dead something' as the smell rose up to my face now. I kept my mouth tightly shut as I inspected my body. I was covered with a mixed combination of dark red, black, and scarlet blobs. The latter trickled down my stomach in independent dribbles creating a crazy pattern through my own short well-tended pubic hair and down through the hairs on my legs. My cock looked crusty with dried blood. I then noticed that I had both of my hands raised in the air above me, as if someone had threatened me with a gun and said, "hands up!" I was in no way going to touch myself. My inner thighs were a dry blood-coated mess, and my left one was by far the worst for some obvious reason! I looked like a frenzied knife attack victim!

Loretta got to her feet and her inner thighs belied description other than they looked completely revolting to match the stench around us!

"Aww, I thought I'd be painting you for longer," she said innocently.

I was dumbstruck. I'd have thought that post-orgasm or whatever she'd had, Loretta would have woken up to our embarrassing reality. If she thought that her perverted practice was painting, then I could not argue with someone so drunk on and convinced of a misconceived understanding of the word. I know that Leonardo Da Vinci used egg whites in his experimental paints, but I was looking at 'Loretta Da Vagina' here!

I looked around despairingly for a towel or cloth of some sort to clean myself up a little and considered grabbing the sheet and using that but thought better of it. I would have had to wrap it around myself for it to be effective and I'd have looked like Julius Cesar during his assassination… 'et tu, Lorettae' popped into my head and I felt my sense of humor inching back or was it derangement? I then thought about putting on my flip flops. What a sight I must have looked standing there like that! Naked and covered in drying blood and shitty gunk, in flip flops with that huge mangey grinding vibrating purple vibrator still growling away on the floor next to my feet, like it was a dying space alien in a dissonant duet with the background 1980s whale music! You can't make this stuff up!!

Loretta stood up in the middle of the mattress looking visually deranged with sunlight catching her body making her look really creepy. Then to my horror she came toward me, but she stopped to bend down to pick up the buzzing grunting vibrator and casually switched it off. Then she let her arms drop to her sides holding the vibe horizontally firmly in her hand looking like she'd just run the last leg of an alternative 400m relay race and had finished last! I broke the silence out of desperation,

"I need a shower" trying not to add an expletive!

"Okay, follow me," she said really kindly and casually, totally at odds with the way she looked!

Off she went walking around the panel partition, totally naked and carrying the vibrator, no checking to see if anyone was around! I just followed, I had no choice!

As we walked through the studio to the shower room, wherever that was I had no clue and didn't ask, we must have looked like we were playing roles in the latest art scene by performance artist Marina Abramović! As I followed Loretta, I could easily see dried blood on her tiny ass, the insides of her thighs and even on her calf muscles! I also noticed that she was still dripping blood occasionally onto the floor as she walked along so I followed her slightly to one side, so I didn't have to tread on it!

We passed the exit/entry door on our right and approached another door shortly after that also on the right. Loretta pushed open the door and flicked on the light. I'd been conscious of someone coming into the studio as we walked through it and what a grim spectacle we must have looked! In the left-hand corner of the windowless room was a small old-fashioned rickety glass shower cubicle with a sink to the right of it. There was a flush toilet in the far-right hand corner about 10 feet from the shower cubicle. Loretta walked nonchalantly to the shower cubicle and pulled a cord to switch on the electric shower, open the cubicle door, and turned on the water. She stood there as before looking like a freaky mess with one hand still holding the disgusting vibrator, using it to hold the shower door open and her other hand testing the water.

She had her back to me and underneath the filth and discounting my memories of her, her body was simply delicious but unfortunately, she paid no attention to her 'business ends'! What a pity women choose this 'look' for political and ideological reasons these days! I literally stank and I did not want to be rude, but I wanted to shower first and then get away from this place as soon as possible. So, I approached her and gently took hold of her upper arm and stopped her getting into the shower first!

"Me first," I said firmly and hurriedly.

"Okay but I thought we could shower together," she said with wide questioning eyes.

I felt sorry for her for a split second then remembered the whole situation and thought there was no way I would be sharing. Firstly, even with her tiny body there was not enough room for two especially if I wanted a good soaping. I got in and closed the door. The water was soothing and then I noticed there was no soap! I took down the shower nozzle and used it close to my skin to wash every crack and crevice I could think of using it as a kind of weak 'jet wash'. I looked through the glass as I became slightly cleaner, and I saw Loretta sitting on the dunny.

She was sitting still stark naked, leaning forward with her elbows on her knees and her head in her hands and occasionally inspecting her fingernails. At one point she put her fingers in her mouth! Fuck me! With the noise of the water, I couldn't hear anything else, and I knew I had to step out into that dingy room again out of the cleansing water. I forced myself to step out and I looked around for a towel. Obviously, there wasn't one, but I always carry a small towel with my 'performance kit' but that was back in Loretta's studio! Dammit! It was never intended for a shower after a 'blood painting'.

I remember thinking clearly that I would never model for a *transgressive* artist again, if that was what Loretta professed to be or not. I promised myself to research the background of artists in the future if I didn't know them before meeting them for the first time. Then I remembered some more of my dad's wise words. "Every man has his price!"

Loretta stood up as I left the cubicle and replaced me in the shower. I had left the water running for her, typically feeling contrite like I always do after being a little impatient with people. I went over to the dunny to take a leak as she busied herself showering. The first thing I noticed was that she'd stood the huge purple vibrator on its end, vertically on the toilet cistern. It looked like some totem to a primitive sacrifice to the alternative sex gods! I also moved away from the shower quickly, so I didn't have to catch sight of more blood being diluted with hot water as Loretta washed herself. As I approached the toilet close enough to look down into the toilet bowl, I saw that she had in the truest sense of the phrase 'taken the piss'! She hadn't flushed and the water was a mess of her urine and blood! Blood droplets were festooned around the porcelain toilet bowl as well as in the water. Oh, my word, why didn't she flush it? This was literally the limit of my repulsion of her, and I felt my temper begin to rise. I quelled it and turned to look at her in the shower cubicle. The site of her filth in the toilet completely stopped me feeling like taking a leak, instant shy bladder syndrome! I instinctively shouted really loud so I could be heard…

"Jesus you cudda flushed the dunny!"

"What?" she shouted back pleasantly.

"The bog. Why didn't you flush it?"

Loretta completely disarmed me by answering so sweetly,

"Oh… so it didn't affect the flow of water to the shower for you when it fills up again."

I felt completely deflated by her considerate thinking! I take after my mum who sees the good in anyone and everyone! Loretta finished her shower quicker than I had done with my own soapless ablutions and I was standing by the door to the studio still dripping wet, naked and cold, to encourage her to hurry up. We both left and I trotted back as quickly as I could once again mindful of the floor for blood spots and anything sharp too. I wasn't going to leave my own blood trail too! I left Loretta in my wake, reaching her studio space very quickly. Just before I rounded the portable panel, Carl stepped from behind an easel about 15 feet from me on my right. How long had he been there I quickly thought, but to be frank by then I didn't give a toss! The curious thing was that Carl didn't give a toss either! He didn't look shocked or even remotely curious. He just looked up, took in my wet nakedness, and looked away.

At least the bloody whale music had ended, but it had been replaced by the persisting thick stench Loretta had exuded!. I clearly heard the stark-naked dripping wet Loretta shout "hi Carl" as she reached her studio space, in an everyday happy-clappy way! He didn't reply, or I didn't hear him as I dressed, cramming my damp legs and arms into my clothes as fast as I could. Loretta slung her ugly sack cloth dress back on and tied it with a red and gold rope tightly around her waist this time. Then she stood there squeezing long lengths of her hair looking thoughtful. To me she looked like a medieval feudal Lord's 'sex serf'!

As I finished dressing and made sure I had everything of mine packed away, not wanting to forget a thing so I didn't have to come back, or see Loretta again, she actually said to me.

"You know, you are the first man I've had sex with who I've not met online this year"!

What! What the fuck! She was actually deluded. Firstly, I didn't have sex with her and secondly, I was her life model! Or I thought that was the arrangement, but in her fantasy world I obviously wasn't! I knew I had to leave because I was feeling my temper rise yet again and I wasn't going to stand and argue with her.

"Yeah…" she said as though I'd acknowledged her. "Yeah, I usually meet guys on the internet and hook up that way. So many men and so few women on there, a girl is spoiled for choice," she continued casually.

She wasn't joking either, she was completely sincere telling me that crap like I was some friendly acquaintance now. What she said was all I needed to know about those hookup websites. I could imagine what they must have been called. 'Period Fetish Land', 'A Period in Time', 'Allied Rugs', 'Hairy Bush Tucker Girls', 'Winning The Poo'! Fucking yuk, pass the DDT!

"I'm having sex with three men currently besides you" she said to no one in particular! "… not with bodies as good as yours though"!

I grabbed my hold-all and left the delusional Loretta to carry on talking to herself as though I hadn't heard a word, and to be honest, I wished I hadn't! Everything about her made me feel uncomfortable and sick in my stomach! I remembered clearly what Valerie had said once, "when you meet someone the first time, right there is the real person". I'd forgotten! As I scarpered I realized that I had dodged a bullet with Loretta! In fact, the initial sight of her inglorious bastard of a crotch had actually been my savior! Every *black* cloud has a silver lining in there somewhere! When I got into the street, I stopped to look up at the studio windows. It crossed my mind that there should be a large hand-painted sign up there just below the windows for all to see…

"TWINNED WITH THE ROBERT MAPPLETHORPE STUDIO"

I'll leave you to research that one!

Unfortunately, I had to see Loretta one last time at the scheduled life drawing on the Friday the following week. Thankfully, she felt like a stranger. She went about her drawing without me ever making eye contact with her and her whole body language was hardly indicative of the whole freaky twisted episode; she'd ghosted me! I've never ignored a red flag since!

Chapter Eleven

The Predator, the Bitch, and the Bastard!

    Looking back now on my experience with Loretta, which thankfully I've tucked away into my personal history of 'lessons learned', it has been clear to me that I think very little about the details of such events. Rather I remember them holistically and the overall creative atmosphere I felt at the time and what ideas and actions they engendered. I don't continue to analyze past events otherwise their influence can negatively affect the future direction for my creative momentum. You can't walk confidently into the future if you are constantly looking back over your shoulder! As I tend to 'live in the moment' because it is the only thing I can influence, the past although relevant is only significant when it was a time of creative inspiration. The negative stories I tend to recount only as funny stories when chatting with people. Life modeling has provided me with a hugely inspiring network of artists and even places have become special.

    Recounting my memories of Loretta are very humorous for me. Some might find my recollections disgusting but they actually happened. I haven't made this stuff up! I have told you how I felt in the moment and described it in detail very much from my male perspective. I haven't looked back and formed my opinions of her from historical hindsight. I have described them from the actual situation I was in at the time. In short, the situation I ended up in with Loretta wasn't her fault. I'm not criticizing her because we are all responsible for our own actions and the decisions we make. To think of Loretta in a negative light would be like trying to excuse myself from the decisions I made and to blame her and to make out I was some kind of victim. Far from it, I was no victim.

    Working in the performing arts with people who are extremely emotional in character by their very nature, I have noticed how so many of them do not move on with their lives after their own perceived injustices were 'perpetrated' against them. They feel 'victimized' and even search to dig up their own personal history in search of past events to repackage them as being victimized. This then has led them to look to blame someone or some event. Indeed, modern society now encourages people to look back and bring it 'back to the future'! A very negative past is dragged back into the present as a means of 'moving on'! Now there's another oxymoron! There's a whole fucking industry thriving on this bullshit. Basically, I learned from an early age that if you look to blame someone and choose to be a victim, you will be stuck in the past. One day you will be on your deathbed and if you are lucky, you will look back and think of all the years you wasted feeling like a victim blaming others for your life, when your perceived detractors forgot about you years ago!

Moving on when I think about Loretta I literally laugh about the experience. I described her as "a wacko," "a drongo" at that time. In reality she's neither of those things. She was simply being herself and nothing she did nor planned was designed to humiliate me. She merely, as I see it, attempted to use an opportunity to satisfy her fantasies and assumed a complicit acceptance of my part in them. I went along with her without complaint. I had witnessed so many red flags but chose to ignore them. Loretta wasn't a horrible or evil person.

Her uninhibited actions and complete lack of self-consciousness made her oblivious to how I might have been feeling. Afterall there isn't a man on earth who wouldn't instantly see her as an extremely attractive and desirable woman. She wasn't malicious at all. In her own mind she didn't even misjudge the situation. Why would she? I went along with it all until the border between her attraction for me and her eroticism crossed over into physical repulsion and disgust for me! In the end, I belatedly took action to extricate myself from her as painlessly and as civilly as possible and moved on… with humor! Had Loretta been a man, inter alia he would have been labeled a 'pervert' instantly.

Whereas in my own opinion, Loretta the woman had sexual fantasies, and she felt comfortable to put her trust in me to pursue and express them within the safe envelope of opportunity that she had created. She naively assumed I'd be turned on by her own erotic form of seduction that presumably had been successful with other men previously. Any thoughts?

The Predator

So let me introduce a real pervert! His name was Bill. Bill was a retired academic who continued to work part-time at a large art educational institution.

His background was fine art and his part-time role in retirement was to promote and organize life drawing for undergraduate students of fine art, graphic design, illustration, and fashion. A noble remit especially as life drawing has mainly been dropped from university art syllabuses. Bill provided an extracurricular option for students. He had built up two quite separate reputations for life drawing among art students and artists in the wider community. This kindly, artistically knowledgeable man was introduced to me in conversation with a highly respected professional artist. He was well-known and respected in the art world, apparently! This was for me a completely trustworthy source and I appreciated her referral with Bill.

I communicated with Bill by email initially. After a thorough exchange of ideas using this method, Bill invited me to model for both of his life drawing groups. The sessions were located in the creative arts premises of his employer providing excellent facilities. I met with Bill shortly before my first gig and he struck me as a little reserved but not in a negative way. In fact, in person he asked no obvious questions of me and barely made eye contact.

The first time I modeled for his undergraduate students proved to be a wonderful experience. Bill and his students agreed that having a trained dancer to draw was a very stimulating challenge and a rare opportunity. I looked forward to a long and satisfying professional relationship with Bill with the idea for me to model about six times during the academic year. The second time I modeled for Bill was with his community group of artists. During the interval he introduced me to an attractive young woman called Sophia. He explained that she was a potential life model, new to life modeling and would be sitting in during the second half of the session so that she could glean an appreciation of what it would entail. I had no problem with this.

At the end of the evening when I was robed up, before I dressed, Sophia approached me voicing her appreciation of my dance themes but stressed her own doubts about her own suitability as a life model. I quickly explained to her in the time available that she could take a more traditional approach to being a life model by sitting and reclining. She explained that she was active in advanced Pilates, and I pointed out that she could easily adapt some positions for life modeling poses as I do with dance. She was happy with this and suggested we go for a quick drink locally after I was dressed for a longer chat. It was only just after 9pm so I was fine with the idea.

I agreed to meet Sophia in the lobby area near the main entrance after I'd gotten dressed. Grabbing my bag and leaving the room to go to meet Sophia I bumped into Bill who was also on his way out. I think he assumed I'd already left but we chatted amiably on our way out.

Entering the lobby area, I saw Sophia standing by the revolving doors and waved to her. Bill noticed me waving to someone and then realized who I was waving to. He said to himself words to the effect of wondering who she could be waiting for. As Bill and I got close to Sophia, she and I smiled and said "hi" to each other.

"Ah you are still here," Bill said, rather stiffly to her,

"Yeah, George and I are going for a drink and a chat" she replied, politely gesturing toward me.

Bill became silent and his mannerisms now became stiff and awkward. He mumbled a few incoherent words, gathered himself and wished us a good night and turned to leave very quickly. His head and shoulders moved in unison as though locked together as he turned. He failed to make eye contact with both me and Sophia. It was an awkward moment for both of us and we looked at each other and shrugged as Bill turned his back on us and left the building. Neither Sophia nor I commented at that moment, but we gave each other questioning looks!

Our chat and drink together later on in the pub were friendly and Sophia was extremely likable but harbored continued self-doubt about her skills and confidence to be a life model. It boiled down to the fear of being consciously naked in front of strangers. I told her of how I adopt characters to get past such thoughts and I raised the fact that she needed lots of tips to overcome her fears as she did not have a performer's background. I won't detail here how I helped her in terms of learning from my modeling experience.

What raised my eyebrows was that she told me that she had been to Bill's studio alone with him twice during the evenings over the previous couple of weeks to practice and to be 'coached' by Bill! My 'spider senses' were activated. After listening to her casual description of being with Bill I learned that he'd recommended she practice poses dressed in her underwear or a bikini! To me, lycra leggings and a vest top would have been more appropriate because that's what I would have chosen for myself. Another surprise for me was that Bill's 'advice' and 'coaching' in no way matched my own personal approval!

I didn't say this to Sophia to my regret! She didn't voice her concern or doubt about Bill's suggestions, so I accepted she was comfortable. Life modeling for the first time in front of strangers can be extremely unnerving for models and some stop after their first gig. Sophia seemed to grow in confidence as we chatted, and I concluded that she just wanted to hear from another model as to what to expect. So, most of our time together that evening concerned the light-hearted and funny things that a life model can expect. I had no reason to be concerned for her.

A couple of months had passed since meeting with the lovely Sophia and I had had four two-hour evening sessions with Bill's life drawing groups under my belt. During these, he was distant with me, professional but not remotely sociable. There was a barrier in his manner preventing us from becoming friends. I work better with artistic people when we develop a slow long-lasting friendship. Nothing in the meantime had connected my working with Bill with Sophia's description of her time alone with him in the art department. However, Bill's attitude toward me had aroused my suspicions about his character. Coincidences began to conspire to bring matters to a head!

I was pleased to hear from a very talented female artist friend, Cordelia who with the help of her family had managed to open a working studio in a trendy part of Brighton. I managed to visit her quite often to chat with her and see her progress and I began to collaborate with her on a few small projects. Cordelia was in her late 20s and very expressive and gregarious. Also, she was extremely and naturally beautiful, reminding me of Elizabeth Taylor in her enigmatic role as 'Queen Cleopatra' in the Hollywood epic movie. She had that rare combination of sheer natural beauty and an incredible unique talent which was reflected in her amazing figurative artworks. She became an extremely successful artist financially because all of her original paintings and the limited edition prints of her originals also sold very rapidly. She also undertook many successful commissions.

Cordelia's buyers and collectors were mostly men and without doubt when men met Cordelia, they were instantly attracted to her. I always said that despite her art being spectacular, her male admirers bought her art because it was like they wanted to 'own a piece of her'! She was aware of this, and it troubled her because she felt she was mainly acknowledged for her looks first and her art second! She was however oblivious to the advances of men and that added to her allure and mystique. She was also dismissive of the obvious and predictable vanilla advances of men mainly because her mind was deeply submerged in her art.

During one of my visits to see Cordy in Brighton, we were having a coffee and a light-hearted chat about how young artists spend their early years struggling to find their own style and how having your own gallery can be a lonely experience at times. She mentioned that she would relish the opportunity to speak with undergraduate art students about her life as a professional artist. Without hesitation I mentioned Bill and his links with the art institute and the students practicing life drawing and I suggested she could arrange through him to give a series of talks. Cordy would have been a wonderful contact for the students and for her to start to build links with local academic art establishments. She agreed that I should email Bill and pass on her details to make contact. I left it at that.

Within a month I was visiting Cordelia again and spent the whole day at her studio. We were so wrapped up in her latest exhibition project it wasn't until I was leaving that I remembered to ask her about whether she had been in touch with Bill. Her face dropped and she looked away from me silently looking very pensive. We exchanged a few silent glances. I remained quiet allowing her time to gather her thoughts. She then began to tell me that Bill had turned up at her studio unannounced. He'd walked around the street level part of her gallery while she had been upstairs painting. She'd seen a man enter on her CCTV monitor and begin to look around. She had no idea who the man was. After a while she went downstairs to speak with him. There was no one else in the studio apart from the two of them. Cordelia introduced herself to him and he did likewise.

She struggled to make sense of why he would simply drop in without notice especially as they'd only briefly contacted each other via email. He had agreed only to pass on to her a few dates to consider for giving a talk to the fine art students. They shook hands when he was introducing himself and his handshake lingered a little too long for her to feel comfortable. She told me it took too long to break and went beyond that which is appropriate for a first meeting, or any meeting! This took place directly in front of Cordelia's latest triptych of female nude studies. Without releasing their handshake Bill had asked Cordelia.

"Are they your tits?" pointing at the artworks with his other hand!

Cordelia is a strong woman and immediately took control of the situation by demonstratively asking him to leave and showing him the door! Good on her! She actually apologized to me for not telling me sooner! Bless her. Her apologizing to me started a cascade of apologies and explanations from me. I sat with Cordy and told her about how Bill had reacted when Sophia and I had connected and should have at least told Cordelia about my suspicions regarding him. I felt awful because I had put Cordelia not only in an awkward situation but one that proved threatening. Fortunately, she and I are still great friends! However, contact with Bill was to occur again shortly after this.

I had been invited to be the life model at a very well-known museum to portray the naked male form inspired by a number of famous artists' recognizable masterpieces both living and dead. Essentially it was an event to celebrate the male nude in the history of art. It was rather like a historical role play for me. I'd be dancing and life modeling separately. I agreed willingly to model at the event and shortly I received email correspondence describing the complete format of the daylong event. My eyebrows were again raised when I read that Bill was to be the lead tutor to be attended by at least 40 artists and photographers both professional and talented hobbyists. I was pleased to note that my contact for the whole day would be Diana, or Dee as she was known. I made contact with her and arranged to arrive early as usual prior to the event starting.

So true to form, I did arrive early, typically to gain a feel for the creative atmosphere. Directed by the ebullient reception staff I made my way to the side gallery on the first floor in the museum where the event was set up. I found it at the far end of the main first floor gallery after ascending a curving ornate wide staircase featuring emotive oil paintings. The atmosphere created was like the figures in the paintings were actually watching you as you ascended, like they were inspecting and casting approval or disapproval. I expected the figures to move between the frames as they do at 'Hogwarts' but they remained steadfastly still! I winked at the Victorian ladies and gentlemen as I went by each of them just in case! At the top I turned right and stared into the perfectly lit main gallery exhibiting an evocative collection of Japanese Shunga art that I clocked for a future prolonged visit. Right up my street!

At the far end of the gallery was a glass partitioned archway leading to the side gallery for the main event. Within this glass partition was a glass door. It reminded me of the glass front of a squash court. At the other side of the glass wall, a woman dressed in the black uniform of the museum, black leggings, and black sweat top, was expertly attaching a translucent temporary film to the glass. This would be used to prevent onlookers staring in during the event. This was obviously the place where I would be life modeling and dancing. Before the glass was completely covered, I observed the setup without wanting to disturb anyone in there.

This side gallery's main space was to the right of the entrance and most of it was obscured as I stood there, but directly in front of me I could see a small stage area. In front of that many artists' easels stood waiting like three-legged pterodactyls. I counted 36 of them. I saw the woman in black inaudibly speak with someone and then she exited the space in a hurry. She smiled and nodded at me without either of us introducing ourselves. She appeared to be a little stressed! I entered the glass door she had just exited from and observed a wide terraced arrangement of temporary seats at the far-right end, rather like 'indoor bleachers'. Six rows of seats starting at shoulder height with a centrally ascending aisle. This would provide the paying audience with a clear view of the stage over the heads of the artists at their easels.

I was slated to perform two short 15-minute dance pieces that I had choreographed, a solo piece from the ballet 'La Bayadere' and a solo dance theater performance to Sir William Walton's 'Battle of Britain'. There would be a short 15-minute interval before I would be life modeling for 60 minutes interpreting historical and contemporary artworks which were to be projected onto a large screen set up upstage of where I would be modeling. I noticed a sound and lighting desk positioned stage right and that the back row of the seating was reserved for photographers. All of the outside natural light was blocked out and the whole space would be lit with various colored spotlights. Each easel had its own little spotlight attached to the boards. I imagined it would be very atmospheric and I thought to 'block rehearse' my dance pieces as soon as the LX guy could run it through. I had two hours until 'curtain up' and all felt good, so I left the performance space and went off to look for the cafe area and to track down the LX dude. All LX dudes are 'dudes man'!

I returned after about 30 minutes and noticed that the glass partition and door to the side gallery had been made completely private. It looked very neat and added a creative allure with the flickering of lights in there. That denoted Mr. cool LX dude was doing his stuff. As soon as I entered, I looked to the far right toward the seating and I noticed movement and two figures actually under the seating scaffolding, one crawling and the other standing. The one standing was Bill. He noticed me and walked over to me with a blank face and little eye contact as usual. His arrogant posture though made it obvious to me he was enjoying the whole experience and looking very 'queen bee'!

Exchanging formalities, he then carried on making final preparations by fiddling with the easels in front of the stage. I decided to leave the LX dude playing with the lights and sound and walked down to the figure next to the seating section. I noticed it was the woman who I had seen when I first approached the side gallery. She was an extremely attractive woman, I guessed in her early 30s, and her long dark hair was now tied up into a very professional tight bun on the top of her head, in a contemporary dance style. Her thick black sweatshirt had been removed to reveal a very tight crew necked T-shirt matching her extremely snug tight-fitting thick black leggings leaving nothing to the imagination. Her look was complete with big black steel toe capped safety boots. Around her waist she had a small 'bum bag' pulled very tight highlighting her hourglass figure. She looked every bit the sexy backstage professional crew member in 'blacks'.

She saw me approaching and stuck out her hand and introduced herself as 'Dee', my contact for the day. She knew who I was without me saying so. I was struck by her air of competence and professionalism. Thank goodness. We struck up quite a long introductory conversation about the setup and Dee gestured toward the LX desk and explained that I could rehearse when the LX guy gave her the thumbs up. As I looked toward the stage from where we were speaking, I caught sight of Bill standing watching us without any excuse for doing so. From that short distance his posture was square on and aggressive, he had that same stiffness in his head and shoulders, a complete change from his initial demeanor. When Dee turned to look in the same direction, Bill noticed and instantly turned away and tried to look busy. Dee had had enough of a look at Bill though to note his previous aggressive stance and she turned to me looking quizzically at me.

"What's his problem?" she asked.

Thank goodness, I thought, I have an ally here!

"Who Bill!" I said rhetorically, and found myself thinking out loud, "you know, I think he's jealous of me when I speak to a woman! I don't trust him as far as I could throw him, and he has the habit of instantly deflating a creative atmosphere!"

"OMG, I knew there was something odd even creepy about that guy" Dee added, "Just now he had me crawling under the seats here to pick up something that turned out to be nothing but an old leaflet and he stood right behind me, well in my space," she continued noticing me nodding in acknowledgement.

"Worse, earlier he had me position each easel while he stood too close behind me there too!" she added. "Creepy!"

"Keep your distance! Let's look out for each other and keep an eye on him!" I said, and gave her a friendly understanding look.

"Come on I'll show you the dressing rooms," Dee replied, starting to laugh and she tapped me on my arm, "more like a dressing storeroom cos that's what it is, a storeroom, but we've cleaned it out for you!"

We both laughed and I could imagine Bill stiffening, but I didn't look.

Dee made a grab for my yoga roll I'd been carrying with me under my arm, and I grabbed my bag, and we walked out of the gallery casually chatting together. I must admit that having Dee as an ally made me feel very positive about the day. Dee and I were united.

"Let's show that old creep we've got him sussed." she said, and I knew she felt the same way as I did.

During the short interval between my two dance performances, I noticed that Dee was standing stage left, in the background. She'd been watching me perform. During my second performance I became more 'stage aware' of her and 'performed directly' for her using her as my focus. Did she know this? I'm sure she did because I saw her face, she was exuding sexual energy after the performance without doubt. There was also no doubt Bill noticed because he was very conspicuous in the background! However, Bill decided to 'get his own back'! Following my role as the life model later in the day I took a Q&A with the audience and the artists. In answer to one question, I revealed the names of the various life drawing groups I worked with. I could see Bill glowering at me! At the end, the lovely Dee was there to greet me as I left the stage and walked back with me to my dressing room where we tucked into coffee and cake.

The very next day I received an email from Bill. I still have it and laugh at his childish rant. He actually lambasted me for revealing the life drawing groups I worked with claiming I'd done so to undermine the attendance at his own groups! He went on to claim many of the artists at the event were personally invited by him from his own groups and he would carefully monitor their future attendance to assess the damage I'd done! What a complete arse! The audacity of the man but what he was really doing was trying to divert my attention from what he really was, a predatory pervert. I took my time replying to him. Normally I would not have replied but I felt it high time that this pervert was at least distracted from his antics. I consulted with Dee over coffee one lunchtime about how I should reply to him, and this is what I emailed back to him. Dee agreed that we needed to put him off his hideous stride with young women.

"It was a pleasure performing at the museum and meeting many wonderfully creative attendees at the event as well as the inspiring staff there who made it all happen on the day. Dee and I would also like to acknowledge on behalf of ourselves and many young women that we have 'got your number'! Desist from your inappropriate behavior otherwise you will deservedly suffer the consequences of your actions."

Dee felt determined to track down a large number of young women who had 'worked' with Bill by using Instagram and Facebook. I'm unfamiliar with such methods as I'm a 'techno laggard' and reluctant social media user. I know that Dee took action and started a discussion group and outed the creep. This took place before the #metoo campaign and thankfully it has expanded and dramatically 'outs' and diverts such men as Bill. Had my sisters ever come across such a man as Bill, they would have surrounded the wretched character and given him a piece of their Aussie Outback upbringing! Bill is dead now and this is where I will leave it.

The Bitch!

It's not just male tutors and artists who have shown me their jealousies and aggressions. I clearly remember the overtly passive aggressions of a female artist and tutor called Simone. In her mid-50s, short and squat, she was a 'retired' theater producer. Well, she called herself retired but in actual fact she'd rubbed up so many people the wrong way in theatreland she found herself with diminished opportunities for work. She was a trained artist and had worked in theaters for many years and had taken the step to become a freelance art teacher and tutor to a number of established life drawing groups. I had heard of her from various sources but we had never met or so I thought, but when we did meet in a professional setting, I remembered seeing her at a theater press night party where she had acted like she owned the place!

I was invited to life model at a select 'highbrow' event organized at a privately owned estate and stately home. A whole day of six hours of life drawing for fee paying attendees, the pay was exceptionally generous and the tutor for the day was… Simone! This didn't concern me. I didn't know her. She had a reputation but I'm always wary of others speaking negatively about people especially if I don't know them. I'm a great believer in 'lies go twice around the world before truth has time to pull its boots on'! I contacted the organizers who were typical 'posh pommies'! Upper-class rich English landowners, the type who don't do much for the reputation of Brits abroad!

Anyway, I made sure they were aware of my Australian roots using my slow Queensland working-class drawl when speaking with the very posh female contact by telephone. I find that despite the British class system, as an Australian I can navigate around the Pommie snobs and interact with them without kowtowing to their sense of superiority and not succumbing to their social filtering. I have never even by default been drawn into their bullshit world! I just look at their Royal family and that's all I need to know!

My main contact was the 'lady of the manor', Felicity or 'Flick' as she suggested I call her. As a boy we had many cats at the cattle station and one of the mangey little buggers was called 'Flick'! Rather than meeting with 'Flick' prior to the event I arranged to arrive on the day at the estate's huge country house deep in the Home Counties of England at 9am, two hours before the start at 11am. I had doubled my hourly rate with Flick and had her send me over a 'purchase order' to make things squeaky clean. As an aside, the richer the client, the slower they are to pay! Flick went a tad quiet when I told her my fee, but she probably drank a bottle of Claret each week far in excess of what I was charging! She paid up eventually!

So much for Flick, I never got to meet her on the day of the event. I think two of her chihuahuas had gotten into a scrape with a Jumbuck on the estate, but what the hell, I've no idea! Anway, I was met by Suzannah, one of Flick's daughters. Managing the vibe I immediately called her 'Suzi'. Suzi laughed at this and confirmed my suspicions about posh pommies when she said laughingly,

"Don't let mummy hear you call me Suzi; she'd have to lie down and take the vapors!" Strange that Felicity accepted 'Flick' but Suzannah couldn't be Suzi! That sums up posh Pommies! One sounds chic but the other too close to the 'council estate'! God forbid.

I liked the lovely Suzi regardless, she was free-spirited, horsey and a bit out of condition with a liking for cigarettes and chocolate! She was a fun jolly English rose and we got on great. In Aus we'd say, "She'll be apples"! She loved my accent, and I teased her remorselessly until she wet her knickers and then she asked me what I was doing later! I told her I was busy, driving home! Of course I got nowhere near the big bloody house. The life drawing event was to be in a row of beautifully converted stables attached to a barn conversion. There was the most amazing modern underfloor heating and Suzi let me into the venue with her key because I wanted to stretch and prepare.

All the original stables had been knocked into one long gallery with the attached spacious barn large enough for wedding receptions to be held there, I believe this was its primary purpose. There was a side room in the barn section, and this was a fully kitted out dressing room, designed, I was told by Suzi, for newlywed brides where they could powder their noses before emerging with a flourish into the wedding reception. My gay mates would love this venue!

I slung out my yoga mat in the middle of the wooden floor in the middle of 18 artist's easels arranged in a horseshoe. The underfloor heating was pumping heat through my bare feet and all dancers will appreciate this glorious sensation. Every dancer is aware of floors everywhere whether performing or not! I began stretching on my mat in that lovely space when the chatty Suzi decided to leave me to it. I heard her leave by the door and within 10 minutes I heard the door open and close again and footsteps approached. I heard another very posh voice, a bloke this time. He spoke in a loud jocular fashion, very friendly. I couldn't see him approach as my backside was pointing his way as I stretched on the mat.

"Hello there!" he boomed. "Don't get up, just popped in to say hello, for my sins I'm the dog's body usually but if you need anything my daughter Suzannah will be on hand to help, just ask. I'm assuming you are the life model, I'm Jack by the way."

"No wuckas, I'm George the life model, thanks, I'm in mid-stretch, love the venue, sorry about your view!" I replied.

"The view?" Jack asked,

"Yeah, my arse, my presentation for you" I said.

"Not to worry" I heard him say while laughing.

"Well, I'm glad it was you, I've met your daughter already, but this position wouldn't be suitable even meeting her the second time!" and I heard Jack laugh some more.

"I'll catch you later during the break" he added, "and don't worry, I'll recognize you" he spluttered laughing!

We both saw the funny side, so to speak. I liked Jack. Jack left without me seeing his face and shortly I heard the door open and close again. I was doing lunges by then so I could look in the direction of the main door. It was some way off and blocked by an internal wall in the small lobby area. That's where I saw the sour-faced Simone emerge! I smiled in her direction as she approached me, and she looked like a bulldog chewing a wasp. Jesus, I thought, how am I going to work with this grump! I was about to speak and introduce myself but Simone simply said.

"Who let you in?"!

That was her introduction, the first time she'd ever spoken to me! So much for her working in the creative arts all her life, the miserable cow! I instantly felt negatively toward her, but like I've mentioned a few times, I wasn't going to react to her because of the way she made me feel. I'd have my chance to unsettle the old goat! As per my habit, I let my feelings subside and carried on stretching, deciding to say nothing sociable to her at any point but keeping everything professional on my part. She did not at any time during the day introduce herself to me and only referred to me as "the model" throughout the life drawing!

Simone wandered off out of sight behind me. My silence had unsettled her. All bullies are cowards! I finished my stretching and went to the dressing room. Walking in I noticed that my kitbag had been moved from the middle of the room where I'd left it, and it was up against the wall at the far end. I instantly knew Simone had done this! Things could only get worse if I'd reacted, so I decided to stick to being patient. My opportunity would arrive to swat this bitch.

Within a few minutes, the lovely Suzi came back with some drinks, coffee and juice and some cake. As I tucked into this kind gesture she told me about the timings of the event, when the artists would break out to take refreshments and asked me what I would like for my lunch. Bonzer, I was back on track thanks to Suzi. Soon Simone came into my dressing room, ignored me, and fawned all over Suzi using an affectation of a posh English accent which made her sound ridiculous. I felt like laughing and I noticed that Suzi was trying to stifle a giggle. I'll get her to giggle I decided! Suzi then politely ignored the rattle of Simone's questions and asked her if she and I had met. All Simone said blandly was, "I met him earlier!"

Then waving her arms around demonstrably in my direction then around the room, she said.

"And please try and keep things tidy in here!"

I was gob smacked! Not even a simple polite 'yes we bumped into each other earlier, didn't we?' Simone made no eye contact with me and Suzi sensed this too. I wanted to tell Simone to 'fuck off' but that would have destroyed any semblance of creativity left; it's like a hand grenade going off in a small space! I then saw my opportunity to shake a giggle out of Suzi by catching her eye when Simone couldn't see me; I made little grimacing faces at her! It's a trick I use for pure devilment to make fellow performers *'corpse'* when we find ourselves in both serious and embarrassing situations. Suzi giggled uncontrollably on cue, and I was happy to see that Simone hated that! She was totally fazed.

I then suggested that Simone must have something better to do than stand around in my dressing room and I could see her seething, but she left with Suzi stifling more giggles. As I snacked, I chatted with Suzi about Simone, and it was clear that neither of us had any previous dealings with her and Suzi had no idea who had appointed her as tutor for the day! She asked me why she was so dismissive toward me and at that point I honestly had no idea. Shortly Suzi left and she promised to catch up with me at the interval at around 12:15 for lunch.

The life drawing began, the artists were settled at their easels and Simone came across as quite chirpy. I wondered if she'd either come to her senses or whether she was naturally 'two-faced' or whether she'd had a personality transplant or even whether she'd taken her medication! All the artists were female. By their chatter they all knew each other chatting in posh cliches and laughing haughtily. I received the odd glance as I stood silently robed waiting for my cue from Simone to begin. In my head I adopted the '4th wall' mentality and rehearsed the characterizations of my poses in my mind.

There was however a palpable sexual frisson in the air! The familiar situation appeared before me yet again, that of a group of women feeling safe in a shared group situation with that female propensity for implicitly sensing an atmosphere and knowing what each and every one of them was thinking! This was heating up the room! I could almost taste their excitement, and the warm space was redolent of a multiverse of perfumes. Looking quickly around the room at them I noticed that without speaking to each other, each had a unique sexual fascination with me. Not for me personally, it was their excitement at the prospect of looking at a male ballet dancer naked all day!

I've often said that ballet is soft porn for rich middle-class women with nothing much better to do! I was extremely tanned all over from my recent sunny holiday to France with the girls and I was in perfect nick as a result of intense dance rehearsals, and I didn't have a single niggling injury. I decided I was going to own this day! I was more intrigued by how Simone would react. I already controlled that space, and she knew it! The audience was mine as well and Simone knew that too! By the sudden change in her demeanor she tried unsuccessfully to bring the artists to order, to go through her introduction. It was obvious she knew she was not being taken seriously. Simone was mostly being ignored. Eventually she went silent, and I could see anger and frustration in her eyes. Then she quickly looked at me and my eyes said, 'they are mine' and Simone's eyes said, 'you bastard'! This little squat angry passive aggressive 'queen bee' already knew she'd lost control, so I saw my opportunity to give her just desserts and at the same time, give the artists what they really wanted!

I walked slowly to the center of the floor and slowly took off my robe without any cue from Simone and the room fell slowly silent. I assumed a good expressive 5-minute pose and didn't spare the sensuality of it! There was complete silence for a few seconds, then a few dropped pieces of charcoal, a rustling of paper on boards, then a quiet little voice said…

"I'd have liked to have been on that beach."

Agreeable laughter broke out and these female artists were a united audience, but not Simone's audience! Other comments followed, all tasteful but daring for these posh ladies whose ages ranged from mid-30s to early 80s.

"Oh, what a treat!" said one.

"Good job, my husband doesn't know I'm here!" said another encouraging more whoops and giggles.

"I will never recognize this lovely specimen of a man with his clothes on."

"I don't know where to look."

"I'm all of a quiver…" followed by…

"Aren't we all, darling"!

This is how it continued in a controlled but unremitting gentle torrent! It was all good-natured and of course I said nothing, but I modeled my ass off! All I did was smile in a professional way remembering what ballet mistresses constantly said during classes.

"Smile, smile always smile… and beautiful backs everyone," very good tips for young dancers.

I gave those artists my best "beautiful backs" and I poured with sweat. Their eagerness to draw with abandonment matched their spirited moods. Nevertheless, Simone gathered herself for one last attempt to regain her control!

Immediately, after the first interval Simone started to instruct the artists on the best way to position an easel when either standing or sitting to draw. She demonstrated with her own easel that it should be positioned with a clear line of sight of the model requiring little movement of the head. This made sense. One quite elderly artist was sitting perched on a high stool. She was sitting side on to me, and I could see her drawing from the direction I was facing.

Suddenly, Simone began a very loud and impatient reiteration of the best position for the easel but clearly aimed at the elderly artist, who in turn ignored Simone. She approached the artist and spoke with her directly. I heard the artist explain to Simone that she was in a comfortable position, and I also clearly heard her say quite firmly that she was "staying put!" Simone should have backed off at that moment but no! The artist then explained her current preferred position was because she suffered from neck and back pain and also had trouble getting off and onto the stool and that she was quite happy. All of a sudden Simone began to move the artist's easel with one foot and both hands! The tripod legs of the easel scraped across the floor. I can only describe what happened next as a fraught few seconds of a squabbling tug of war! Voices were raised and I'm pleased to say that the elderly artist won the battle! Simone was left with tears in her eyes and her silly intervention ended when a posh voice from one of the other artists spoke up with,

"Please, leave her be!"

Simone gave up and retreated. She looked embarrassed and flushed. The control freak was kaput! For the rest of the day, she had the sense to say little and to instruct even less. In fact, I took requests from the artists regarding poses and length of each pose! What little tutoring Simone did was strained and looks were exchanged between this phalanx of women whose day was not to be ruined. I had 18 allies that day! Here was an obvious case of Simone acting on feelings and then suffering the consequences and the power of silence on my part. Simone for all her theater experience failed to read the audience. There was a palpable togetherness between those women, and I was flattered to be part of it. To Simone's credit, if that is the right term, she knew when she was beaten.

During Simone's contretemps with the easel, I had made eye contact by smiling and raising my eyebrows with an artist directly to my right. I found out later her name was Caron. We both began 'corpsing', we could not control our giggles. It was excruciating! Corpsing is an irrational and uncontrollable and certainly unprofessional attack of the giggles that you fight to contain and fail! It can happen at any time on stage, on film set and especially during rehearsals. It is extremely tiring too! It can be hilariously funny entertainment, and I simply love film clips of 'outtakes' of actors corpsing. If you want to see the best example of corpsing, just type into a YouTube search

'Ricky Gervais Keith Chegwin outtakes extras'

And for the best example of live corpsing there's none better than searching for this on YouTube

'Archives: test match special 'Leg over' incident ft Brian Johnston and Jonathan Agnew'

Both will give you a hilarious insight as to what Caron and I went through that day! Keith Chegwin used the phrase "sweating buckets" to describe what corpsing does to you, and here I was doing it in a room full of sexually charged women! It is not a place where you want to find yourself as a male life model in the professional sense! On this occasion the whole space descended into uncontrollable hysterics. There was only one person not laughing, Simone! This made the situation even funnier! At the end of the day, I accepted the applause and thanks from the artists, but I dedicated the day to them. I simply handed over the creatively fun atmosphere to them and they turned the day into a unique experience for all of us.

I merely left the center following the applause (very unusual following life modeling) and returned to the dressing room. I joined everyone later for a refreshing drink. I didn't stay long however because it wasn't about mingling and networking for me and those artists were tucking into so much wine anything could have happened! I stayed for as long as the conversations and laughter rolled then I left. I would describe my relationship with Simone that day as 'having creative differences'. Some months later I discovered that Simone wanted to choose her own life model that day but 'Flick' being the lady of the manor, had insisted on me! I never really found out why! I had my suspicions though. Valerie was very coy when I told her about my day!

The Bastard!

Artist Tom had told me a few years previously about the 'power of walking away' and coupled with silence and staying calm, it has a powerful effect and maintains your dignity. Always keep things civilized and if you have to speak,

speak with gentle humor. However, things can go wrong with this approach if you let your feelings get the better of you. *'Here starteth the lesson'*!

At the start of a very long day of life modeling with a small group of six elderly female artists, whose wealthy patron had provided an established studio venue for them, they politely asked me to begin with a 90-minute standing pose without the usual quick warm up sketching. I had no problem with cutting out their need for warmups but the thought of a 90-minute pose was daunting. It is an incredibly long time in any position and usually such a long pose is done in repose, lying down on your front or back on a comfortable sofa or mattress. For a standing pose I would need to be extremely well balanced as well as comfortable and I would need to take at least two breaks during that time. It's a fact that most life models will 'sag' during a long pose.

It is very important to be open with artists and inform them of the likely consequences of any pose. Arms, legs and even the torso can move unconsciously; 'no man is a statue' so to speak! It is for the model to inform the artists that if this should become obvious to them, they should speak up. This is essential for the longer poses, but 90 frickin' minutes, holy cow that's a crook deal!

As a dancer, I am obviously on my feet. That's what dancing is. Some might say 'hey what about all that rolling around the floor in contemporary dance, isn't that dancing?' Yeah, it is but I tend to agree with Graham Norton's definition, that contemporary dance is more like 'care in the community'! Anyway, I digress. Being trained in ballet, I am aware of my posture and supporting groups and pairs of muscles. I also have a strong understanding of my Musculo-skeletal relationships so that I am able to activate my body correctly to minimize stresses and strains on my ligaments and tendons. Someone who is unfit or overweight or lives a sedentary lifestyle, will find that their body defaults to supporting them with their tendons and ligaments, not by their major supporting muscle groups. This leads to acute and chronic pain. Pain is the body's way of saying 'stop this right now', whereas aches are the body's way of saying, 'it's time to rest please'. Aches are indications that a muscle is in repair mode. Muscle fatigue is simply a lack of oxygen and increased lactic acid.

Over a long dance performance, of course, every muscle fatigues eventually. However, we can push through aches with sheer willpower. Even so, 90 minutes of standing still was going to be a trial of mind and body but my awareness of my muscles allows me to switch on and off the differing pairs of supporting muscles. This gives one pair a rest while another pair takes the strain. I alternate pairs of muscles throughout the longer poses. The quicker I need to alternate between pairs of muscle groups, means I am tiring more quickly.

This 'day of the 90 minute standing pose' that I had agreed to, fully disclosing what to expect from me regarding changes in muscle observations for them, I simply began using a relaxed upper body with my center of gravity over an 'open fourth' ballet position of my feet. This is the most comfortable way for me to engage my largest supporting groups of muscles in my legs and glutes. It also has the effect of portraying latent movement. The artists also agreed to my request for gentle piano music as I posed which is arranged for ballet barre exercises of differing tempos. This would allow me to focus my mind on ballet rather than wishing that time would speed by! Silence for me actually adds tension to my body, and I tire even more quickly! Simply put, silence makes time appear to drag!

Twenty minutes into the pose all was going well and all of us were happy. I was then suddenly aware of the door to the studio being opened along with a lot of clattering. The door slammed shut and the clattering and banging continued until a strong looking thickset elderly man came into my view and began to set up his easel, which he wasn't efficient at. This resulted in an extended period of noise and distraction for everyone else. What surprised me more was that none of the women spoke up until the studio became relatively quiet once more before one of the ladies said quietly.

"Good morning, Edward."

That was it! Nothing more was added. Edward didn't reply and no one else spoke. Unfortunately, there followed a series of events that when linked together forms the basis of an accident waiting to happen! Edward continued to clatter around with his easel and drawing media again, mumbling and swearing under his breath and he had set up directly in front of me. I couldn't help but observe every bloody thing he did! Coming in late he'd heard zilch about the format of the life drawing and the strengths and weaknesses of my long pose. It wasn't long before he began to complain in an elderly curmudgeonly way about the soft piano music that was irritating the upper-class twit! To my surprise and angst, one of the ladies switched off the music that was linked via her smart phone to a Bluetooth speaker somewhere in the studio. Then Edward began to complain about the lighting, the heat in the studio despite being trussed up like a 'Michelin Man', his drawing position and finally he began to complain about me!

"You've moved!" he blurted out, "you've moved again" he said a split second later.

I didn't say a word and I hadn't moved either. To reply would be unprofessional and Edward obviously took this to be a weakness on my part, not professional tolerance. None of the ladies attempted to speak on my behalf.

"How long is this bloody stupid pose for?" he grunted.

No one answered. Edward continued, obviously encouraged to complain continually and all I could conclude was that the others were hoping their silence would silence him! However, he began to insult me personally.

"Where did you get this amateur from, he may as well be wandering around? Hasn't anyone explained to him that a life model needs to keep still? How long is this stupid pose for."

At last, a kindly calm voice behind me spoke up,

"90 minutes, Edward. We are almost 30 minutes in now. We are going to have a short break in 15 minutes for George to stretch, maybe we could change the pose, and you could start drawing then?"

Edward grunted his disapproval, continued with more insinuations of my 'incompetence' which resulted in my hackles beginning to rise!

"We are lucky to have a ballet dancer to model for us," one of the other ladies added calmly.

"I don't care what he is!" shouted Edward, "he keeps bloody well moving."

I bit my lip and finally at around the 45-minute mark the rest break was announced. One of the ladies proceeded to mark where my feet were located with masking tape before I robed up so I could recapture the pose later if that was required. I could sense sympathy and support for me from the women artists and I was offered tea and biscuits, but no one confronted 'der fuhrer Edward'!

I won't bore you with the details further, but Edward began to complain continually during the break. He wandered around confronting people but fortunately he didn't approach me. My temper was beginning to rise dramatically, and I lost my creative vibe completely as I drank my tea and munched on the biscuits. As I did this part of my biscuit fell onto the floor as I bit into it. Suddenly a dog shot over and gobbled up the biscuit! I didn't even know a dog was in the space! At this one of the ladies literally hissed at me not to feed her dog! I felt the need to explain but it fell on deaf ears with her dirty looks heading my way! My only encouragement and support came at last when one of the other ladies said to everyone what a wonderful challenge and blessing, they all had with my prolonged standing pose which she described as unique. Edward just sneered and laughed!

"We'll restart in five minutes" someone said shortly.

One of the other female artists eventually came up to speak to me.

"Are you performing or modeling anywhere else currently?" she asked sweetly.

"I'm in rehearsals right now" I replied "I'm in a mixed program in two weeks…" I replied unenthusiastically.

I didn't elaborate and give her details of the performance and venue because superstitiously the negative vibes surrounding me were tarnishing my creativity! What I wanted was for someone to acknowledge that Edward was out of order and spoiling the life drawing for everyone. Worse, here was a man criticizing me while I was completely naked! The annoying way English people avoid what is right in front of their faces as is their habit raised my hackles even further. The English use politeness to cover up that they are ineffective and weak. Any irony is completely lost on them when they describe this as a 'stiff upper lip'! At that very moment Edward walked by and began to insult me within my space! Square on to me then pacing back and forth as though trying to garner an audience he said,

"What are you talking to him for? Where did you find him?"

I blew my lid! This bastard was cracking the shits with me and unloading his bollocks at me directly. It was time to defend myself as no one else was going to!

"You fucking cantankerous old goat, you've ruined the whole atmosphere and fucked up the whole day" I ranted. "You fucking old coward, you've tried to humiliate me while I'm naked and vulnerable. I'll tell you what, I'll get dressed and we can take this outside you fucking miserable cunt!"

And guess what! There were audible groans as the English traditional so-called upper classes closed ranks with a series of disapproving descriptions of my language! It was ripe! Edward wasn't the problem, I was! Typically English, ignore the problem and look for bad manners! This made my anger reach boiling point! Sir Cunt Edward just stood there looking like Coco the Clown with a silly grin on his face. I actually wished at that moment that he would try to punch me! I responded by getting dressed as calmly as possible as I listened to those women complaining about my bad language. As I left, I walked past the tubby streak of piss.

"Are you coming outside?" I asked, and I was serious.

Edward just went and sat next to one of the ladies without speaking. He had a blank idiotic look on his face. I supposed because he was a coward and suddenly someone had called him out so he 'ran off to nanny'! I decided to go out and drive off and leave this quagmire to stink without me. As I put my hold-all into the boot of my car, I heard footsteps behind me, and I turned quickly thinking it was Edward! It was one of the female artists and she came to a rapid halt probably because she saw the anger written all over my face. Slowly she approached me and spoke.

"We didn't know that Edward would be attending, and we should have mentioned that he has been diagnosed with dementia!"

Holy fuck! I ran through some rapid questions in my head as to why they hadn't thought to tell me discreetly at any stage but thought better of it and stayed quiet. What did jump into my mind was the fact that I had been brought up by my parents to take responsibility for my own actions regardless of others. In the end I'd broken my golden rule, not to make decisions based on feelings and emotions! I thanked the woman for explaining but I didn't apologize. Apologies were wide of the mark that day. It was a day of not confronting a spiraling situation until it was too late. We'd all played our part. I simply said,

"I won't be returning, I've burned my bridges."

It might not have sounded like some sort of muted apology but this clear situation of burning my bridges, making a clear and irreversible break, was the only option I had in order to begin to mend the complete destruction of a creative day. I needed to leave, and I did. The group sent me a cheque in the post for my time that day. They paid in full! I donated it to a men's mental health charity.

I leave you with this to decide. Who was the real bastard that day?!

Chapter Twelve

The Hen Party

Traditionally for me the months of July and August are quiet on the work front. It's a time I usually head down to L'Ile de Noirmoutier on the Vendée coast of Western France. I holiday there with a 'flight of ballerinas'. There's a particular basic campsite tucked into the sand dunes. There's a shower and toilet block with water pipes located around tiered sand dune camping pitches. It's not glamping, it's more like slumming! We spend the beautiful warm evenings chatting under the stars with our tents and our canopies strung out creating our own 'gypsy camp'. We eat lots of cheese, baguettes, salads, fish, and drink lots of cheap wine. We are best described as scantily clad becoming more like a camp of 'Robinson Crusoe-like' characters as the days and nights progress. There are usually nine of us in total, me and a gay friend, Colin and seven delicious ballet nymphs who thrive on chocolate, coffee, and cigarettes! They are as a group completely cuckoo and carefree, letting their hair down, gradually becoming more and more uninhibited away from the stresses and discipline of ballet companies. The wonderfulness of our stay is always accompanied by daily visits to the nearby nudist beach during the day where we sunbathe and skinny dip. The campsite and the nudist beach are both populated by lots of other itinerant summertime creatives including opera singers, dancers, and classical musicians from all over Europe.

Our journeys to the Ile, or the 'Isle de Nudity' as we call it, are usually done in cars or the odd flight, singularly, in pairs or in small groups turning up over a number of days when work commitments free us up. We are all usually gathered as a whole group by the third week of July, and we stay until the final week of August. Before joining the merry throng as arranged, I delayed my trip that year because I received a very generous offer from an upmarket events company to dance and life model for a large 'hen party' at a large secluded countryside events location in the Scottish borders just over the border from the English county of

Cumbria. Hen parties traditionally consist of a group of women, obviously, friends, relatives, acquaintances, and colleagues of the bride-to-be, going on an organized piss up for one evening organized by the chief bridesmaid. It's an established excuse for a group of women to let their hair down. The Hen Party is the female equivalent of the male 'Stag Night'.

Hen parties have now turned into 'Hen Weekends'! Gathering together from Friday afternoon onwards, the hens indulge themselves in prearranged activities over the whole weekend at specific venues and then depart at varying times during the following Sunday when hangovers and blood alcohol levels permit! These weekends are therefore typified by the drinking of copious amounts of alcohol and the individual and group behavior of the women becomes more and more uninhibited and even outrageous! I couldn't resist the offer of a booking for no other reason than the extremely generous pay I would receive for two hours work spread over one Saturday afternoon including travel and subsistence expenses. I would be paid to perform a 30-minute ballet barre exercise with an accompanying string quintet during a silver service lunch. This would be followed later the same day by a 90-minute tutored life drawing class with me as the life model. This was booked for the bride-to-be (BTB) by her head bridesmaid (HB) through the events company as part of a package of surprise treats for all. The whole package was kept as a complete secret for the BTB.

The appointed life drawing tutor was by good fortune, a good friend of mine. His name is Barry. He's a retired art teacher and following retirement he took up figurative painting and teaching art to adults, including tutoring life drawing classes. Barry's talent and skills as an artist and his experience as an art teacher meant that the life drawing would be run professionally and Barry always filled me with confidence. I always enjoy being with him, he is funny, entertaining and a brilliant raconteur. Cementing our friendship is a shared understanding of a life-changing experience. I adore his outlook on life. Life for him is for living and I share that understanding. I have been asked on many occasions if I would be a life model for Hen parties and up until this time my response was always to suggest that they hire a male stripper! When I discovered Barry was to be involved, I instantly knew that this Hen weekend would be focused on figurative art, not overt titillation!

Driving up to Scotland was a joy that day. The weather was fine, and I made a few stops at idyllic villages in the beautiful county of Cumbria. I still managed to arrive early at the venue which is set in the rolling countryside of the Scottish

Borders, 'Reiver Country'! Cumbria and the Scottish borders were famous for cattle rustling in times past and that was something Queensland ringers knew a lot about! I almost felt at home except the rolling hills around Queensland are not as green, or rolling, or anything like this place really! I drove into the grounds of the venue and parked up quite a distance from the main building entrance. I usually have a wander when I'm early rather than introduce myself straight away to reception staff to stretch my legs and clear my mind.

I eventually made it to the reception area in my own time, chilled and in a positive mood, where I was processed by two bonzer Scottish lassies. Soon I met up with the 'chief hen' the head bridesmaid (HB). Her name was Isabel, a lovely tall intelligent slender woman aged about 30 in my estimation, and soon we were joined by my mate Barry, and we settled down for a surreptitious coffee to chat about the activities for that afternoon. The staff had let us use the room behind the reception desk, a totally discreet area where we could organize our thoughts without the rest of the hens seeing us together. Plus, I would be allowed to change there before making my entry for the actual events.

Isabel departed to get back to the rest of the hens, with Barry and I leaving the room together a short time later. We had decided to wander around to familiarize ourselves with the venue looking like guests rather than the entertainment. It gave us time to chat together and catch up on all of our news. To the right of the reception area was a spacious hallway leading to a huge ballroom. On the left walking toward the ballroom was a cantilevered staircase beginning near the entrance to the ballroom. The ceilings were high, ornate, and grand. The ballroom, similarly, grand and ornate with huge chandeliers, was set up intimately in spite of its huge size to accommodate six small rectangular tables in the center of the dance floor. The tables were set up to seat two diners' side by side. The seating arrangements ensured that all the hens would be facing toward the large windows where the string quintet's instruments and music stands were set up with space between the musicians and the dining tables for me to locate my portable ballet barre where I would perform. During my performance, a silver service lunch was to be served to the BTB and the hens.

Following lunch there would be a breakout when the hens would depart for an organized event elsewhere in the house while Barry and the staff would set up for the life drawing. Twelve chairs with twelve drawing boards, easels and drawing materials were arranged for the hens. There would be enough time once the setup was complete for Barry and I to take a short trip to the local village pub for our lunch and continue our catchup. In another part of the large house the string quintet were having a chillout. I dropped by to introduce myself and we had a brief chat about the five pieces of music they would be playing. All I had to do was to get an idea of tempo to match it with the type of barre exercises I would perform. There was no need for a rehearsal as I could easily improvise.

Just before lunch was served at 1pm, I changed into my ballet gear discreetly. I was to make my entrance with my portable ballet barre after the first course. A member of staff 'stood guard' at the large double doors to the ballroom who would give me my cue to enter. I could hear the wonderful quintet playing from my reception hiding place. I was dressed in a white ballet vest top and white tights and black ballet pumps. I'd put Brylcreem in my hair, I'd done my basic stretches and absorbed the music. At around 1:20 I received my cue and taking hold of my ballet barre I made my way to the ballroom. None of the hens could see me as I entered through the double doors, but the quintet observed me and played a gentle introduction as I approached my allotted space to set up my ballet barre between them and the hens. Very professional uniformed female waitresses were beginning to clear away the plates from the first course very quietly and proficiently. As I set up my barre everyone suddenly noticed the look on the BTB's face. It was a look of complete joyful surprise. There followed a spontaneous round of applause from the hens, the secret being revealed finally. All of the hens had been told what was about to unfold shortly before lunch except the ballet-loving BTB.

The quintet struck up on my nod and I began. A wine waiter unobtrusively topped up wine glasses as soon as they looked empty, and the quintet upped their volume to create more of a performance atmosphere. It was normal barre work for me. It's designed to loosen and stretch so I was under no pressure. I added flourishes to everything to connect with the audience of hens. I performed tendus, pliés, relevés, rond de jambe, développés, petit and grand battements and combinations of all shifting from 'à terre' to 'en l'air' when relevant. All very simple stuff but the hens were mesmerized and they took quite a while to eat their main courses. It was all very elegant and civilized. As I finished and the quintet gradually played out their last piece, I completed my part with a double pirouette and a 'reverence'. The applause began. I joined in to show my appreciation for the musicians. They took their bows and plates began to be cleared, and amazing desserts and cakes were wheeled out on two serving trolleys. As I was about to leave the ballroom, I heard one of the hens shout out humorously…

"Hey Kelly, how can you possibly get married now?"

There was a peel of laughter, and I turned to catch sight of Kelly, the BTB shaking her head animatedly with her head in her hands drumming her center table with her elbows. The atmosphere had been set. I was going to enjoy life modeling later… or was I?! It was to begin at 5pm.

Just before 5pm I stood waiting outside the double doors of the ballroom. The early evening light was perfect, and the ballroom chandeliers were lit, and the peripheral lights were adding extra atmosphere. I'd changed into a thick brown robe that the hotel had provided, and I wore my own flip flops. The hens were already seated and from where I stood out of their sight, I could hear Barry discussing the life drawing format for the 90 minutes scheduled. At his nod, I flicked off my tatty flip flops and walked in, barefoot. As soon as I entered there was a ripple of chatty excitement and a smattering of gleeful applause. Kelly the BTB was beaming. I walked to the center of the room with the hens no more than 10 feet from me in a wide semi-circle. Barry told the hens that I would be taking up a standing ten-minute pose. Their eyes were glued on me and a few hens had their hands over their mouths. They weren't paying much attention to the charcoal and drawing boards. I dropped my robe as soon as Barry started his timer with a beep.

As this happened the atmosphere in the room became a torrent of raucous and embarrassed exclamations as well as excited squeals and laughter! The overall atmosphere was supposed to be professionally artistic even for these beginners. However, during the time between their lunch and the life drawing, while Barry and I had been back to the local pub for another chin wag, the hens, unbeknown to us, had had a cocktail mixing and tasting demonstration! Barry had found this out from Isabel at the last minute! He had no chance to tell me. What difference would it have made? The show had to go on! In simple terms the hens had had a piss up and they had obviously imbibed way too much booze!

I've described the state of the hens politely! Holy crap, the atmosphere was turbulent, and it wavered in and out of raucous! Barry came over to me from where he had positioned himself to one side. Under his breath in a hoarse whisper, just loud enough for me to hear him above the intoxicated chatter and giggles he quickly and clearly told me…

"Don't worry, I'll take control if things get out of hand, leave it to me. The staff are aware and two of them are just outside! I suggest we keep the poses short, and we will play it all by ear!"

I nodded my agreement and to be honest I felt fine with Barry in charge. I didn't have to tax my body, and I trusted him implicitly. To believe that this was the same group of civilized women who had watched me earlier and had appreciated a silver service lunch with a string quintet you would be in no position to be convinced! The atmosphere became beyond raucous. The sound level was verging on hysterical. I felt like I was Justin Bieber at a private girl's school! Sexual references were tossed around in a constant ad lib! Barry indicated to me silently mouthing "60 minutes" and I read his lips instantly. He wanted to inform me that these inebriated over-excited hens would not be receiving the planned 90-minute drawing instruction. To her credit, Isabel, the HB had stayed relatively sober and worked with Barry as best as she could to keep the hens focused. 'Good luck with that' I thought!

In a way I was in a bubble watching the gradual but relentless breakdown of female decorum! My mental approach was 'hey ho I've got Buckley's chance of clawing this back to normal, so use the difficulty by showing off a bit'. It was naughty of me stirring things up a little with provocative poses and I began to enjoy this new experience! I began subtly to sexualize my poses and made eye contact with the hens individually! This was unprofessional and I mitigated this with the belief that I was going to be sexualized by the hens anyway, so I asserted my masculinity! It seemed as though I had become the audience, and the hens were performing a crazy act for me, and I was being paid for it!

I was, however, dripping with sweat. It started under my arms and ran slowly down my back and chest and either dripped onto the floor or ran down my stomach, groins, and thighs. This attracted a verbal response from one of the hens to my left as I faced them. The loudest and gobby one of the 'coop' she was a chubby girl, the largest of them with an accompanying loud voice! She effectively started the banter with…

"He's literally dripping with sweat… phwoar!"

Not exactly contentious but it encouraged the others. Comments, very loud, signified that the situation was likely to get out of control! Some but not all of the comments I can recall, in no particular order, were constant and continuous combined with giggles and laughter!

"Oh, my fucking god, I need a new boyfriend!"

"I wonder if he's single?!"

"I want him full frontal next!"

"Look at his ass, I've never seen a bloke in the flesh with an ass like that!"

"Fuck, imagine sinking your nails into his bum."

"Nails? I'd sink my teeth into that… oof, if it didn't break them!"

"Gorgeous chest and abs, imagine licking them!"

"He's got the perfect happy trail and money muscles…huh!"

"I didn't know a man's body could have so much to admire."

"Look at the curves in his groins, I know he uses them for something, but I'd like to find out what!"

The hens began to hold up their drawings, and despite Barry's clear tutoring all I saw was a gallery of penises in charcoal! The hens continued.

"I always knew a man needs a strong hammer to bang in a long nail!"

"Don't you think he'd be like a Duracell battery in bed!?"

"He'd go all night!"

"God I'd fuck that!"

"What a piece of meat!"

"He could be your very own porn star!"

"I hope he isn't gay cos I want his babies!"

"You'll have to share him!"

"Fuck babies I just want his spunk all over me!"

The ribald comments were relentless and overlapping and the laughter was maniacal! Occasionally a hen would get up and try to approach me, but Isabel and Barry managed to contain it! On occasions there were short pauses of complete silence only to be broken by more comments, laughter, and increasingly lewd comments. At one point Barry slowly walked up to me from behind and said.

"I'm… er, losing… the room. Better get ready to run Georgie!"

I was on my marks. Barry wasn't joking! To his credit he'd certainly 'read the audience'!

There were a few compliments thrown into the mix from time to time, basically references to me having an "amazing body." TBH my body is as it is because it reflects what I've been doing nearly every day since I was six years old, dancing! My body in adulthood has rarely been uninjured in some way. Also, when I'm mingling in social situations, dressed obviously, hardly any women pay me any attention, certainly not sexual. I put this down to being 'short'! I'm

5′ 8″ tall and 152 lbs. I have no visible fat which makes my muscles look highly developed in the buff but totally unlike a 'gym monster'! I also prefer to be 'out of the limelight' in social situations. One thing I have noticed throughout my life is that large women want to hug and mother me, gay men 'come on to me' and straight women think I'm gay! I think that is so cool but probably explains why women are not obviously attracted to me in social situations!

Barry had managed to encourage the hens to draw of sorts for about 45 minutes. He then came up to stand next to me and told me it was time to "make a break for it!" I quickly walked over to my robe on the floor, grabbed it and made a naked running bow, RSC-style and simultaneously worked my way into the robe. It must have looked comical because it kicked off cheers, groans of disappointment and laughter! I darted for the double doors leading out of the ballroom and a female member of staff was waiting to hold one of the doors open. She had a huge smile on her face. She had previously entered the room discreetly to be ready for the hens should they go completely mad and to assist Barry and Isabel with crowd control I suppose.

As I passed by her, I could hear cries of "MORE!" and "ENCORE!" and "COME BACK!" I left Barry to it; I would catch up with him when I was dressed and unrecognizable in my clothes and my beanie hat! I knew he had planned a 'show & tell' at the completion of the life drawing session plus a casual 'photoshoot' of the hens displaying their drawing skills! Judging by the number of 'penis drawings' I couldn't help but have some sympathy for Barry, but I knew he'd enjoy himself and keep the hens buzzing.

Entering into the long wide hallway I walked toward the reception desk and the venue manager stood waiting controlling her own laughter. She ushered me quickly into the room behind the reception desk and I thanked her, exchanging a few jokes with her too.

"You just about survived then!" she said in her gentle Scottish accent.

"Only just!" I replied laughing and grateful for the security of the room.

I quickly changed and leaving my hold-all in the reception room, I headed back to the ballroom to see what was up! I could detect a more civilized babble but there was still an excited atmosphere in there! Barry was in control though. What a lovely man to have kept the room buzzing allowing the hens to enjoy the day without upsetting anyone. Rather than enter and distract him or set the hens off 'clucking' again I held back and moved sideways a little, parallel to the large double doors. One of the doors was wide open. I did this slowly attempting to catch Barry's eye if I could. He did see me, and he didn't overtly react. He just raised his eyebrows quickly and nodded toward me.

I could tell he was indicating 'see you later'. Suddenly as I was about to turn on my heels and head back to the reception room, Isabel recognized me despite my beanie! I dodged from her view but realized she was on her way to speak with me, so I waited for her out of sight from everyone else. As she emerged from the ballroom, she slowly closed the door to cut us off from the sights and sounds in there. The door was heavy, and she required both hands to pull it shut. As she did this her cute lean butt in very tight-fitting black jeans was in full view. The back pockets accentuated her sensuous lean cuteness. She then turned, giving me a look that conveyed secrecy! She skipped over to me and spoke.

"Are you leaving?" she asked with her big eyes a little shiny from the alcohol consumed but she was definitely not pissed.

"Hi, er no, not yet just popped along to catch Barry. There's no rush. We are going to the local pub to have a bite to eat later" I replied.

There was a long pause between us and then Isabel touched my arm slowly, looking coy but controlled!

"You have an amazing body; hope you don't mind me saying?"

I shook my head and thanked her, trying to look cool. Then I remained silent. There followed another long pause until Isabel spoke again but hurriedly.

"Look, we are all going by minibus back over the border tonight into Carlisle, will you be in town?" she said, trying to choose her words carefully.

"Er, I've not made any firm plans to be honest." I said.

Isabel pursed her lips and putting her feet together she wobbled her hips slightly while trying to choose the right words.

"Well... we could meet up in Carlisle, you, and me and... come back here with me in your car? Say... 11pm ish. All the others would come back here at 2am when the minibus is booked to bring everyone back? We'd have loads of time!" Time for what I thought!

Was I surprised? No, no, really. Alcohol is great for releasing inhibitions but what I mostly thought about from Isabel's polite proposition was the most likely scenario!

'I'd be totally sober, drive over to Carlisle and meet her at a place she had managed to let me know of by text message. Would there be a signal? Who knows! She'd have no idea about the exact location of the bar she'd be in, and I would also be totally unfamiliar with the town, especially driving around at night in a confusing array of small one-way streets. But hey, I'm nothing if not versatile right! By 11pm she would be drunk, far more inebriated than she seemed right now. She'd also have to tell Kelly, the BTB, that she was leaving to meet me, and Kelly would probably 'go off on one' as Isabel was important for the group as the HB.

All the other hens would find out pretty quickly and stack the shits with Isabel! The hens would also be drunkenly advising her not to meet me with descriptions of me being 'a mad axe murderer'! Let's face it all men are mad axe murderers to young women these days! If we did manage to meet up and then come back to the big house, quite frankly she'd be in no fit state to shag anyone! Not to mention the propensity for women to mess men around with their sudden changes of mood and mind! So fuck all that for a game of soldiers!'

[In parentheses, I didn't think of the following at the time but in retrospect my response to Isabel's 'proposal' was what is part of my mind's 'muscle memory'! Firstly, her suggestion excited me, it gave me a *feeling* of an exciting outcome. Rather than make a decision based on my *feelings*, I instead automatically turned my *feelings* into an *idea*. That *idea* made me think about the situation rationally. Then I turned my rational *idea* into an **action**; I clearly indicated my positive acceptance of getting together with her but packaged it in a brief 'yes or no' decision for Isabel. I essentially gave her the power to say yes or no. It both tested her commitment and her willingness. I effectively said yes and now! As in any improv class at any drama school I didn't say no… I said yes and… So what was the outcome?]

"That wouldn't work well, Izzy but…" I said, pausing, looking reflective, and smiling.

She smiled when I said her name and hit her with the alternative by saying,

"But I'm free now… no time like the present!" I added with a slow shrug of my shoulders.

Izzy looked shocked for a split second as her brain computed it all. Then she looked thoughtful, and her eyes widened, and she began to grin naughtily. Touching her chin she said,

"Follow me!"

Quickly she indicated the wide staircase behind me and trotted off toward the soft maroon carpeted ascent. She didn't look around as I followed her. I didn't look around to see if we'd been seen. I wasn't naive enough to think that that pretty young woman wouldn't change her mind but at that moment it was time for me to 'enter stage right'! We both speedily made our way up the stairs, me following her a few steps behind checking out her slender thighs and calves and the way her little ass flexed as she ascended two steps at a time!

The long high stairs turned left at the top to an open cantilevered landing giving a view down into the hallway below. Turning left again on the landing we quickly walked back in the direction of the ballroom below us. I noticed Isabel glancing down a couple of times toward the ballroom doors over the banister rail. I suppose it was to check if anyone was coming out of there and likely to look up and see us. I doubted that as we were very high up above the hallway. At the end of this section of the landing we turned right into a broad carpeted corridor with bedrooms either side individually named rather than numbered. We walked the full length of the corridor, and I noted the names of the bedrooms as we did so. At the very end we came to the bedroom named 'Rosebud'! 'Jeez, how appropriate' I thought.

Izzy opened the door with a swipe card she'd gouged out of the front pocket of her tight black jeans, and we entered the room. She walked in ahead of me unnecessarily quickly and I closed the door with a secure click of the lock and twisted a small button on the inside door handle that I knew would prevent someone else swiping in. She turned around and stood looking at me as I quickly took in our surroundings in that exquisitely furnished and lavishly decorated room. There was a four-poster bed between two windows against the far wall opposite the door. I then turned my attention to the still and silent Izzy. 'Here's where she backs out' I thought! However, changing her mind wasn't on her mind!

"Look" she said, thoughtfully "I share this room with Kelly, we all double up two to a room. I'm gonna go back down and let her know I'm gonna be up here a while. I'm also gonna tell our mate Louise too cos she's a teetotaler and she'll distract Kelly and the others from getting too curious and stop them disturbing us!"

Without waiting for me to reply, she opened the door fumbling with the little button I'd used to prevent swipe card access. She gave me a little embarrassed devilish look and disappeared away to the left, letting the door close quietly behind her. She was away for approximately 10 minutes, which is a long time in a quiet strange environment on your own with only your thoughts keeping you company. So to kill time and distract myself I went over to the set of drawers under the window on the right to make use of the selection of complementary teas and coffees on offer and prepared myself a brew. I noted that the bathroom was at the far left of the room and the door was open giving a view of the shiny clean surfaces from the natural light that was cascading in. I then looked out over the grounds of the house. I didn't get undressed, I'm neither stupid nor presumptuous especially where women are concerned. God knows who might have come in and of course Isabel could change her mind. As the kettle boiled, I texted Barry with a quick and exact update of where I was. Shortly he messaged back saying he'd be here at the venue for at least an hour and then head over to the pub. If his car was in the car park, I was to look for him in the hotel bar.

Suddenly Isabel returned with a quick swipe of the lock and a firm push of the door. She tried to push the door closed more quickly than the door would allow and then turned to look at me.

"Okay, all sorted now, we can relax," she said, taking a deep theatrical breath and exhaled with her arms above her head. Her small pert breasts pressed against her tight cotton top.

She smiled at me.

"My heart is racing though!" she added.

"It's all your running around," I replied, finishing off my cup of tea.

Isabel, still standing by the door, looked confident and intelligent. She had a quaint attractive sinuous posture I grew to recognize when she looked thoughtful. It was time for me to 'press the flesh', test her intentions, to take the initiative. I put down the empty cup and walked over to the bed dragging off my beanie hat and took off my Levi jacket and literally chucked both onto the floor. I then turned around to face her and dragged off my vest top, then my suede sneakers and joggers, and sat on the edge of the large bed keeping on my black Homme briefs and took off my socks. I lobbed these onto my jacket and looked up at Izzy who hadn't moved. I looked at her face and she had a naughty grin! A good sign.

No doubt there. I said nothing. She walked over toward me with restrained enthusiasm, slightly shaking her head. She was wearing a pale blue long-sleeved stretch cotton top with a wide deep V-neck. It showed off her elegant neck and delicate collar bones. The tight sleeves highlighted her slender arms. It was quite long and pulled down covering the waistband of her tight black jeans to the level of the front pockets. Her breasts were small and 'perky' under the tight top and it was obvious she wasn't wearing a bra. She didn't need to. On her tiny feet she had very wide trendy closed toe flip flops and no socks. She looked casual and sexy.

She looked at me standing in front of me and I moved myself further onto the bed without breaking eye contact with her. I turned my body ninety degrees to her and lay on my left side propping up my head with my left arm. Izzy slowly pulled her top off over her head smiling and she giggled a little. I saw her pert breasts with large perfectly flat pink nipples larger in proportion compared to her breasts. A stunning erotic image! She had a flat belly, not toned, just naturally slender and she began to unbutton her jeans and pull down the fly zip. She had to wriggle out of them and as she did this, she looked just a little self-conscious, probably because I was showing no emotion on my face as I drank in her youthfulness. She then said,

"Phew, I've seen you naked already and it's like I'm starting all over again!"

"It's a whole different world when you are naked," I replied.

I smiled nodding slightly appreciating her, as I watched her slowly get herself out of her jeans. She didn't look completely confident, but she was definitely feeling her way into the vibe! I didn't speak so as not to break her thoughts and to hold the tension between us; she was exuding submissiveness so I wasn't about to say something that could undermine that. Her hair was long and free-flowing, very dark almost black, cascading in thick shiny locks. Her small breasts suited the narrowness of her torso. Standing at the side of the bed in a blue lacy high-leg thong she looked totally elegant, revealing my love and obsession, a thigh space! Her arms hung by her sides with a natural space between them and her rib cage. It gave her a 'coat hanger' look, healthy and natural with her pale smooth shiny skin.

Her hair was parted slightly off center naturally to the right and hung either side of her eyes framing them beautifully. She had a high curving forehead and the hint of a widow's peak to the left of where her parting originated. Her eyes were slightly watery and almost purple in color! I learned later that she wore blue-tinted contact lenses. The effect was stunning in this early evening light combining with her milky skin. She had a long face, and her chin came to a near point, narrow complementing her aquiline nose, not big but pronounced and highlighted by the frame of her hair.

Everything now seemed to speed up. It was as if she suddenly realized we might have limited time considering the propinquity of her boozed-up friends downstairs. They might just suddenly decide to become too curious and come looking for her. As she continued standing in front of me she backed off a couple of paces and shimmied her slender hips and hooked her thumbs into the sides of her blue lace thong and began to inch it down slowly, dragging the lacey sides against her skin with the front lagging behind during this sexy process. She was teasing me but not a slow tease because the front of the thong quickly popped over her pubic mound until the thong was a horizontal band on her hips.

I just looked and thought wow! From this point she had to bend toward me to take the thong off, but she turned around with her back to me and bent over with straight legs to take off the thong. The curve of her spine began to reveal the vertebrae through her skin as she bent over. She then slightly parted her legs and bent over completely and flexibly until I could see her inverted face between her legs, her long hair reaching the carpet and her pussy and asshole right there smooth and exposed for me! She was showing off! She then flicked her body vertically upright again very quickly, spun herself around smiling broadly and did another shimmy with her hips. She threw her thong onto my pile of clothes between us. I was electrified by all of this, and I was becoming ever harder! Her pussy was completely waxed smooth, and her delicate thigh space revealed her delicate protruding labia, and her left side was protruding comparatively longer than the other. Gorgeous!

As Izzy stood there, I was reminded of how tall she was. When we first entered the room, she was obviously taller than I am, she was easily 5′ 10″ if not taller. It didn't bother her obviously. I didn't even think about it until now. I started to take off my briefs to release the sideways pressure of my hardon and let's face it she'd seen me naked already and I couldn't wait to taste her. I was feeling the need to speed things up too as she did. Izzy tilted her head to one side looking really cute and I used this as a signal to encourage her over to the bed.

"Come on over here right now" I said, grinning,

"Yes sir" she replied, and saluting me in fun, she did a hop, skip and a jump and playfully plonked herself onto the bed next to me.

Our skin met. She was cool and smooth and delicate and firm. We began to kiss, and I immediately put the flat of my hand onto the left side of her pelvic bone that looked sharp, sexy, and shiny. As I did so she slid her top left leg backward remaining squarely on her right side revealing her silky inner right thigh. We were subconsciously encouraging each other all the time due to the prospect of having less time than we both wanted! Her mouth was small, and I had to adjust my open mouth smaller to accommodate hers.

Her tongue was tentative at first and I showed her a little encouragement by making my tongue deeper but keeping it relatively still, letting her tongue search mine and very quickly she responded, pushing her tongue deeper into my mouth and we began an equally passionate search of each other. She was breathing heavily through her nose, and she began to hold the back of my head, and the pressure gestured for me to roll with her as she rolled onto her back. I instinctively nestled my thigh between hers and pressed my upper thigh firmly onto her pussy. I began to tense my thigh muscle and pressed it harder against her as I did so. She had the smell of sweet alcohol on her breath with the hint of a cigarette which I found sexy.

Removing my thigh slowly from her pussy I replaced it with my hand cupping it. I applied a slow massaging pressure with my palm, and she began to open her thighs and attempted to draw both of her knees upwards, so I removed my thigh from between hers, completely freeing her up to spread her legs wider. I popped my right forefinger into her warm slit finding wetness immediately. I circled the opening of her cunt and at the same time I moved to position my head to kiss, lick and suck her warm sweet-smelling breasts concentrating on each nipple in turn. I noticed her abs were flexing through her slender flesh. I became compelled to go down on her and to taste her. This had been on my mind the instant I saw her standing naked before me.

As I moved down her body with kisses she moaned slightly from anticipation and approval quickly lowering her right knee. Reaching her pussy with my head I placed my legs between hers and encouraged her to raise both knees, spreading her thighs wide with her feet off the bed. I held her in this spread position by bracing the backs of her thighs with my forearms. I noticed a little shaving rash on the top left of her pubic mound; she'd have been unaware of it, and it turned me on to know it was mine to discover. I licked her slit and her pretty labia and sensed her feeling too sensitive, so I applied more pressure with my tongue. Suddenly conscious again that we might be disturbed I delved into her cunt with my tongue and lips. I felt her wanting to place her feet back onto the bed and allowed her by removing my supporting arms and she began to buck in rhythm to my licking, bracing herself with her feet now on the bed.

My neck was in a stress position. Her ass was tiny and slender and not enough of it to support her high enough for me to eat her out with passion. I stopped licking her and quickly grabbed a pillow from the top of the bed and encouraged her to raise her ass and I placed the pillow under it.

"Lift your tush for me," I said, softly, she looked a little puzzled for an instant "I'm going to put this under your butt, trust me!" I added.

Isabel pushed down with her feet again and lifted her pelvis then brought her ass firmly down onto the pillow. Perfect! I began to eat her ravenously. God, I wanted this woman all day and all night, I wanted to taste her cunt in every position but that unnerving feeling of limited time kept niggling me! Izzy began a slow prolonged moan and suddenly bucked up and down, so I eased the pressure of my tongue. It was obvious she had orgasmed. I stopped licking her and kissed her all around her groin and pubic mound, tasting her on my lips and mouth and smelling her sexual heat. An unmistakable healthy feminine essence.

I then knelt up to look at her with my hands on her knees to keep her thighs spread. Her pussy was pinkish slightly swollen and glistening with wetness, a mixture of her girl juice and my saliva. Cutting this short I began to lie next to her again to give her some come-down time and then I suddenly thought about the pressure of time again, so I knelt between her thighs again. My cock was hard, and I inched myself forwards and hooking her legs with my arms I put her into a deep stick. She easily and flexibly adapted to this, and I marveled at her long legs with each of her knees either at the side of her head. I plunged my cock deep into the willing, accepting, soaking wet tightness of her pretty cunt. We gently fucked, sometimes she stared at me really hard, other times she looked away as though she couldn't believe what was happening.

I had no intention of cumming because I wanted to enjoy her. If we were to be disturbed, I wanted to take in as much of her as possible rather than rush to my own orgasm. If I'd rushed to cum I'd have needed 20 minutes to become hard again so I opted to fuck her and absorb her every essence, sight, sound and movement. As we fucked Izzy began to whisper something, I couldn't quite make out her words, she spoke in a truncated sentence of mumbles which confused me, but we continued to fuck, and she continued to move in rhythm with me. Her lovely small, pointed chin rocked gently forwards and backward as I planted my full length into her with slaps of my balls against her asshole. I stared down at her constantly watching every expressive detail of her face. I didn't have time to ask her what she was saying unfortunately!

Suddenly there was a rapid knocking on the bedroom door! Not loud but consistent. It sounded more of a warning than a demand to enter. We both stopped fucking, but we didn't release each other as we craned our heads to look toward the door. We heard the door handle outside begin to be used a few times. Someone wanted to come in! The knocking continued but not urgently. Izzy and I unraveled our bodies, and she jumped up in a bit of a huff…

"Shit, what now!" she hissed in a whisper.

I liked how she reacted. It indicated she wanted to keep the sex going rather than have an excuse to stop. Izzy wanted more. It was obvious that this woman did not want to be disturbed as I didn't but it seemed inevitable all along and yet it still annoyed Isabel. She reached the door naked and beautiful, and I smiled appreciating her natural slender physicality. She stopped before opening the door realizing her nakedness and she looked around quickly as though looking for something to cover herself up with. She gave up on the idea as more knocking commenced. She had her hand on the door handle, and I was admiring her cute firm little ass with side dimples. Rather than being concerned about the consequences of her opening the door, she then turned the little deadlock button on the door handle and slowly opened the door a few inches hiding her nakedness to one side. The door didn't burst open thankfully, but I could hear a whispered conversation between Izzy and whoever was outside. Then I distinctly heard Izzy say,

"Oh, okay, come in, but hurry!"

She backed away from the door allowing the person outside to open it as she quickly ran back to join me on the bed. In came Kelly, the bride-to-be! She allowed the door to close on its spring and just stood there at the door staring at Izzy and me. I made sure we were close skin on skin and hooked my leg between Izzy's thighs to wrap her up as close as possible.

"This is interesting," said Kelly, looking at us for quite a while with wide eyes.

"Fucking hell, for fuck's sake, have you been fucking, have you?" she gabbled, walking closer to us.

Kelly was obviously a little drunk!

"Err...." I started to speak when Izzy quickly interrupted me,

"Yeah, what do you think we've been doing with no clothes on? Peeling grapes for each other!"

"You are a fucking lucky bitch" Kelly half slurred in reply, grinning and looking very happy!

"Carry on then, I wanna watch!"

"What!?" Izzy exclaimed as Kelly stood next to the bed looking at us both.

"Look it's my hen weekend and I want to see my bestie getting laid," Kelly said with clear intent. "Wow, you both look amazing; it's so fucking horny oh my god!"

The idea had never occurred to me, but I was still horny. Seeing Kelly didn't put me off, but I wasn't in any mood to fuck her! She wasn't my type, and she was drunk, and my current situation was complicated enough right there and then and besides I fancied Izzy and wanted more of her! It was obvious that Kelly and Isabel knew each other well. There was a familiar sisterliness about them both. That relaxed me.

"Come on Izz, fucking hell, this is amazing, this is a one-off chance in a life time, this ain't gonna happen again… please fuck, keep fucking, I gotta watch!" Kelly continued with pleading eyes.

"Arrrgh" Izzy said, glancing at me.

I smiled at her and laughed a little and then Izzy laughed too. We both looked at the wide-eyed pleading Kelly who by now had her knees pressed onto the bed from where she stood. I unfurled myself from Izzy and lay down on my back and Izzy responded by crawling to the bottom end of the bed close to my feet and knelt there dragging her fingers through her long dark hair and looking at Kelly.

"Okay that's his hard cock right!" Izzy said, gesturing her hand toward me and laughing in the direction of Kelly.

She then stretched out her arm comically and pointed at Kelly, then her own mouth, then at my cock and then lowered her head still kneeling and began to suck my cock! Kelly responded by kneeling down on the floor to watch at a better angle muttering "'oh my god," constantly! I was super hard and watched Izzy rather than pay Kelly any attention. Kelly gradually and slowly began to stand up from where she was kneeling and slowly began to unzip her jeans! She reached into them with the flat of her right hand and began to play with herself! I was so horny; the whole situation wasn't threatening, and it had become playfully amusing in many ways. Kelly was big-boned and slightly overweight but not unattractive and went at frigging herself like she didn't know she could be seen! She got really into it! The phrase 'dance like no one is watching' sprang into my mind, only I replaced 'dance' with 'frigg'!

Isabel used every part of her mouth, lips and teeth while sucking me. She seemed to zone out that Kelly was there watching us. She pushed my cock into her cheeks either side of her mouth over and over grinding it with her teeth with skillful pressure. I could see the erotic sight of her cheeks being forced outwards made more erotic by Izzy occasionally glancing seductively at me with her purple-blue eyes and long very fine eyelashes framing them. Wow! She was watching for my reaction, and I propped myself up onto my elbows to watch her.

I nodded gently every time Izzy looked at me, showing my pleasure. It was obvious that Izzy wanted to demonstrate all of her detailed sucking repertoire for me knowing that Kelly was watching. It was a performance for Kelly and me! Izzy was acting her role with Kelly there. This differed from her sensuousness with me when we'd been alone together. Then Izzy suddenly stopped her 'cock sucking demo' and positioned herself straddling me and reached down with her hand between her slender thighs and grabbed my cock and slid me partly into her pussy then sliding me in fully and began fucking me cowgirl!

"Oh wow, show me, wow!" Kelly muttered, still frigging herself.

Kelly's jeans and underwear were now around her thighs allowing her free access to masturbate with her whole hand! She too was waxed smooth I noticed! Kelly then walked around to the foot of the bed to stand behind Izzy.

"This is so fucking surreal" Kelly said, still frigging herself her eyes glued on the sight of my cock inside Izzy!

She was mesmerized by the sight of us fucking.

"I'm so glad you weren't pissed," I said quietly, staring up at Izzy as she plunged herself down on me.

"Fuck no!" she replied, slightly breathlessly, "I had a few but you can understand why someone has to stay sober with this lot."

"I love cowgirl" I said, bringing us back into the moment "it's a first for me though, cowgirl with a voyeur!" I couldn't help smiling, "I won't cum though with Kelly here," I mentioned.

"Neither will I," Izzy said. "But I don't care," she added with quickening deep breaths.

She really ground down on me with every downward thrust...

"I'm really enjoying myself though, kinda getting into it!" she whispered, smiling.

We could hear Kelly talking away in her reverie behind us.

"I've known her for years," Izzy whispered, "and to be honest I've always been a bit of an exhibitionist at the right time in the right place!"

That would be an interesting conversation I thought but then I tried to put Kelly out of my mind and marveled at this incredibly beautiful woman riding me. Her belly had four little horizontal parallel lines of creases as she hung over me, fucking me, highlighting her healthy slender abs and her long hair was hanging down and flicking around in front of my face. I started to play with her hair, pushing and pulling my fingers through its shiny length. Izzy knelt up with a straight back which stretched out her long lean flat abs. Very sexy. Her navel was a vertical slit appearing quite high due to her slenderness and I noticed she had quite a long torso, her head seemed a long way from my face making her seem far from submissive, dominant even. She was tilting her head back attempting fruitlessly to knot her hair behind her head. She fiddled with this as I felt my solid stiffness in her gripping cunt! Her hair held for a few seconds then as she leaned forwards toward me again it all slipped and cascaded before my face again due to its frictionless shininess.

Izzy looked around herself casually, straining herself around to look at Kelly who presumably still had her fingers inside herself. I couldn't see from my position. I had to laugh quietly when Izzy said,

"Kels, do you have a bobble?"

"A what?" a suddenly distracted Kelly replied,

"A bobble? Oh, never mind," Izzy concluded.

Izzy attempted to knot her hair again, but it was a futile exercise!

I loved seeing the smooth milky toned skin of her hairless armpits as she did this. I reached up for her pink swollen flat nipples and squeezed, twisted, and pulled at them to entertain myself and to distract Izzy. Responding, she leaned further back slightly letting her hair fall back behind her shoulders and I could see the nape of her neck straining as she tilted her head as far back as she could and began to flick her pelvis forwards and backward. She was fucking me again. Her speed became extremely frenetic, but she kept my cock deep inside her delicious cunt rocking on me. The sight of her clit flicking in and out of sight as she did this was extremely erotic for me and I began to feel the initial itch of an orgasm in me!

I looked up at her face occasionally to see if she was watching me looking at her, but she was mostly facing straight ahead with her eyes closed. I admired the beautiful line of her slim pronounced aquiline nose with their slim elongated nostrils flaring with her breathing and motion. One nostril was slightly narrower than the other one adding a detail I hoped no other man had ever noticed! Beautiful asymmetry. Her lips were pursed together as she continued to breathe heavily through her nose. Then I heard Kelly speaking.

"Fucking hell Izzy, go for it oh my god go girl!"

All of a sudden Izzy slowed and stopped fucking me and tilted slightly sideways and drew up one leg then balancing herself with one hand on my chest and the other out to the side she drew up her other leg. She righted herself then into a squatting position over me balancing herself with both hands on my chest. She began a deep slow pumping up and down sliding my vertical cock into her full length and almost letting me slip out of her before burying it again. She did this with increasing speed and confidence. I was slightly distracted due to the thought that if she became too excited, I could easily slip out of her. As she moved up and down, if I'd slipped out of her, she could easily have 'broken' my cock! It's a serious injury requiring major surgery! I'd read about that shit in GQ!

The thought brought me back from cumming, but this position had the desired effect for Kelly who verbally shouted her own approval encouraging Izzy again! I looked at the amazing sight of my cock rapidly appearing and disappearing as it penetrated Isabel's pretty little oyster of a pussy! As I continued watching her, I became aware of Kelly's hand slowly appearing between Izzy's legs as she fucked me. Kelly wrapped her finger and thumb around the hilt of my cock among the white cream that had gathered there, squeezing it, and attempted to wank me in time with Izzy pistoning up and down!

"No, no!" Izzy exclaimed, when she realized what Kelly was doing!

Kelly removed her hand quickly, saying something I didn't catch and then Izzy buried me deep inside her cunt holding herself there. I was surprised to look up and watch Izzy climax almost silently. Her face was scrunched up tightly, her nose wrinkled up, her eyes were squeezed tightly shut and her head quivered, and she let out a little open-mouthed rushing sigh!

She must have suddenly realized post-orgasm that her thighs were aching, and she began to balance herself as before and flicked out each leg in turn to return to straddling me. She was skillful and thoughtful as she did this, so I did not spill out of her! She then brought her head down next to mine burying it into the bed and placed one hand on top of my head. She was breathing steadily but audibly through her mouth now.

"Fuck, fuck, I've just cum too" shouted Kelly suddenly!

Both Izzy and I sniggered listening to the glee coming from Kelly as she pranced and danced around the room like a little girl on Christmas day!

"Fuck I've had two of those scary fuckers now" said Izzy quietly into my ear "ping ping, wow!"

Izzy was paying Kelly no attention at all while she came down from her orgasm, but Kelly continued to voice her excited approval! Izzy wriggled her body occasionally with me still inside her,

"Did you cum?" Izzy asked me softly.

"No not yet, I will though, jeepers I was close a couple of times, I will get there no trouble, you are fucking amazing" I answered, genuinely complimenting her.

"I'll sort it" she replied quietly, "gimme a couple of minutes."

"Hey Kelly, what you doin'?" Izzy said, lifting her head and looking around for Kelly.

Kelly had disappeared into the bathroom to my right as I lay there with Izzy. Kelly's voice echoed from there as she answered,

"Taking a pee, hang on."

There was then a short flush of the toilet and Kelly emerged from the bathroom without wearing her jeans, no T-shirt, and no underwear, she was completely naked except for one sock! Her broad full thighs met at the top and she had a jiggly belly and very large breasts which hung full and rounded. In her hand she had something red and lacy, and I assumed it was her underwear. She was about 5′ 4″ tall with thick shoulder length mid-blonde hair. She was slightly overweight but not unattractive. She walked over to the door and for a second both Izzy and I thought she was going to leave the bedroom!

I think Kelly had no idea why she'd walked over to the door to be honest, obviously still slightly drunk! I got to see her shapely full firm ass and visible love handles and thick thighs. Facing away from us she rested one hand on the door and wobbling, she attempted to use her other hand to hook her underwear back onto her left leg. She attempted this many times, cursing as she did so and located her foot finally. Izzy and I genuinely howled with laughter at this sight which had the effect of bonding us because when we looked at each other there was a connection as we laughed. Kelly was the outsider, we were close.

Looking back at Kelly she finally bent down and pulled up a very large red lace pair of knickers that covered her ample ass. The comparison with Izzy's boyish firm ass and Kelly's large, inverted heart-shaped ass was not lost on me. She then turned around and the lacey front reached high up over her ample belly. She then stood looking around the floor pulling them up even higher in a funny drunken way! I had a moment to think of both of these women in that moment with me. This whole situation had turned us all on unexpectedly. Izzy and Kelly had chosen to use the opportunity to be spontaneously adventurous, obviously made easier with alcohol of course.

I wasn't going to make any demands beyond the point we had all reached. I really wanted Izzy to make me cum though mainly because of the memory and images of her 'rapid blowjob audition' earlier which was indelibly imprinted on my brain's erotic lobe! In fact, I ached to have time with her alone again. I knew we had a connection, and she would feel the same, but I wasn't going to rock the boat between her and Kelly. I'd be patient and see how it panned out. I wanted that slow visual spectacle of erotic sensuousness with eye contact again, but I was prepared to wait in tune with my tendency to be an 'anticipation junkie'!

There was then the sound of voices rising from along the bedroom corridor outside the room and both women suddenly looked at each other and stared at the bedroom door. We all expected the voices to get closer and conclude with a knock on the door. The voices though, stopped and quietened abruptly following an audible slam of a door in the distance. Nothing was said but we all relaxed again. Izzy was still straddling me, and I was still hard, and our eyes met. She looked at me with serious eyes as she seemed to sense my urgency for her. I also sensed she wanted to have a quick chat with Kelly because she repeatedly looked toward her as Kelly shuffled around the room. This did not stop me making little thrusts into Izzy to keep her focused and I loved her reaction to each of them as she squeezed her vagina for me!

Kelly walked over to the bed in her big red lace knickers and one sock, then she sat on the edge of it with her back angled toward me and her facing more toward Izzy. She could easily speak to both of us from where she was positioned and she smiled at both of us. Her inebriated state had ebbed slightly, and she was very calm. She appeared to be in a gentle mood, but her eyes revealed that she was not totally sober, and she looked sleepy and started speaking, choosing her words very slowly.

"Is he, err, still inside you, like?" Kelly asked Izzy.

"Yep, happy right where he is, feels ace," she replied, casually.

"Did he cum inside you?" Kelly continued,

Izzy looked at me briefly as she answered, I slowly shook my head as I lay there without speaking.

"No, he hasn't, yet. Maybe I have other ideas, no rush eh!" Izzy replied.

They talked together a while and giggled a lot. It was as if I was given permission to listen in. They were both comfortable with me being there! Their chat began with them remembering what had just happened accompanied with a lot of humorous fake contrition and conspiratorial giggles. Occasionally Izzy looked at me and squeezed my cock inside her with her vaginal muscles as if to remind me to stay hard. That wasn't a problem for me, just by looking at her naturally beautiful lean body kept me interested! She played constantly with her long shiny dark brown hair as she chatted away.

Her pert breasts were gorgeous, and her pink nipples were still swollen and occasionally I stroked and squeezed them and both Izzy and Kelly would watch me do that and yet continue to speak to each other uninterrupted! These women I sensed were both relaxed and still horny. They were in no rush to go off to be with the other hens it seemed, probably because they were in charge of the hen weekend, and they were enjoying this private time they had to themselves away from the others. I thought what a great time Barry would be having regaling the hens with his hilarious stories and wicked sense of humor! I soaked up how visually erotic this scene was sharing it with Izzy and Kelly. I was gagging to cum but remained patient. I sensed Izzy had plans for me; a patient girl too, I liked that!

Neither of these two women showed any signs of regret or guilt. Kelly at one point said that she would have joined in, but that Izzy had "possessed" me! She then countered this by saying that she was getting married in two weeks to which Izzy laughed and replied that she herself most definitely wasn't! Kelly looked a little envious, but I suspect not of Izzy, but envious of her considerably greater choices in life. Getting married I suppose closes down the life you had and can seem suddenly confining to some people. I continued to stay silent and watch these two lovely modern women chat about friendship and memories of growing up together and going to the same university. I learned that Izzy had been in a relationship all through her university years which ended three years after graduation after living with her boyfriend in London where they both worked. Whereas Kelly had jumped, it seemed, at the first opportunity of a relationship she had had and was getting married two years after first meeting her boyfriend.

They both laughed about their relative situations, a shared humor that two very close friends have when they are taking the piss out of each other. I enjoyed the distraction of still being hard and inside Izzy! Izzy couldn't help laughing as she described her "outrageous" observations watching her best friend masturbating while watching us fucking. There was irony too in her playfully rebuking Kelly for being a voyeur although Izzy owned up to being turned on by it! We all laughed at this. There was no attempt to normalize the whole situation; they reveled in its spontaneity. It was a melting pot of a fantasy factory! Izzy also spoke of wanting to "make up for lost time" after being in a monogamous relationship for so long and wanting to have as many "sexual adventures" as she could. She'd been with the same man for six formative years of her early life and had just grown bored during which time she had changed so much. She wanted some adventure. It had been a feeling that had grown within her relentlessly.

I had worked out that these women were both 29 years old as "becoming 30" cropped up a few times between them like some 'sword of Damocles'! From my take, I would describe them as being in some age-related, biological clock quandary that I thought was no longer relevant to modern women but apparently it is, it's just been ignored! Izzy had planned to split from her long-term boyfriend six months before actually doing so. I always understood that women tend to 'monkey-branch' between long-term partners. They don't initiate the relationship split until they've secured another relationship to swing neatly into! Men are clueless about this.

The shock to men as a result of this I had learned from a couple of straight male friends who had their hearts broken as a result of sudden and inexplicable splits with their female partners. In parenthesis I wasn't the best shoulder to cry on really! I just listened to them because I could have told both of these fellas individually, that I knew why they'd ended up in their situations. They'd committed to a relationship because they'd become 'pussy-whipped' as artist Tom had described so eloquently for me some years before. I could have said to each of them "I could have told you so" but that would have been needlessly cruel. All I advised was that the next time they considered jumping into a relationship, come and speak to me! Even that is pointless because 99 percent of men think with their cocks!

As Izzy and Kelly chatted freely about men and their relationship history with each other I thought about artist Tom again. Thank goodness I'd met him some years before. Also, as a bloke I've never experienced anything remotely like the 'biological clock'. My long-term relationship was with Valerie, and it certainly wasn't conventional nor 'plain vanilla'. We grew our relationship from its beginning rather than either of us trying to change it into something conventional that would have ruined it. Fourteen years down the line with Valerie and it still felt new, fresh, and exciting. The fact that she was now 68 years old made no difference to how I thought about her; except it did! Her diet, exercise and lifestyle put '30 something' women into the shade for me! Also, I couldn't wait to tell Val about this experience with Izzy and Kelly! I knew it would turn her on and lead to incredible sex! Thinking about Val made me fully hard and caused Izzy to be distracted from her chatting with Kelly because she looked at me and playfully slapped my arm saying,

"Easy Tiger, I haven't finished with you yet!"

It took this unconventional situation, being naked with two naked women in a hotel bedroom in the middle of nowhere, to make me think about myself in that moment. I reckoned that sex has always made me 'introspectively expressive' and this book has given me the opportunity to express and record my thoughts. It's an opportunity to encapsulate what for me is an artistic appreciation of sex rather than just a sexual experience. I am often alarmed by the implicit and explicit conflict that sex creates for both women and men. Conflict that is borne out of jealousies, possessiveness, restrictive communications, an unwillingness or inability to express ideas, materialistic approaches to a relationship and all the mismatched expectations that eventually percolates out. Artist Tom made it quite simple for me to understand. People do not understand that relationships are a 'business transaction' between men and women and that they are simultaneously unequal and diametrically opposed! This causes a festering conflict, and it is usually the woman who recognizes the conflicts in detail and plans out her future life before removing herself.

While I was in deep thought while Izzy and Kelly continued to chat, I was suddenly brought back to the present by Kelly. There had been a pause in their conversation, and I heard Kelly then say,

"Shall I go?" in a little docile voice while looking between Izzy and me.

"Yeah… if you like," Izzy said, smiling at her then looking at me raising her eyebrows playfully.

Kelly reached out and held Izzy's arm giving it a little squeeze and then looked at me, briefly patting me on my chest digging her nails into my skin slightly.

"And you my man of balletic grace, be good to my bestie," she said happily with slightly inebriated eyes!

Kelly stood up and Izzy and I watched her walk very slowly toward the door. We both drew in an audible breath and spoke out simultaneously…

"You'd better get dressed first."

"Oi you can't leave like that!"

Izzy and I both laughed, and Kelly stopped and turned mechanically to her right and tottered off to the bathroom again. She emerged topless and wearing her jeans and the one sock! She silently walked to the bottom edge of the bed and bent down to retrieve her bra and T-shirt. She put on the T-shirt and kept her bra in her hand. She turned around and placed her ample ass onto the bed and bending down again fumbled with her shoes, expending far too much energy for such a simple task judging by her heavy breathing and cursing. Izzy and I stayed silent, smiling at each other, and watching Kelly. She then stood and waved her arm at us without looking at us, she headed to the door. Kelly opened it, looked at the bra in her hand and tossed it over her head back into the room. She then peered out with her head then slipped out, letting the door close quietly.

"At last," Izzy said, shimmying her pelvis into my hardness, "where were we?"

"The door!" I said lifting my head off the bed and pointing at it.

"Oh yeah!" Izzy said and began to lift herself off me and then stopped, "It'll be okay, I don't want you to come out of me." She said.

"Lock it!" I reaffirmed "you know she's pissed, and she could choose to come back any time and bring who knows who else. Her swipe card could be in her jeans!"

Izzy nodded and slowly, ever so slowly and seductively raised herself off me. I watched how she literally watched as my cock slipped out of her pussy all wet and shiny! She did it with erotic purpose. I became entranced by how her longer, more pronounced left labia delicately slid over my hard shaft as she pulled away from me! My cock suddenly popped out of her and dropped onto my stomach. I squeezed and raised it, testing my hardness! Her elegant long lean body jumped off the bed like a milky white Bambi and she trotted over to the door and flicked the deadlock on and returned the same way all in one movement. She plopped her knees firmly into the bed between my legs as I firmly took hold of my cock and rubbed it slowly and gently up and down with the fingers of my right hand. I harvested the thickened white girl juice into the web of skin between my thumb and index finger and raised it to my mouth. Izzy watched me intensely as I tasted her delicious aromatic mild bitterness.

Izzy began playing with her hair and then grinned confidently. I wondered what she had on her mind! I grinned back. She slid backward on her knees and stood up at the base of the bed facing me where I lay on my back, legs akimbo, and then she walked around to the window to her left and began clinking around in a small handbag. She returned to the bottom of the bed pulling her fingers through her hair and with her smooth armpits and pink swollen flat nipples in full view of my lustful eyes. She seductively pulled her long hair into a ponytail and fixed it into a loop with the hair bobble she had just retrieved from the handbag. She looked sexy and casual, and her shiny hair was effectively not going to fall over her face! I grinned knowingly!

Keeping my legs spread and knees pulled back, I knew what was coming but I powered them flat quickly onto the bed then raised them up and spread them again as a signal for her to crawl toward me! She got the message, slowly crawling onto the bed eyeballing me! With her spine arched down as deep and as flexibly as any yoga expert and her little boyish ass in the air she took hold of my cock and pulled it back toward her face beyond the vertical away from me! She increased the angle, and I felt deep pleasure at the root of my solid hard cock from the pressure. She fully intended it! She placed her mouth around the tip and gave out a little sexy 'humming hmm' all done for effect, and it worked! She owned me! From the angle we were at, I could look her squarely in her eyes with me supporting myself on my elbows. In that light, I then noticed she was actually wearing tinted contact lenses, explaining the purple hue of her eyes. She removed her hands, and we were connected only with her gripping lips around the tip of my cock. Izzy then slowly, without breaking eye contact with me, moved herself forwards by leaning into me, taking more of my cock into her mouth. She went deeper and deeper and I squeezed my pelvic floor muscle to increase the tension in my cock feeling it pushing hard into the roof of her mouth. She kept coming closer, taking more of me into her mouth until I was aware of pressure that told me I had reached her throat. There was a little flicker and widening of her eyes. She then began to pulse her body forwards and backward and she loosened her lips and widened her mouth. I could see her white upper front teeth and see my cock inside her mouth.

Her lips were fully stretched, and her face became naturally expressionless as she made little coughing gagging sounds as she pulsed the tip of my cock into her throat. She began to blink regularly and her eyes watered, but she didn't stop. At one point she actually gave a little cough but again she did not remove me from her mouth. Saliva appeared on her bottom lip and at the corners of her mouth. It was an erotic vision! She began to look abandoned and excited, and I wondered whether this was an act to seduce me or whether she was genuinely unaware, but to be frank I didn't care either way, as she breathed heavily through her mouth and nose simultaneously.

She uttered a mumbling sound through her nose as though trying to talk with her mouth full and this was also extremely and intensely erotic! Her eyes were saying 'is this what you want!' Oh, my word!

Raising the angle of my eager cock slightly into a more vertical position, Izzy, still without using her hands and still able to make eye contact with me, she became motionless and paused. I noticed her dark fine eyebrows and her narrow aquiline nose again from her angle with me. It made her look as though she was preying upon me! This was extremely sexy. Two little rivulets of her saliva ran down the shaft of my cock as I could feel and hear her tongue playing around with the tip of my cock, which appeared at the sides of her mouth occasionally. The amount of her translucent saliva increased and followed the same rivulet lines as before but clearly flowed faster and ran down and around to the hilt of my cock and down and around my balls and on into the crack of my ass. This, combined with the sounds she was making was intensely visually and explicitly erotic and unforgettable! I sensed what was coming as she repositioned her arms and shoulders and slowly losing eye contact with me, she took more of my cock into her mouth.

I could see the top of her head and the thick shiny loop of her hair within the bobble and then the vision of my cock disappearing out of sight into her throat! The pressure and knowledge of what she was doing blew my mind! Her nose squished into my lower stomach; she was so deep! She held this position becoming very still until her body suddenly convulsed and bucked and she tried to extract me from her throat in a controlled way but suddenly with a chorus of gags, coughs and splutters she freed my cock from her throat very rapidly. She dipped her head and partly pulled away from me and she grabbed my cock in her right hand as she gathered herself with a big swallow! She coughed a few more times elegantly, and with her long delicate fingers she massaged my saliva-rich cock between her fingers and delicately spat more saliva onto me as she continued to clear her throat. This must sound like she was flustered but she wasn't. She used every opportunity to maintain our erotic momentum with every single consequence of her deep throating me!

Izzy put my cock back in her mouth and expertly deep throated me again over and over. It seemed as if she'd completely abandoned any discomfort for herself in favor of this incredible erotic act, we were both in tune with it. Her deep throating became mesmerizing for me and a few times as she withdrew me from her mouth, her little gulping gags were accompanied with many thicknesses of silvery translucent gossamer strands of saliva which looped from her lips to my cock as she regulated her breathing. As I watched this most amazing vision, I said.

"Don't swallow," almost appealing to her, "Spit on me again, spit your saliva all over me… and kiss me after you make me cum!" Her eyes widened in naughty acknowledgement.

I wanted the intimacy of the connection of our mouths meeting to cement the incredible eroticism of what Izzy was doing to me. Was I falling for this young woman?! It certainly felt that way at that moment! Izzy looked down at the erotic artistic mess we had created, saliva strands linking us and then she looked at me quickly grinning, teasing me. She slowly moved toward me like a cat on the prowl and without breaking those shimmering iridescent bonds, she cascaded them slowly up and along my belly until they broke and fell onto me. She then knelt upright and massaged my cock with both hands staring at me, moist lipped, twirling and swirling her fingers in a circular movement transporting my senses. The swell of a huge orgasm began to build inside me,

"Look, look now" I said quickly.

She followed my eyes and we both saw that I was beginning to cum gently at first then a thicker pulsing pouring stream out of me, down from the tip of my cock onto my shaft and into her delicate long skillful fingers. She continued to lightly massage my shaft. There was no sudden blast from me. The perfection of her touch edged out my cum in a solid flow now as Izzy gazed at the sight of me cumming. She then slowly and delicately put her lips around my tip again and rotated her tongue almost without touching me, so gentle, it was almost as if she was breathing on me. My orgasm continued slowly, deeply, and prolonged. I was tingling from my navel to my knees, my thighs especially were tingling! I could hear myself groaning, fuck, I'd gone into sexual heaven!

I glanced at her quickly and she looked back at me questioningly; her eyes were saying 'do you like this?' Tasting me, savoring me, she took the last of my flow into her mouth and slowly swallowed. There was no hesitation in her face and her fingers rubbed the skin of my shaft up and down without putting any pressure on my super-sensitive tip. I looked at the way her looped shiny pigtail bobbed gently now with her eyes out of sight as she ate my cum. I reached down and put my hand on her head and with my fingertips, I gently pulled at the loop of her hair within the elasticated bobble, and it spilled softly and deliciously onto my belly and into the delicious wetness on my skin.

"Kiss me!" I said, Izzy didn't respond. "Kiss me!" I repeated and then she came toward me lips parted.

Izzy came forwards and slowly lay on top of me, our juices wet between our skin, and she kissed me. We searched for and ravenously shared and devoured the warm pollen-like essence of my cum. It felt like we were long-term lovers, like we knew each other instinctively or was it me feeling like I was falling for her again! We kissed continually for a long time, and I was slowly aware that the light had changed in the room. It was darker now as the daylight began to fade away from the windows. There were no lights on in the room and it was filled with soft shadows. Izzy slowed our kissing and said in a soft whisper,

"Dammit, dammit, dammit!"

I was thinking she was indicating it was time for us to end this incredible connection and go our separate ways, but she began to speak again,

"I didn't need alcohol to be like this with you, you know. Do you think we could ever recapture all of this again?"

I didn't think of what to reply, I instinctively replied,

"God, yes we can, of course we can, no excuse these days it'd be so easy to stay in touch, wouldn't it?"

Not a very romantic thing to say but I wanted her to understand how connected I was with her. I wanted her!

"Yes, it would, I'd like that" she said looking at me again, smiling "That makes me happy."

That made me very happy! Izzy buried her face into my neck.

"Erotic, unconventional and fun, keeping the connection of this newness going." I heard myself saying.

"Keep reminding me of that when you sense my life is getting stressful," she answered, hugging me tightly.

"And by the way," she said after a short pause.

"What?" I asked completely unsure of what she was going to say.

"Your cum tastes really good," she said with a soft giggle.

"Yeah, it does, doesn't it!" I replied, and we both laughed gently hugging each other, "Mixing you and me together, it's unique" I added, and I meant it.

After long minutes of us entwined together, never wanting this moment to end, I finally carefully and slowly uncurled our limbs. I knew if I didn't get up and dress first, it would leave me feeling worse about going our separate ways if Izzy was to get up and get dressed before I did. So I slowly stood, clicked on the ornate brass bedside lamp and dressed slowly facing her, allowing her to look at my body and to show her I was in no rush to leave her. I understood that she had duties to attend to and stuff to organize with the hens elsewhere in that venue! She watched me dress fully as I watched her watching me dress. Her long, lean naked body on the bed was a languid, sexy, relaxed, elegant, sinuous 'S' shape where she continued to lie unmoving.

Her thick dark healthy hair cascaded over her shoulder nearest to me free now from the partial confines of the pigtail. Izzy was a masterpiece of subtle asymmetries. I'd absorbed all of her throughout the time we'd been together. Her slightly differing shaped nostrils, the way she subconsciously brought her right shoulder forward when she was aware people were looking at her. She'd subtly dip her chin toward her shoulder and turn her head slightly toward it when she walked; probably this was a self-conscious reaction to her height. Her very long fingers and small feet were both elegant and slender, the extreme pointiness of her knees and hyper-extended elbow joints evident when she stretched her arms above her head. One of her eyebrows was slightly higher than the other and one eye was detectably wider than the other when she stared intensely at something. I was definitely falling in love with Isabel!

In those few seconds of momentary sadness, I felt at us having to part, I could only hope that if we didn't see each other again, that any men she might choose in the future would also notice her beautiful unique combination of asymmetries and appreciate her unique inner and outer beauty. She saw me staring at her and her face was questioning my silent thoughtfulness. I broke the silence.

"I can smell you… and I can still taste you" I said softly, as I finished getting dressed, and I could!

Then Izzy spoke with her eyes sparkling in the soft diffused light from the bedside lamp,

"I'm not gonna shower before getting ready to go out tonight!"

We both laughed, we both knew it to be true!

Chapter Thirteen

Great Characters, Scrapes and Embarrassing Moments

Deciding on and describing some of the wonderful people I have met in the art world as a life model is difficult in the sense of choosing who and finding the words that best describe them. By its very nature art tends to attract and create the most flamboyant, insular, extrovert, introvert as well as the bizarre people as you might have noted earlier. So, I will attempt to tell you about the people who have made some of the deepest impressions on me. As I write, I am not at the end of my adventures in art by any means. It continues and I hope it always will. There is much to discover on an ongoing basis. There's a poem that had an immediate and long-standing influence on me. A Japanese Haiku poem by Kobayashi Issa.

'Oh Snail
Climb Mount Fuji
But slowly, slowly'

To me it is all about the journey in life. The journey is always more interesting than arriving at your intended destination. To reach a destination can leave you in a state of 'Okay, what now?' Reaching a destination too quickly or rushing to a destination is rather like a rocket firework. It goes up quickly, explodes in a shower of sparks and then falls down to earth to its original start point or worse! I remember as a small boy, I saved all of my pocket money for weeks to buy a packet of bangers. I even paid an older boy to go into the shop to purchase them for me. I then rushed home and set them all off one by one and I remember standing looking at the burned remains and thinking 'what now, what a waste of money!' The journey to owning those bangers was thrilling but I focused too much time and energy to one dedicated objective that not only did I end up with nothing, I'd missed out on other opportunities along the way I could have spent my pocket money on something of long-term value or use to me.

I am since that day, 'a snail'. I take my time in all my endeavors, interests, and loves to take a 360-degree view of what is going on around me at any given moment. As a result on one level, I have met many interesting people and ended up in more creative situations than I could have imagined. The 'rocket' fails to meet these people and opportunities or ignores them as irrelevant. I have never reckoned on single narrow targets or objectives because on a journey, however specific and desirable the destination might seem, by being the snail you become aware of opportunities *during* the journey.

People make a building what it is, a home, a gallery, a theater, whatever the physical edifice might be, people give it atmosphere and an identity with the possible exception of art galleries where the art creates the atmosphere. However, artists create the art. Organizations too are always a reflection of their leaders. A leader does not necessarily command people. In the arts, leaders inspire others. These are the best leaders who facilitate creativity, teamwork, and ideas. Ideas lead to actions. Sometimes leaders have no idea they are leaders! Art has been the connective tissue in my life, mainly figurative art but not entirely.

For me, art that attracts and inspires me has a story within it. The art that attracts my attention and imagination has not only a story in the moment, but it engenders in my mind a 'backstory' as well as generating an idea of where that story is leading to next, a 'future story'. This is my 'holy trinity', in the moment, back story and future story. When these things come together, I am inspired. My mind goes to places I could not have imagined otherwise.

In my own creative life, I aim to create a visualized appreciation of movement latent or otherwise, from my toes to my fingertips accentuated by my eyeline. This is inspired by visual artists, painters, sculptors, and musicians. I aim to create stories with my body. That is the definition of dance for me. It's not about dancing to the music, it's about creating a story from the music. Dance movement is fleeting but the effect of dance has a lasting effect in the imagination and memory for people. I adore life modeling because although it is static I attempt to project a static representation of movement that artists can capture. Transitions between movements is the journey from one position to another. I try to project these for artists and the best artists are those that capture that movement or as one artist told me, "Capturing the life in a movement."

Artists who are able to capture life in a transition, a pose, or the actual moving figure are my favorite artists.

The Jean Jeanie, Angelos, and Robin

One of these artists is my great friend, Angelos. Angelos is a Greek name, but his predecessors and ancestors originated from all over Europe, parts of Asia and South America. A slender and extremely tall charismatic man, he is also a truly talented professional figurative artist and art tutor. His many talents also include being an expert musician playing many musical instruments from strings to wind. Angelos is an extremely likable and garrulous character, and this is reflected in his life drawing groups. Artists of all levels of talent flock to his tutored life drawing classes. They are attracted not just by his expert tutelage but also his artistic storytelling about his life in the arts covering all forms of visual art and artists. Women love him, men want to be him. I just call him 'Angelimo' which means 'my angel'! I also love his heavy Greek accent. He always calls me 'Georgio' with an elongated 'Geeee-orrrr-gio'!

I met Angelos because I am a snail not a rocket! I was heading home one evening and on the way to the bus stop I suddenly thought about my mum and in my mind, I heard her saying.

"Don't walk around on autopilot. Stay in the moment. Try to travel back from a destination by using a different route compared to the one getting there."

Hardly profound but very influential. It has the effect of making you think about where you are 'in the moment'. The result is that you often meet people you would never have met otherwise. People lead to opportunities and opportunities lead to creativity. Wasn't it Frank Zappa who said that,

"… the mind is like a parachute; it only works when it's open!"

On this particular day as I do most days, I thought to myself, 'why am I heading home now?'. I had no time constraints or deadlines, so I physically stopped myself and stood to one side of the street. Instead of walking to the bus stop I turned right into another smaller street and began walking again in a completely different direction and importantly, in a new creative frame of mind. Suddenly I was venturing into uncertainty and unpredictability and therefore it was exciting. Within 30 minutes of consciously taking routes that would make little rational sense to most people I ended up walking past a small regional theater. It was open so I decided to pop in and buy a coffee and sit and watch the world go by.

It was a lovely bright dry early evening, so I took my coffee outside into the theater's small garden area. As I sat sipping my coffee and looking around, I saw a group of animated attractive older women who were talking and laughing together. I then picked out a wonderful Ulster accent among them. I looked in their direction and caught the wonderful sight of the magnetic Jean! I'd always called her 'The Jean Genie'. I immediately called out her name. She and her friends turned to look at me. I hadn't seen Jean for over ten years since we were on stage together, typical for those in the performing arts and to be honest, that is no excuse!

"Georgie!" Jean exclaimed in complete surprise.

She immediately got up from her chair and ran toward me with her arms open. We met in a fun laughing embrace and as I hugged her, she said, "Spin me around!" So, I did!

I put her through a little salsa dance and her friends immediately clapped and cheered with delight.

"She's such a tart!" I heard one of them say, laughing.

After about an hour of chatty catching up, Jean told me about the art classes she was attending with a local Royal Academy of Art trained artist called Robin. Jean was adamant that I should meet him as he ran tutored life drawing classes in the area. She promised to pass on my details and make the introductions, the rest as she said, was up to me. I'm happy to say that Jean and I have been in regular touch since. It's important here to reiterate about not spending your time on autopilot! Had I drifted mindlessly to the bus stop my life would not have improved creatively.

I met with the erudite, quietly spoken, friendly Robin and he gave me the opportunity to model for him and his regular life drawing class of extremely talented artists. In fact, it was Robin who then put me in touch with Angelos! And so, it goes. I am blessed with a life knitted together by truly talented art loving people. Robin and I always meet early before the life drawing classes begin. Robin's and Angelos's love for figurative art and their knowledge of the greatest inspiring figurative artists across the ages forms the basis of their teaching for each of their classes.

They both use examples of the most formative figurative artists to tutor in the techniques for shading, movement, perspective, and proportion, or as Anglos would say, "prop-po-shun"! I love these men. They both introduce different media for each of their classes taking their students on a journey in figurative art. They cover the techniques for pen & ink, feather & ink, coffee & brush, charcoal, pastels, pencil, graphite block, oils, and water colors, even drawing in oils in the inspirational style of the British painter Euan Uglow. I could listen to these two amazing men all day long and never tire!

One particular funny story when modeling for Angelos was during one of his tutored life drawing classes detailing the techniques required for 'proportion'. It went like this. I was in the middle surrounded by a very large group of artists. We were well into the first hour and I was undertaking a long relaxed standing pose. Angelos, as is his wonderful habit, was wandering through and around the artists giving them detailed tips and instruction. With one artist who was struggling, Angelos helped her by referring to me, to reference where she was going wrong, speaking very loudly.

"Ah, you see his left *nipple*? From this perspective it is higher than his right *nipple*. Both *nipples* are at an angle you see? Left *nipple* is in line with the right armpit, and the right *nipple* is below the right elbow. So put *nipple* here, *nipple* there, and we use each *nipple* as reference for mapping. So constantly go back to each *nipple* for reference, okay? Always *nipple*, *nipple*, *nipple*!"

I could sense the buildup of restrained mirth around the studio space. The way Angelos pronounced 'nipple' was *'neeeeple'*! So, I dare you to go back and read Angelos's instructions again by pronouncing 'nipple' as he did! Replace 'nipple' with neeeeple'! I sensed there was a need to release the restrained mirth, it was beginning to bubble up! As a life model I do not speak unless spoken to but on this occasion, I was compelled to speak up and literally help the artists who were completely distracted! I knew the group well so there was no problem in my mind. So, I said…

"Oh, for goodness's sake, if you mention 'neeeeple' one more time I will faint with embarrassment!"

The laughter exploded. The artists were released from their spluttering diminishing self-discipline! The laughter exploded, long and loud. Some of the artists had tears in their eyes! It was made even funnier by Angelos's reaction to the sudden laughter. He looked mystified. Everyone was looking at him as we laughed. The laughter reignited when he said…

"What? What I say?"

"Neeeeple!" I replied. "Neeeeple!" I repeated!

It was a wonderful moment.

Moving on to Robin's life drawing classes. He intends them to be inspired by Rodin, Degas, Modiglione, Uglow and Scheile to name but a few. Robin is keen to use artists who were rapid sketchers and inspired by expressionist shapes and dancers, particularly exemplified by Rodin and Degas. Robin on one particular occasion chose Egon Schiele as inspiration for his evening life drawing class. As an artist Egon Schiele captured expression in his contorted and highly stylized drawings and paintings. He was a very influential artist in the expressionist figurative genre. The figurative shapes are sometimes simple and sometimes complicated. But as a model, attempting to emulate the physical shapes of Schiele's art is pure agony.

I call him 'Agony Schiele'! Ballet dancers by their very discipline tend to be masochists because the balletic techniques required to portray effortlessness and lightness requires much disciplined repetition in training. In class, during rehearsals and during performances it is bloody painful and very exacting on the whole body. Of course, audiences do not see or sense this. Dancers use all of their large muscle groups but nevertheless the body succumbs to fatigue but as dancing is a dynamic art form, the movement provides relief for muscles as they interchange to support and balance the body. At no point as a dancer have I experienced or needed to endure a persistent emphasis on the body's pressure points. I'm sure some ballerinas might disagree with me in some instances! However, pressure points in the body are what 'sports masseuses' concentrate on in my own particular experience for relief of pain and helping the healing process following injury.

So taking up poses to emulate the expressionist shapes of Egon Schiele is quite frankly fucking agony. I believe Robin knew it would be a difficult evening for me as the model but hey, I'm a ballet dancer right! Everyone knows ballet dancers are contortionists, right? Wrong! Ballet dancers are extremely flexible, it is a requirement as well as a result of their training. Let me explain! A 15-minute Schiele pose on one knee, the other leg angled at 90 degrees, weight on one knee and through two angled wrists, with one elbow bent and the other straight and the head and neck at juxtapositions to the torso! Oh, my word! Within five minutes every joint and pressure point is screaming "STOP, STOP NOW!"

Bearing in mind my USP is the extended expressionist standing pose, anything involving being off balance without supporting muscles being activated to keep me upright means I'm in trouble! Aches I can contend with. Muscles tire and therefore tend to ache. Aches can be relieved in muscles. I have ballet inspired knowledge of which muscles to rest and which to activate to provide respite from aches, but pain is another kettle of fish! Pain is acute. Pain is the body's way of saying "stop doing that shit right now! It's time to put a stop to what you are doing!." But as a life model out there in the center you can't stop! You are a 'professional masochist' to boot! So there I was modeling in the style of Egon Schiele for a 15-minute pose and the sweat didn't just pour from me, it dripped from me constantly! How the hell was I going to get out of this hell of a pose! Fifteen minutes began to seem like an eternity.

Five minutes into the pose and I felt a growing crescendo of physical pain which also engendered a tortuous psychological odyssey! I was compelled by the pain to speak up. Firstly, I attempted to communicate with Robin using 'telepathy' that I was in the throes of imminent collapse! My mind was running wild by now. Then my arms and legs began to quiver. Surely Robin could see my pain!? He did! He spoke up addressing the artists.

"As you can see, Schiele was adept at expressionist figurative art. Twisted body shapes and expressive lines characterize Schiele's paintings and drawings. He was an early exponent of *Expressionism* inspired by Gustav Klimt who was mentor to Schiele."

My brain searched feverishly for a sense of humor! Robin was paying me a compliment really. I'd captured Schiele but my mind and ligaments were definitely 'expressionist' on another level. They were expressing sheer agony or should that be *'Schiele Agony'*! All of my muscles were working but not in the way they had been trained and as a result all the strain was being channeled through my joints and on a rising scale! My muscles were quivering in an attempt to cover and relieve the pain in my joints, but they were unable to do so. Then I discovered a growing pain in my sacrum, coccyx, and my lower spine. They are places for nerve endings to gather and relax but I'd put a ticking time bomb among them! I spoke up. I had to! I was ten minutes into the 15-minute pose by now.

"Er Robin, folks, I'm not gonna be able to carry on!" I said appealingly through clenched teeth, not looking at anyone.

I'm sure that my eyes were closed! There was a murmur around the studio from the artists. I thought it was disapproval. Robin spoke calmly.

"Okay everyone, just one more minute."

One minute! Could I do it? Yes, I could! I summoned every last drop of mental energy and in my head, I counted down from 60 seconds and then…I collapsed with an audible groan!

"Fabulous," "fantastic," "well done," "you really captured it," "thank you" were some of the comments from the artists and Robin. I received much praise from my artist friend and graphic designer, Kevin Greenhill who allowed me to use his life drawing of me for the front cover of this book.

I lay stretched out on my yoga mat arms out front and toes pointing in submission to my pain! My joints began to scream, and my muscles went into spasm!

"I really didn't think you could hold the pose for that long, George… just the job!" Robin said.

"It's evident that Schiele was a very quick sketcher, and it is thought he used early photography to capture expressive poses and made his drawings from those." Robin continued.

"Holy crap! Yes" I exclaimed "I've just proved the use of a camera!"

Everyone laughed and clapped, and I lay there quivering! Apparently, before I'd commenced the pose when I had gone off to take a pee, Robin had explained to the artists that they'd better draw quickly as a 15-minute pose was excessive. Five minutes would be the limit, and this would be an exercise in rapid sketching to capture expression! I really like Robin. He's a friend, but he'd forgotten to inform me! I had to laugh. His calm words and the way he speaks is 'guru-like' but it was at odds with the lack of guru-like calm in my twitching body! It was 'me' lying there certainly not me in character. I was George Harman, and I was among friends, thankfully so I recovered my dignity at least. Robin's group of artists have become part of my 'art family' and I count Robin and Angelos as two of my closest friends and they are professional artists too. Bonus!

Steph

This leads me on to Steph. She's a self-taught artist and many things have happened to her in her life that could have resulted in her not being the genuine ebulliently positive woman that she is. She is therefore inspirational. I met her through a referral, and I wasn't at all surprised by the vast mercurial creativity that exudes from her. Life modeling for Steph's tutored life drawing classes is just like being part of a large family of like-minded souls. She has a loyal following and as soon as I modeled for her group the first time, I was confronted with eager and friendly questions about my life. This group engages with the model verbally and encourages it. It's like therapy! With Steph's group it works well. Her group is the only group of artists for whom I model mostly as myself, rather than in character.

When you reveal things about yourself and career, I think most creatives would feel that it brings on 'impostor syndrome'! When you bare your soul and put everything into your art you lay yourself open to judgement that feels personal. Visual artists including film actors and directors have their work visually available to all forever! As a performing artist you don't leave anything physically tangible behind except memories for the audience. Those memories can of course be negative, so it is a fact of life we are all open to judgement regardless of the modern-day mantra of *'don't judge people'*! However, judgement is a part of life, of being human. I once received some advice to deal with 'being offended' by people in whatever way. Apart from growing a thick skin engendered by having four older sisters which toughens up a boy for life, I would advise taking the following advice to heart.

"If anyone tries to bring you down, they are already below you."

I have received a few negative comments about my style and presentation as a life model both firsthand and second hand and here's some more advice…

"Offense is never given; it is only accepted."

In fact, what anyone thinks of me is none of my business! The people who have criticized me one way or another are 'drains'! People can be negative by nature and they tend to suck creativity out of any room or company that they are in. I've overheard some vitriolic criticism of art, artists and actors, even the local butcher! I once heard some stuck-up fat cynic say…

"I can't stand Ian McKellen, I've no idea why he's so popular"!

Fuck me sideways! If some arsehole can criticize one of Britain's national treasures it simply tells me very clearly that it reflects the character of the critic themselves rather than a reflection of those they criticize. So, when you are criticized just think, even Sir Ian isn't immune from those drongos so you are in very good company indeed!

We are all imbued with the propensity to be cynical. Cynicism is a disease of the soul and a knee jerk reaction from personal ignorance. I advise you here to exorcise cynicism from your soul. It takes time but like exercising a damaged muscle, you can become stronger by removing the damage that cynicism does to your life. Putting it bluntly, if anyone is ever insulting you, you should be aware that it is their shit, and they are looking to dump it on you. When you see this stink coming, sidestep it, stay civilized and walk away. There's a time to be personally skeptical but please do not be cynical! Also remember this, I reiterate, when you first meet someone, that is who they really are! Thanks, Val x

I really recommend a wonderful quote from the film 'Layer Cake', words delivered by the late great Sir Michael Gambon in the role of Eddie Temple, putting life into perspective; I often quote it when I hear friends moaning about something ephemeral…

"You're born, you take shit, you get out into the world, take more shit, you climb a little higher, take less shit. 'Til one day you're up in the rarefied atmosphere and you forget what shit even looks like. Welcome to the Layer Cake, son."

The film is about the criminal world of drug gangs, but hopefully you will get my gist! God bless you Steph, you bring all my worlds together in one place.

Right time, wrong place!

One of the oldest and longest established life drawing groups in the UK is located in a quintessential ancient English town. It was a gem of a find for me. The group meet together in the same 'time warp' venue spanning over 60 years. The venue is privately owned and run as an events location by an amazing dancer called Noel. The multi-talented organizer of the life drawing is the magnetic and erudite softly spoken, Rupina. I'd heard of the group in conversations with many artists who recommended I introduce myself to Rupina as a potential life model for the group. I contacted her by email and received a polite reply asking me for references! I was more than happy to attempt to gain qualification! I was also told that Rupina would be making polite enquiries about my suitability in the meantime! Even better. I'm happy to say I passed muster and began to model for this wonderful group "on a trial basis." I love this approach, it is professional, careful, considered, and courteous. I can report that I am now a regular life model for Rupina. I am blessed once again to be included into another group of eclectic art lovers.

One of the highlights of this group is the 'tea break'! The conversations and stories about the arts are informative, enlightening, and funny as well as genuinely educational. One very crisp and chilly Thursday morning I had begun to model with the timer set for the first 10-minute pose in the warm perfectly lit first floor studio, when from my standing pose I was in a position to look out of a window. Directly across the narrow street was a bedroom window of a nearby house. I was close enough to be able to see some Venetian blinds ever so slightly tilt to a discreet angle. It was evident that someone was standing behind them believing they were hidden from sight! The artists around me were concentrating on their drawings and unaware. I was being spied upon by a peeping Tom! Male or female I couldn't tell. Whoever they were they were extremely practiced in keeping still not unlike myself! As every trained commando knows, 'movement gives the game away'! For me it was instantly amusing because I'm a bloke. It would elicit a different response for a female life model. I was quite happy to let the voyeur get an eyeful, but I knew I'd have to laugh at some stage and until then it would affect my concentration and performance. Using the difficulty, I decided it wasn't the professional option to remain silent. I therefore made a joke of it. Speaking up would not be out of place here.

"Darling Rupina!" I began, impersonating Sean Connery!

Every artist looked up toward me from their seat looking surprised!

"There sheems to be an uninvited audiensh in the upper shircle acrosh the shtreet!"

There was an immediate peel of laughter and murmurings of a familiar recognition of the situation. Rupina immediately shot out of her seat simultaneously slapping her thighs with both of her hands.

"Oh, the peeping Tom," she sighed humorously.

This beautiful elegant tall figure of a woman gracefully walked toward the offending window not unlike a ballerina as she skillfully circumnavigated the other artists. With a sweep of her arm, she closed the curtain. She made no fuss, and her grace canceled the distraction without affecting the artistic ambience.

On another occasion a new female 'artist' joined the group taking up one of the arranged chairs just before the life drawing was about to start. She wasn't late but she'd left it to the last minute. It was one of those situations when everyone thinks that someone else knows who the latest additional artist is, expecting someone to introduce them before the off. Other than this growing omission nothing seemed particularly out of place. We all assumed we had a new member joining the group. I dropped my robe to begin and suddenly the 'new artist' rose to her feet with a resulting clattering of a falling pen and notebook.

This pen and little A6 notebook should have been a clue to her attendance! Everyone stopped and looked at her standing staring at me!

"Oh! oh, ooooh!" She uttered. "I th…th…thought th…th…that th…th…this was the creative writing class!"

Our laughter didn't begin immediately while this declaration sank in! Then we all spontaneously exploded laughing. Then immediate silence as everyone suddenly felt it rude to laugh but this sudden short silence started everyone laughing again. I couldn't keep still! I had to reset my pose! She gathered her things in a complete fluster, dropping her coat she'd hung on her chair, then she dropped her bag as she made for the door, stubbing her feet into chair legs and fumbled for an eternity with the door handle before exiting without a backward glance! It took us a while to settle again. Then Rupina came to the rescue with her calm dulcet tones,

"Please continue everyone… if you can!" We calmed down. "I think she'll need to sit down with a strong… cup of tea!" We all roared with laughter again!

We all looked at Rupina's calm face and then she started to giggle as well, we all fell about the place crying with laughter. The tea break entertainment was the best ever! Life Modeling can be great fun.

Thank you, Rupina, for adding joy to my life every time I join you all.

Husbands!

I would say that the vast majority of people who choose life drawing as a regular hobby are women. I have no explanation for this. I have come across husbands and wives both attending life drawing classes together occasionally. On the whole, partners tend to have separate hobbies and show little interest in each other's activities. During an interval at a beginner's life drawing class I wandered around the room to have a quick dekho at the drawings that the enthusiastic students had produced. It was fascinating to look at the many individual styles.

Before the break I'd posed standing for 20 minutes and now on my own, I stood looking at the work of one young woman in her absence, who'd been drawing with colored pastels using an easel. She had really caught my proportions, perspective and movement, except her grasp of proportion had completely failed in one area! She had drawn me with a minute if not minuscule penis! As I looked, she returned to the studio. Trust my luck! As she approached, she looked slightly embarrassed and as I indicated that I was going to grab a coffee she stopped me and apologized to me!

"What are you apologizing for?" I asked,

She continued to look extremely embarrassed, but her eyes were appealing to me in supplication!

"Er, it's my husband you see! He's an extremely jealous person and I know he'll check out my drawings when I get home so I've made adjustments to you!" she said, quietly and coyly without humor.

I started to understand but I had nothing to add. I didn't know whether to smile, joke or whatever!

Then she bit the bullet and said, "if my husband had a body like yours, he wouldn't be jealous of any man!"

I left it at that! Yeah okay, I did feel like a 'shag on a rock'!

On another occasion in a tiny village hall in the middle of nowhere, I modeled for a group of well-to-do wives of rich farmers. I was clearing up my gear at the end of their tutored class, wearing my bathrobe and flip flops. All of the artists had packed up and left. I suddenly heard the door open and there stood a very tall gentleman farmer. He was dressed in a tweed flat cap, a long Barbour jacket over a bright yellow waistcoat and a thick pair of dark brown corduroy trousers tucked into those expensive Hunter wellington boots. He looked a little disheveled and his wellies were muddy. He stood with his hands deep in his jacket pockets, staring at me intensely and silently! I stopped clearing up my kit and turned to face him. I'm not a polite Pommie so I didn't ask the usual passive aggressive question that the English use… 'can I help you?'.

I was naked under my bathrobe and my footwear was unsuited to defending myself because this well-built farmer didn't look too friendly. So, I thought on my feet as usual and quickly thought, 'do I squarely match his aggressive posture' or do I play 'the gay card'! I played the camp gay card!

"Oooo hello lovie," I said, in my best impersonation of Julian Clary, "You're a bit late for the class, maybe I'll get to see you next week?" I said, with one hand on my hip 'teapot style.'

My robe wasn't tied, and it fell open at the front and at this sight the silent farmer turned on his heels with an audible squeal of his Hunters and left without saying a word. In fact, he couldn't get out of there fast enough! 'Thank fuck for that' I thought!

The following week I was setting up to model for the same group, when I recognized a beautiful woman coming into the room. She was one of the artists. She quickly approached me and began to pour out apologies! My mind didn't compute at first and then I clicked. She was the wife of the gentleman farmer who had stood gawping at me the previous week.

"I'm so so very sorry" she said in her posh Pommie accent, "you see my husband never took any interest in my art before but one morning he unrolled some of my life drawings from here and was struck dumb and a little peeved that you are a male life model! He seemed to think all life models were supposed to be women! I didn't tell him you were a man and a dancer, why would I? I had no idea he would show up here. I'm so very embarrassed. I hope he didn't alarm you?"

Bless her, she looked very concerned for me, all the more surprising was that her English stiff upper lip was wobbling! I didn't know what to say other than comfort and reassure her that everything was fine, and I hadn't given it a second thought, but I did add…

"There wasn't a problem. I had no idea who he was or what he wanted but he left after my friend Julian spoke to him!"

"Oh, that's good," she answered, taking in every word literally that I'd just said, "but it's made him a little more attentive toward me," she added, raising her eyebrows!

Every cloud has a silver lining!

Kit and extracurricular Caboodle

During my early days as a life model, I literally just turned up without a bag of what I learned to be necessary kit. I often carried my hold-all containing all the things I needed for theater performances or rehearsals which included a towel, a snack, a drink, and a change of underwear, plus a small bag of toiletries and 'medication'. Very quickly I realized I needed to supplement this with quite a lot more necessary kit to be prepared for comfort and mishaps! I learned by experience to be prepared for any contingencies!

I hope I'm not about to bore you with the following list of kit that I carry with me for any form of live performance or rehearsal including life modeling. It is a question I am asked from time to time.

- A small fan heater
- An electric extension cable
- A thick cotton bath robe
- A pair of flip flops
- A small pillow
- Two yoga mats, preferably black for modeling
- Two long black fleece blankets

In my contingency kit bag

- Deodorant and small towel
- Aloe Vera lotion
- Nose spray
- Eye drops
- Sudocrem
- Savlon
- Micropore
- Paracetamol
- Ibuprofen
- Tweezers
- Nail clippers
- Dental floss
- Toothbrush and toothpaste
- Vaseline
- Liquid soap
- Insect repellent
- FirstBite and sting ointment

All of this fits neatly into my time-served vintage designer label bag I bought at Camden Market. I've been described playfully as looking like a carpetbagger! I leave it to your imagination why I carry these items but it's fairly self-explanatory.

At one of my earliest life modeling gigs as in London, I appeared without any essential kit. I was directed to change in a dusty if not a dirty disused toilet! Some places I have changed have been storerooms and large walk-in cupboards!

The more thoughtful groups provided blankets, mats and cushions. In short, they were not clean and very often dusty, plus they often stank like secondhand clothes shops! On more than one occasion I ended up with itchy rashes and fits of sneezing! One lead artist in a group setting, actually opened up windows during an extended pose resulting in me shivering and covered in goosebumps! Regardless of the outside temperature, being naked in the UK is a cold and drafty experience!

The worst inconveniences to befall a life model are minor inconveniences for the clothed. Some of them but by no means all include, insects particularly wasps, drafts especially around my feet, sudden glaring sunshine in my face, sudden changes of the light, artists walking on my mats and blankets, artists coming in late and then inanely explaining why they are late (no one fucking cares), artists walking too close to me especially from behind, artists continually fumbling with their easels, artists who take photographs of me while I'm naked (they don't even ask), insensitive crude remarks (very rare) and bloody chatterboxes! Some of these affect other artists and can shatter a creative atmosphere.

Talking of chatterboxes, the worst ones are chatty tutors, not those tutors who talk about the arts but those who chatter about irrelevant subjects! In one very large class of beginners I experienced three tutors tutoring simultaneously due to the size of the group. Too many cooks sipping the broth perhaps? Barbara, Alice, and Adele. They were competing with each other but at the same time attempting to keep things polite but there was a strained atmosphere! They ended up talking among themselves across the room about their techniques. The beginners became an afterthought! Following a strained disagreement about the correct height of easels, they became quiet and eventually struck up pointless conversations about pointless subjects. I modeled my ass off for the artists. As usual, the sublime becomes ridiculous! The conversation turned to vacuuming! I've no idea how! Adele actually asked my opinion of vacuuming! I used the difficulty to return the atmosphere to an artistic perspective.

"… I like vacuuming because you can observe an instant result rather like an artist drawing!"

There was a murmur of understanding around the studio; nothing to do with vacuuming carpets! This both transmitted and relieved some of the growing frustrations among the artists. I'll leave that parked here for a while!

At the end of the first session that morning everyone left the studio including me for refreshments except the tutors who remained in the studio. I needed to return to the studio at one point to retrieve my cellphone from my coat that was hung just inside the entrance. I was hidden from the main space close to the door by a short entrance corridor where the coat pegs were located, leading into the studio. From there I was distracted by overhearing the three tutors speaking to each other. This is what I heard.

"I don't know about you, but I'd like to put some instant results on the model's tight backside!" Barbara said.

"You are such a 24/7 Domme," I heard Alice say in reply.

They were all in serious agreement! I listened in until I thought I might be discovered! The three of them continued to conjure up a scenario to have me model at a life drawing class for a group of BDSM enthusiasts! I heard their humorous references to me being tied to a St. Andrew's Cross and then caned and whipped. The three of them laughed lasciviously. They were fucking serious! At that point I quietly left without them seeing me! Personally, I have no inclinations, predilections, proclivities nor idiosyncrasies for BDSM one way or another. Whatever floats your boat. I did have to research what a St. Andrew's Cross is however!

Barbara, Alice, and Adele were perfectly pleasant people, but I had to concentrate extra hard for the rest of the day and remained silent as I modeled, never quite dispelling the thought that these three women had a BDSM fetish. The plain looking Barabara was a Dominatrix! I've met the three tutors individually on many occasions since, but I got my revenge a few weeks later at an art exhibition. I bumped into Barbara during the exhibition's private viewing. In general, polite conversation she asked me,

"How's life modeling going recently?"

I saw my chance to rattle Barbara!

"Oh, I've not done much over the past few weeks because of some bruising," I replied.

"Oh dear!" she said, looking concerned "have you injured yourself dancing?"

"Nope," I said, looking casual, and lying to her, "I was caned senseless at a BDSM party in Mayfair and the welts and bruising on my back and ass look like an experiment in chromatography… you can still see the bruises!"

She stood there in front of me like a statue. I love the power of silence when I hit a bull's eye! I can still imagine what thoughts were going through her mind!

Her eyes were a sight to behold! I bet she remembers that art exhibition but it's my guess that she'll remember diddly squat about the artworks that hung there!

Chapter Fourteen

Manon, not the ballet! 'Erotique Cordiale', the French BDSM submissive and her cuckold husband

BDSM fetish art tutors, and grudgingly compliant husbands, have therefore created vivid memories for me. However, it's got to be a crazy life when you can recall an occasion when both combined to create an adventure during the course of your day job! BDSM isn't something I felt any need to explore after meeting 'Barbara the Dominatrix', but like most things that crop up unexpectedly you tend to notice them more in the future. It's like my car. I'd never noticed a blue Alpine A110 on the roads of the UK, but after I bought one, I noticed them everywhere! Well perhaps not everywhere but whenever I see one I recognize it instantly and they seem to be more common than I first thought! It's basically a heightened awareness. So, it was with BDSM! However, this takes a little bit of an explanation. I've never been a husband, nor had I ever felt inclined to indulge in BDSM. Yeah, there are aspects of it that are included in any healthy adventurous relationship including within a marriage hopefully, such as mild restraint and spanking. Some married couples take it to an extreme, of that I am aware! As I've mentioned before, whatever floats your boat!

An annual residential event covering a wide range of creative subjects is organized and convened every year at an extremely large country estate deep within the English countryside. It is an extremely popular 'highbrow' and 'go to' event for dilettantes and experts in the art and literature worlds. Subjects covered include Egyptology, Ancient Greek drama, cartography, the life of Magellan, Roman literature, you get my gist. These individual courses are extremely popular and tickets for the event are sold out very quickly. Of course, there is also a life drawing course over the scheduled three days, entitled 'The History of the Nude in Art'. Attendees are attracted from all over Europe and North America.

I had been invited to be a life model at this event for six straight years. It's an honor. As well as life modeling I also speak to an eclectic audience about the 'anatomy of a dancer' and an entertaining humorous brief history of ballet! The three-day event offers a three-night accommodation option on site in the splendid luxurious period buildings located on the estate.

I love the slow-paced culture of the event especially as it takes place during July in the middle of the English summer. This means there is a long evening twilight creating a slow changing panorama of the English surrounding countryside. This provides the opportunity for all the residents to take drinks outside, to mingle and chat on the beautifully cultivated lawns that surround the huge mansion house. A wonderful feature is the 'ha-ha' which invisibly separates the gardens from the agricultural lands spreading out into the distance. There is a maze of beautifully converted outbuildings turning them into meeting rooms and accommodation. It all combines for a wonderful creative atmosphere, and I get to enjoy grace and favor food and accommodation!

The leisure facilities are equally amazing. Two swimming pools, one large one small, saunas, steam rooms, a large jacuzzi and a large gym. These are all available to the residents and the tutors and presenters. As a dancer, these facilities are a necessity but sadly all too rare for me! I have always used the facilities each year at this amazing venue to recuperate from any residual muscle strains and injuries as well as making use of the saunas to stretch at the start and the end of each day. It's like an all-expenses paid vacation for me. I prepare well in advance liaising with the organizers and life drawing tutors. I approach the event with a deep sense of relaxation. The format of the life drawing is very straightforward with a ballet theme. Right 'up my Strasse'!

During one of my scheduled short talks to a well-attended early evening audience alongside an experienced figurative art tutor, I talked about the anatomy of dance and movement. The audience numbered around 50 in total. I illustrated my talk with dance, wearing ballet gear under a spotlight. This proves very popular for a wide range of attendees. That year I danced a short repertoire from the ballet 'Manon'. This was arranged or should I say 'forced' on me by the ballet-loving art tutor who was sharing the stage with me. It was of course done with friendly pleading on his part to the extent I had little choice. He was an expert scholar in the work of Edgar Degas. The talk was completed by 6pm and an early evening 'break out' was scheduled for drinks and canapés before dinner 7:30 for 8pm. I took the opportunity to go for a swim and a sauna. I don't like eating canapés in a dance belt and tights anyway! I shot back to my room, put on my blue Speedos, grabbed a towel and wrapped myself in a luxuriously thick cream cotton bathrobe. I rummaged around my bag for my trusty 'massage kit' which is nothing more than a tennis ball on a rope! #MOTL

I was surprised by the lack of guests in both swimming pools when I arrived there. I decided on the smaller 12m pool because it had a small jacuzzi attached to it and an intimate sauna right next to that. The pool water was cool when I entered it so I had a brief swim and elected to head for the sauna due to my tightening muscles! Prior to this I took a short shower in the open cubicle provided and took note of the location of the sauna's glass door nearby. I could see my reflection in the glass quite clearly which masked any chance of seeing into the sauna to check for anyone who might already be in it. I hoped to be alone.

I grabbed my towel and my tennis ball on a string that I'd left on a poolside recliner with my bathrobe. As I reached the glass door of the sauna, I became aware of two other people in there. I walked in and quickly closed the door. I nodded toward the man and woman sitting there and said a polite "hello". They both responded with a pleasant "Bon soir" with obvious French accents. They sat at right angles to each other on the bottom level of the three-sided double tiered wooden benches on my right. The man sat facing the glass door and the woman was to his right facing the opposite wall. I decided to sit on the top tier facing the glass door. They both glanced at me politely and continued their quiet conversation and it was obvious as I first suspected that they were both French.

I spread out my towel and sitting down I was taken by surprise how hot the wooden benches were on my feet. I was pleased I'd brought my towel in with me to sit on. Below me to my right I could see the top of the French guy's head and his shoulders. He continued facing the glass door as I was. The French woman sitting to his right was in full view for me and I glanced below occasionally in her direction as they spoke quietly. I had no interest other than heating up my body and getting to work on my pressure points with the tennis ball. The woman could easily look up to see me from her position and each time I glanced over she would make eye contact with me. There was no connection in our glances.

As they spoke, I picked up the odd French word. In ballet we use French terminology but that would be of no use here. I had my 'schoolboy French' that only improves during my yearly French vacation. I'd call it 'pigeon French' or

'Franglais'! There was nothing in their conversation to prick up my ears and cause me to eavesdrop.

After a short while, I realized that I hadn't turned the large sand-filled timer on the wall as I'd entered. The heat was so stifling I knew I had to get to work on my stretches and pressure points as soon as possible. I shuffled my seated position further back until I could sandwich the tennis ball between my back and the sauna wall. The attached string allowed me to position the ball exactly where I needed to apply the pressure. Using my weight, I pressed against the ball in a slow pulsing motion. The woman noticed this immediately and the man glanced around for a quick look. The tone of their conversation changed, and it was obvious they were talking about what I was doing as I heard the French word "balle de tennis" mentioned.

After this and as a result of encouragement from the woman the man politely gesticulated with accompanying stilted English as to what I was doing. They were genuinely curious. The French are far less reticent than the English. I attempted to explain by gesticulating with my hands and using my body and mentioned "mon dos" and pronounced "muscles du dos" in a French accent and also mentioned "danceur de ballet" and "modele de vie." I didn't know whether I was making sense, but we all smiled at my attempts! Suddenly the woman spoke to the man quickly and animatedly with reference to me. I soon decided to lie flat on the top tier to locate the ball on my lower back, meaning I would be facing the roof of the sauna with my feet behind and above the French couple. I made my polite apologies and received a polite wave and shrugs of acceptance.

The French couple continued their conversation but not as before. They spoke rapidly in whispers, in higher and lower pitches. The woman did most of the whispering and interrupted the man many times. I couldn't understand the detailed meaning of their conversation. It was obvious to me she was being extremely firm with the man and at one point spoke in a normal voice and she interrupted him with a rattle of hissing whispers! The whispered conversation continued then at a pace, and I could only assume that they whispered, thinking that I understood enough French to understand them, but I couldn't!

I did hear the English pronunciation of "steam room" and "la chambre" and a few other French words that also had no significance for me. I was distracted though by beginning to feel the extreme heat on the top tier as I rolled my lower back over the rapidly softening tennis ball! Suddenly the man stood up and I tilted my head to my left automatically and he looked at me and nodded, I presumed at his farewell. I heard the woman say "salut" more than once! He left quickly, closing the glass door carefully and I sat up feeling the heat! From my position I could see him walking away from me through the glass door and he turned left into the steam room. I saw the door open before he entered.

With the man out of sight I automatically looked down to my right at the French woman and our eyes met. She smiled in what I can only describe as a 'French way.' There was more to it, more communication, just a little more obvious than subtle. I can say that her 'French look' was far more communicative than an equivalent English female would show. It was the first time I had clearly seen her face. She was very attractive, not pretty. She had shoulder length dark blonde hair with a fringe highlighting her brown eyes. There was nothing striking about her in terms of being glamorous, but she looked healthy and slender. She sat with her hands just underneath her thighs and her knees were squeezed together held high because she was on tiptoes. Her shoulders were bent slightly forwards. which made her look friendly and approachable. Her lightly tanned thighs looked narrow and deep.

Her back was straight despite tilting forward, her shoulders square and her chin jutting forwards slightly. Her face was narrow, with a small nose and thin shapely lips. Her small breasts were flattened by the one-piece sky-blue bathing costume. I noticed that the costume was styled like a pair of shorts at the thighs, reaching her mid-thigh level. I couldn't help thinking how sexy she would have looked in a high-leg style of bathing costume or bikini! The one-piece bather was a bright mid-blue with black piping around the neck, shoulders and around the thighs. The other thing I noticed was that the material of the bather was very thick, almost like the neoprene material of a scuba diver's suit. It hugged her skin lightly making little indentation pressure on her skin. She looked sporty and extremely healthy. She could have been anything between 32 and 42 years old, I just had no idea. She had a mature look and a flawless complexion. Her neckline, arms and legs were shiny with perspiration from the heat of the sauna. She looked at me without turning away!

There's something more communicative with a woman when you don't share a common language. Nonverbal communication is far more informative and descriptive but when coupled with a common language NVC can be used to deceive. Without a common language there was no doubt in my mind that this intelligent attractive French woman was interested in me now her male partner had left. I rearranged my brain so as not to default to the Anglo-Saxon way of looking away to show politeness. I matched her gallic stare. I say stare, we weren't staring at each other, it was more like she was saying 'I am thinking how to make this work'! I thought of the man she had been with.

I suddenly wondered why he had left her alone with me after their hurried one-sided 'conversation'. There was a little rancor between them. She didn't become aggressive; her tone was assertive, and he showed no displeasure or unwillingness to leave the sauna. Maybe, I thought, he was a friend or her brother or simply a colleague. I just didn't know, and I tried to put him out of my mind but there was a niggling doubt in there! She spoke to me in a clear voice,

"Je m'appelle Manon"

Holy fuck I thought. Is she taking the piss, making the connection with my performance 30 minutes previously or was this a complete coincidence? Regardless, I love the name Manon. I just went along with it.

"Hi, je m'appelle Georges" I replied, pronouncing my name the French way. "Il fait trop chaud ici" I said very slowly, thinking about each word in turn.

Manon laughed and gently lifted her right thigh to remove her hand and gestured outside the sauna room.

"Le jacuzzi, uh?" she said.

"Oui!" I replied.

She stood up in one strong movement and I climbed down grabbing my towel and wrapping my tennis ball and string in it. Manon laughed a little. She was about 5' 4" inches tall and naturally slender. Her toenails were polished and shiny with what looked like clear nail varnish and her upper arms were naturally well-formed not gym-toned. She looked amazing in her modest expensive beautifully colored swimsuit. I said in English.

"Follow me."

I opened the door glad to be stepping out of the dry heat. Manon followed and I watched her slowly close the glass door. The jacuzzi was immediately on our right just higher than the pool level. I dropped my towel bundle onto a small shelf next to the jacuzzi and stepped in quickly. I did this so I could check out her body some more! The jacuzzi felt comparatively cool compared to the sauna and I stood with my hand out to help her in. She thanked me, swished her hair, and fixed it around both ears with one hand as I held her other hand. I released her hand shortly and sat down slowly into the calm water, and we looked at each other. Subconsciously I thought she would sit opposite me, but she sat right next to me and as she did so, her left thigh rubbed my right thigh for a split second.

I was about to break the silence between us with some pidgin French when the bubbling cycle started, saving me from making me sound comical. The sound of the bubbling grew louder and we looked sideways at each other. The bubbling water suddenly squirted up between our bodies in a few small fountains which made us both jump slightly. She laughed a delicious slow laugh, and she reached out under the water with her left hand and held my wrist. I put my arm onto my thigh as she held it, and she left her hand there. Her fingertips were touching my thigh. Within a few seconds I lifted my left arm out of the bubbling water and pointed toward the steam room door.

"Connais... Ami?" I asked.

"Non, mari" she replied.

She didn't hesitate and sounded very casual without smiling. The word she used sounded like 'marry'. I wasn't sure of its exact meaning, but it was clear they were an 'item', partners. I'd been thinking to ask her about the event here and what she was here to study but I couldn't think of the words. It would have sounded lame especially as she still had my wrist in her hand under the water. I looked at her. Her face was no more than 18 inches away from me and she held her strong gallic gaze with me. It was unmistakably one of sexual interest in me as I looked deeply into her dark eyes. Then I felt her left hand loosen around my wrist and she slid it down the top of my hand and interlocked her fingers into mine. She mentioned something in French that I didn't understand, and she gently lifted my hand and placed it onto her left thigh. She squeezed my fingers and pressed them down onto her own thigh firmly. Her voice deepened and quickened. I still couldn't understand her.

I reached across with my right foot and hooked it under her left calf muscle. I don't know whether I thought of her partner just before he walked out of the steam room or whether the sound of the door made me think of him, but the timing was significant. Things moved very quickly!

As her partner emerged, he looked over to the two of us in the jacuzzi. I had the sudden inclination to remove my foot from her lower leg and let go of her thigh, but I didn't for two reasons; he couldn't see them, and I didn't want to! Manon made no surprise move either. She just looked his way, and her stillness wasn't a result of her being surprised, it was a statement! If I'd been her partner, I'd have thought why is she sitting so close to that guy! I thought he would walk over to us, but he stood still looking at her. At no point did he look at me. He was wearing baggy swimming shorts. He was about 6 feet tall and surprisingly pale with a slightly sunken chest and black hairy nipples! There was a tuft of thick black hair between his pecs and his arms and legs were toneless and tubular. His hair was jet-black and short. His posture was weak.

Manon raised her voice over the sound of the bubbling water and spoke at length to him. He gestured toward her bag and robe hanging up on a coat hook halfway between us and she rapidly shouted,

"Non, NON… NON!"

That's telling him, I thought! He accepted what she said, turned his back and walked slowly away without a word and turned left into the passageway to the men's changing room. I was not exactly dumbfounded but many thoughts ran through my mind that concluded with 'she wants me, and he's got no fucking say in the matter'! To be honest I lost respect for both of them instantly! He was a wimp and why he was with her was beyond my understanding. I decided to just get up out of the jacuzzi and go back to my room and get changed for dinner. I looked at her thinking what to say and all I could say was along the lines of,

"Ma chambre, maintenant avant manger ce soir"

I stood up and so did she. I walked over to the open shower recess. Manon followed me. I pressed the shower nozzle and tested the water with my hand and suddenly I felt Manon standing next to me. She felt the water too. I stepped into the water, she did too! The shower recess was wide and quite deep, and I turned to face her showering trying not to look surprised. She stood watching me and then moved right up against me and rinsed her hair. She looked amazing! I didn't understand why she hadn't gone straight to the female changing room. I finished and decided to wrap myself wet in my robe and leave the pool by the door leading to the spa reception area. To be honest I didn't want to bump into her pathetic partner in the changing room! Manon did the same, she followed me! She obviously took my pigeon French for a suggestion for both of us. Two things ran through my head, 'Use the difficulty' and 'improv, just say yes'!

I stopped at the exit to look at Manon , and I felt for my flip flops that I'd put into my robe's pocket. I pulled them out, dropped them onto the tiles, and slid my feet into them. She came up next to me and took my arm in both her hands looking appealingly at me with wide eyes! There seemed something a little desperate about her or was it that she wanted to be clear with me that she wanted to be with me and get away from here as fast as she could? I had no idea, and I didn't care.

We both walked out of the pool area with her linking her arm into mine. What the hell I thought, I wasn't going to cause a scene. Turning right we walked about 20 feet to a small narrow staircase that had probably been the original servants' stairs to the upper floors. I walked up them with Manon by my side still linking her arm with mine. Neither of us spoke. We walked through a fire door at the top and I went to turn to the right as the sign on the wall opposite indicated a range of numbers for the direction of my room. Immediately Manon said,

"Non, non, s'il vous plait, Monsieur, allez… ma chambre avec moi, je veux etre ton salop!"

I knew what salop meant! She was totally different compared to the cool French woman I had met in the sauna. She wasn't acting desperate she was determined but respectful! I wanted to ask her if her partner would be showing up. I didn't want 'Monsieur Cuckold' to be present, simpering at her feet! The whole situation felt very strange as though I was in some sort of stage play! Did I have visions of another 'Loretta situation'? No, I didn't! Not then anyway but in retrospect I recognize that there were a couple of potential 'red flags'. If Manon had any desires or plans for me my natural curiosity was leading me as always.

There was no way I was going to Manon's room! That was for sure. She could either follow me or fuck off to her room by herself. I started to walk the other way in the direction of my own room along the soft carpeted corridor. Manon hesitated and said something placatory in French and came quickly up to me as I walked. I don't know why I reacted the way I did after she leaned hard against me, almost pushing me into the wall. She then pulled down hard on my arm with both of her hands. It was as if she was trying to annoy me, so I grabbed her hair gently, and firmly directed her to one side away from me. She turned wide-eyed, open-mouthed and gasping.

Adjusting my grip on her damp hair, tightening it but not pulling, I kissed her! She melted as we kissed deeply, she was breathing in a deep stuttering way. I enjoyed her hot breath and searching tongue. She was a great kisser. Our mouths fitted together perfectly without any adjustment or awkwardness. I kept my eyes open, hers were closed. She was giving herself to me. I broke away from the kiss, took her hand, and walked the short distance around a few corners to my room. I used my swipe card to open the door with one hand without fumbling, and she pressed against me hard as we entered as though to encourage me to grab her again!

In the middle of my bedroom, we kissed again, she was eager, and I called her, "Ma salop" and she bent slightly at her knees saying, "Oui, oui" repeatedly.

I slipped her out of her bathrobe letting it fall to the floor and I removed mine. Taking hold of the shoulder straps of her bathing suit I peeled it down over her body dropping to one knee to help her out of it. She placed one hand on the top of my head to steady herself. Her pussy had a neat wide dark trimmed triangle of pubic hair. I stood up and looked at her breasts, pert and round thoroughly pale with a strong bikini top tan-line and small erect flesh-colored nipples. I stood back slightly to look and admire her. She had a tan-line around her lower half too just above her pubic bone. She had natural flat abs. She obviously looked good in a bikini, and I would have liked to see her in the pool area in a bikini, I thought, but she'd taken the modest option choosing her blue bathing suit today. Or so I thought!

She gently sagged a little at her knees and started to feel her own breasts, excited and a little self-conscious. Her face was submissively saying 'tell me you like me, Sir!' (but not in English obviously!) I flicked off my flip flops and slid out of my Speedos. We kissed again and I slid my left hand around her slim waist and firmly but slowly spread my fingers and stroked the skin on her back upwards until they were tangled in her hair. I firmly tugged on a handful so that her head bent backward fully. With my right hand I held her pelvic bone feeling it and then moved it up toward her left breast.

I squeezed it, kneading it firmly as Manon breathed shallow and hard, swallowing through her gasps a number of times. Her mouth was watering, and I savored her saliva, I knew it was indicative of how wet her pussy was right now, and I felt the desire to taste her wetness but restrained myself. She was a little jumpy in my arms, muttering French words talking into my mouth as we kissed! She wanted something but I didn't know what and I wasn't going to relinquish control to her. She could leave any time she wanted if that was it but until then I was in charge!

I felt her twist in my arms, and I pinched hold of her nipple and pulled. She winced saying.

"Oui, Oui… oui, oui…!" breathing hard through the words.

I then released some of the pressure relieving her, then immediately pulled even harder and twisted it between my thumb and index finger fully stretching her breast outwards. She squirmed, winced, and breathed harder. Her knees bent and banged into my legs. I held her tighter. I maintained the pressure on her nipple until she pushed hard against my chest to ease off her pain, gasping. I'd found her pain threshold. She slowly pulled away from me and walked toward the bed. Then I noticed the faded welts and bruising on her upper back and ass cheeks. I was simultaneously aroused and a little shocked. Surely her husband wasn't capable of doing this to her! There was no bloody chance of that! Was it abuse? Was it kink? Bloody BDSM, I suddenly fucking clicked!

"Maintenant, Monsieur! s'il vous plaît," she said, walking over to a pair of my jeans which were folded over the top of a chairback by the writing desk.

She picked them up and attempted to pull my belt from the belt loops, but it was too tight. Still trying to pull it out she walked over to me and handed me my own jeans muttering and gesturing appealingly for me to remove the belt. I did it easily! I half smiled at her wondering, then I finally understood Manon! She stood naked in front of me about 6 feet away with her arms by her sides clenching her fists looking into my eyes. She gently rose and fell on tiptoe as I took in her simple beauty. Her natural slenderness made her look young, fresh, and lithe. Her brown eyes were wide and unblinking. Her dark pubic hair within the pale skin of her tan line was defined and gave her a 'layered look'. I noted that she was smooth below her clitoris. She saw me looking and spoke to me in French, words I didn't understand and then she walked over to the bed and stood in front of it placing her hands on her head with her back to me.

I enjoyed looking at her slender hips, her healthy skin, taking in the erotic sight of her thigh space from behind and her pert small heart-shaped ass. On her lower back she had a very black tattoo in a gothic style which read **Dolens Libenter**. I memorized this and checked it out later! It's Latin; I'll leave you to research its meaning! I've heard of a 'tramp stamp' but this was a 'BDSM stamp'! I moved closer and examined the faded bruising and welts. I know all about bruises as a dancer and these were probably four to five days old and a long oval-shaped bruise on her ass was much darker and edged in yellow. Whatever had made that bruise had been vicious with a huge impact. It was obvious she wanted to be belted and bruised some more by me this time! To be honest I'd never done anything like this, so I'd be testing myself as well as her!

I stood to one side of her very quietly and scooped her hair upwards and then held it there for her to hold onto, gathered at the back of her head. I then placed my lips on the back of her neck and sucked, gently at first then hard and harder still. Her shoulder blades moved inwards and outwards as her elbows moved forwards and backward in response to the pressure of my sucking and she gave out moans of pleasure and little gasps. I intended to bruise the back of her neck with a deep love bite which would be hidden under the cover of her hair. The love bite was soon a deep dark clearly defined crimson. She became more wanting and needy. I encouraged her forwards with the loop of my belt in my right hand and she quickly bent forwards and then lay flat on the bed. Her feet were just dangling over the edge.

"Okay" I said quietly, "Maintenant!"

She squeezed her glutes tightly and relaxed them, repeating this about four or five times waiting for the blow! She was anticipating me to strike her ass! So, I aimed between her shoulder blades, raised my arm, and brought down the looped belt with such force that it surprised me, let alone Manon! She let out a sudden very loud prolonged yelp which she suddenly stopped. With a deep audible inward deep breath, she came up onto her elbows blowing little breaths from her pursed lips. I tapped her on her head with the belt and she lay flat with her arms stretched out above her head again. I heard her say,

"Un… merci Monsieur." very quietly.

Oh, my word she was counting out loud and thanking me!

I'm not going to count out and describe each blow! I alternated between both butt cheeks together and separately as well as her back, and the backs of her thighs. Her thighs were fresh untouched bruise-free virgin territory! I avoided her kidney region. Halfway through she raised herself up onto her hands and knees, kneeling for me to carry on, and I concentrated the strikes on her ass. I stopped when she had counted out to *cinquante*! It was a nice round number, but she was so heavily bruised the bruises had merged and her skin was swollen red with purple centers. Her skin on her back and butt had lifted into swollen ridges in places. Her natural skin color was barely recognizable! In some areas of her back and butt the bruising had already turned purple! There were other areas of her flesh that looked close to blistering and on the edge of bleeding where the blows had crisscrossed the same area many times! I'd had enough!

She lay flat on the bed again and spoke in a satisfied way in French that I couldn't understand. I'd noticed that after about the first 12 lashes her yelps and screams became muted and instead, she would let out a loud 'hum' and inwardly absorb each blow! During the lashes while she was kneeling with her butt presented, she would rock forwards and backward at each stroke rapidly soaking up the pain until she became still again. She then arched her back downwards and lifted her head, preparing herself, as a physical signal for me to administer the next stroke!

She seemed to be satisfied with "cinquante" and looked at me smiling with wide teary eyes! She raised herself up onto her hands and knees again and stuck her ass out and then placed her head back down onto the bed! As she did this her skin obviously stretched causing her pain.

"La la la la la la la la la la la!" she whispered, and then she said with very accented questioning intonation.

"Monsieur?"

I knew what she meant so I knelt behind her and fucked her! I couldn't match the intensity of the belt, but I didn't hold back! She writhed and squealed as I touched her back and ass cheeks so I stopped to test her consent, but she encouraged me verbally to carry on, so I spanked her ass bruising without mercy. She literally screamed, shouting in a continuous combination of French and English…

"Oui, yes yes, yes, Oui je suis ta salope, fuck, fuck, Monsieur, putain, baise ta salope, Monsieur," she repeated combinations of this many times.

I know she said all this because she screamed the words so many times they are imprinted on my mind! I also remember pushing my thumb firmly into her asshole as I fucked her, stretching and pulling her anal muscle. God knows what people in the neighboring rooms thought! Me spanking her bruises must have been excruciating but she channeled the pain into screams and contractions of her vagina and anus! She became abandoned slamming her bruised butt into me as I fucked her. I noticed her using her left hand to play with herself a few times, but she wasn't able to keep that up with her aggressive thrusts as well as my own! If she orgasmed I didn't recognize the moment because there was no pause or change in her verbally or in her momentum throughout. I did cum though, explosively! I'd spanked during sex many times before but not to this level of intensity! I just went along with it willingly!

There was no ordinary connection between us it seemed. This was purely a kinky physical act for both of us but a definite and determined need on her part. Looking back, I thought about the 'BDSM' abbreviation. There was no strict *bondage* then or over the next 2 days and nights but there was *domination* on my part. Not a requirement on my part as in I felt no need to dominate her but by definition I was doing so! *Sadism*? Yeah, I inflicted pain and bruising on her body, consensually, it was a new experience and to be honest I was 'experimenting' with the phenomenon! *Masochism*? Manon was most definitely a masochist and a submissive one at that! She literally needed it to 'get off'!

It was her preferred method. She was consumed by it, and it was as if her inner second personality took her over. She reminded me of a heroin addict needing a fix! Her husband was part of her sexual preference but not in the role of administering to her needs. He simply tolerated and even accepted her preferences. I often wondered if he knew what she was like before they were married or afterwards. I can say that I would not have entertained a relationship with Manon let alone marry her! They were obviously well suited. He got his kicks from her kicks I suppose!

Judging by her experience and the amount of faded bruising I saw on her butt before I 'topped her up' she was most likely never bruise-free! I saw her in my bathroom, examining her bruises by standing on a chair that she'd taken into the bathroom, and she photographed herself with her bruises using the bathroom mirror and her smartphone! This lasted for ages! I could hear the shutter tone dozens of times! She took copious photographs of herself this way, probably to send to her husband… thanking him! Weird! But hey, whatever!

Manon left my room after about 90 minutes. I'd missed dinner so I ordered room service. At about midnight my room telephone rang, and it was Manon. In stilted pigeon-English she asked if she could come to my room. I said yes because to be honest I really fucking fancied her… both of her two personalities! Also, I liked the idea of waking up with her and enjoying each other slightly more conventionally when we did, but there was nothing vanilla about Manon! I must admit to getting dressed and I put on my shoes before she arrived just in case her suffering cuckold husband came along with her for whatever reason! She came alone and she snuggled up next to me in bed. So, there was a connection between us then! We didn't make it to breakfast the next morning either! I ordered 'breakfast in bed'! I saw her and her husband together a few times during the communal breakouts and at dinner over the two remaining days. Manon always spent the nights with me and ate breakfast with me at my table for the final two mornings while her husband sat eating on his own at the far end of the dining hall. He never complained!

Is this the end of my adventures in art? No, it isn't! It is though, the end of the beginning! Take it easy, and keep it real, until next time. Cheers.